"Think of *Hunter Chef in the Wild* as more than just a pathway toward making delicious food outdoors. It's also a battle cry howled in defense of living close to nature. As you collect and prepare these ingredients, you'll feel as alive as a wolf."

Steven Rinella, *New York Times* bestselling author of several books including *The MeatEater Outdoor Cookbook*, and host of the television show and podcast *MeatEater*

Seasoned outdoorsman, hunter, and angler Michael Hunter takes readers on his adventures in the wild across North America. In this highly anticipated book, Hunter shares his passion for nature, hunting wild food, and takes cooking outside in over 80 recipes—freshwater fish (bass, trout, walleye, salmon), saltwater fish (tuna, swordfish, halibut, salmon, ling cod), seafood (clams, lobster, octopus, mussels, geoduck), fowl and small game (snow goose, pintail duck, quail, pheasant, rabbit), and large game (bison, wild boar, muskox, elk, deer, bear, beaver), along with vegetables, and cocktails and desserts fit for a campfire, including:

- Grilled Brook Trout
- Coho Salmon Candy
- Grilled Octopus with Romesco Sauce and Salsa Verde
- Smoked Pintail Duck
- Hot Rabbit with Braised Collard Greens
- Canned Moose Meat
- Bear Ragu with Smoked Cheddar Polenta
- Birch-Syrup-Glazed Bison Short Ribs
- Elk Smash Burgers, and much more

Hunter Chef in the Wild includes a variety of cooking methods—grilling, smoking, spit-roasting—along with instructional guides: How to Cook a Whole Fish, How to Cure Salmon Roe, How to Harvest and Prepare Geoduck, and How to Roast a Pig.

Featuring stunning nature photography, *Hunter Chef in the Wild* is a must-have book for outdoor adventurers and everyone who wants to get outside, cook over fire, and eat wild food.

HUNTER CHEF IN THE WILD

**Game, Fish, and Fowl
Recipes and Techniques
for Cooking Outdoors**

MICHAEL HUNTER

PENGUIN
an imprint of Penguin Canada,
a division of Penguin Random House Canada Limited

Canada • USA • UK • Ireland • Australia • New Zealand • India • South Africa • China

First published 2025

Copyright © 2025 by Michael Hunter

All rights reserved. No part of this book may be reproduced, scanned, transmitted, or distributed in any form or by any electronic or mechanical means, including information storage and retrieval systems, without permission in writing from the publisher, except by a reviewer, who may quote brief passages in a review. No part of this book may be used or reproduced in any manner for the purpose of training artificial intelligence technologies or systems.

Penguin Canada, a division of Penguin Random House Canada Limited
320 Front Street West, Suite 1400
Toronto Ontario, M5V 3B6, Canada
penguinrandomhouse.ca

The authorized representative in the EU for product safety and compliance is
Penguin Random House Ireland, Morrison Chambers, 32 Nassau Street,
Dublin D02 YH68, Ireland. https://eu-contact.penguin.ie

Library and Archives Canada Cataloguing in Publication

Title: Hunter chef in the wild : game, fish, and fowl recipes
and techniques for cooking outdoors / Michael Hunter.
Names: Hunter, Michael (Chef), author
Description: Includes index.
Identifiers: Canadiana (print) 20240432991 | Canadiana (ebook) 20240433009 |
ISBN 9780735244511 (hardcover) | ISBN 9780735244528 (EPUB)
Subjects: LCSH: Outdoor cooking. | LCSH: Cooking (Wild foods) |
LCSH: Cooking (Game) | LCSH: Cooking (Fish) | LCGFT: Cookbooks.
Classification: LCC TX823 .H86 2025 | DDC 641.5/78—dc23

Cover and interior design by Lisa Jager
Typeset by Daniella Zanchetta
Front cover photography by Jody Shapiro
Back cover photography by Michael Hunter
Food photography by Jody Shapiro

Printed in China

10 9 8 7 6 5 4 3 2 1

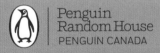

To Marlow. I see the adventurer in you.

Contents

1 Introduction
5 Fire Set-Ups

15 Freshwater Fish
47 Saltwater Fish
75 Seafood
115 Fowl and Small Game
149 Large Game
213 Game Barbecue
243 Vegetables
267 Desserts and Drinks

304 *How to Make a Euro Mount*
309 Acknowledgments
311 Photo Credits
312 Index

The Recipes

Freshwater Fish

21	*How to Cook a Whole Fish*
25	Grilled Brook Trout
29	Fire-Roasted Kelp-Planked Steelhead Trout
30	Smoked Carp
33	Grilled Baitfish
34	Grilled Lake Erie Whitefish
37	Fried Perch with Gribiche Sauce
38	Arctic Char Torched with Soy and Honey
41	Blackened Catfish with Creole Sauce
43	Brown Trout with Sweet Pea Risotto

Saltwater Fish

51	Grilled King Salmon with Roasted Garlic Compound Butter and Sautéed Sweet Peas
55	*How to Cure Salmon Roe*
56	Pacific Albacore Tuna Donburi
59	Rockfish with Caper Butter Sauce and Pickled Shallots
63	Halibut with Cucumber Kohlrabi Slaw and White Wine Cream Sauce with Herb Oil
65	Ling Cod with Red Pepper Butter Sauce and Grilled Tomatoes
69	Coho Salmon Candy
70	Baked Salt-Crusted Trout
73	Grilled Swordfish with Roasted Tomatoes and Olive Tapenade

Seafood

78	*Uni—Foie Gras of the Sea*	96	Grilled Geoduck
81	Smoked Uni Butter and Bison Tenderloin	99	Grilled Oysters Rockefeller
83	Lobster Rolls on Squid Ink Buns	101	Grilled Octopus with Romesco Sauce and Salsa Verde
86	Lobster Boil	105	Grilled Squid with Peperonata
89	Pizza Oven Baked Clams	106	Seafood and Rabbit Paella
90	*How to Harvest and Prepare Geoduck*	109	Gooseneck Barnacles
95	Sashimi-Style Geoduck	111	Mussels in White Wine Cream Sauce with Grilled Baguette

Fowl and Small Game

121	Snacking Sticks	138	Smoked Duck Wings with Maple Hot Sauce
122	Goose Jerky	141	Grilled Quail with Honey-Lime Glaze and Corn Salsa
125	Crane Steak au Poivre	143	Barbecued Pheasant with Alabama White Sauce
127	Buffalo-Fried Quail	145	Hot Rabbit with Braised Collard Greens
131	Smoked Pintail Duck		
133	Crispy-Skin Snow Goose		
137	Whole Roasted Woodcock		

Large Game

- 155 Boar Bacon Fig Poppers
- 156 Fire-Roasted Antelope Chops with Rosemary and Tzatziki
- 159 Sausage-Stuffed Grouse with Maple Candied Yams
- 161 Bison Tomahawk Steaks with Chimichurri
- 164 Mule Deer Tataki
- 167 Wild Boar Peameal Bacon
- 168 Wild Boar Peameal on a Bun
- 171 Muskox in White Wine Cream Sauce with Orecchiette and Kale
- 173 Muskox Sausage and Rapini Pizza
- 176 Pulled Goose Leg Barbecue
- 179 Roe Deer Caprese Salad
- 181 Spit-Roasted Beaver with Birch Syrup and Blueberry Glaze
- 185 Cold-Smoked Cured Swan Breast
- 189 Grilled Wagyu Porterhouse Steak
- 190 Elk Backstraps
- 193 Elk Heart Skewers
- 194 Elk Liver with Serviceberry Compote
- 197 Elk Osso Buco
- 199 Venison Patties
- 203 Canned Moose Meat
- 205 Canned Moose Poutine
- 207 Bear Curry
- 211 Bear Ragu with Smoked Cheddar Polenta

Game Barbecue

- 216 *Whole Wild Boar Breakdown*
- 218 *How to Roast a Pig*
- 223 Chopped Wild Boar Barbecue
- 224 Asado Roast Pig
- 227 Birch-Syrup-Glazed Bison Short Ribs
- 228 Bison Brisket
- 231 Smoked Wild Boar Shoulder
- 232 Smoked Cougar Ham
- 235 Elk Smash Burgers
- 236 Bear Ribs
- 239 Spit-Roasted Porchetta

Vegetables

- **247** Campfire Chanterelle Risotto
- **248** Fire-Roasted Cauliflower with Baba Ghanoush
- **251** Charcoal-Roasted Whole Cabbage
- **252** Fire-Roasted Heirloom Carrots and Onions with Hummus
- **255** Charcoal-Roasted Beets with Yogurt Dressing
- **256** Fire-Roasted Sweet Corn
- **259** Charred Zucchini and Stracciatella Cheese
- **260** Fire-Roasted Whole Squash with Burrata Cheese
- **263** Campfire Brussels Sprouts and Bacon
- **264** Grilled Artichokes

Desserts and Drinks

- **271** Duck Fat Caramels
- **272** Chaga Ice Cream
- **275** Grilled Peaches and Vanilla Ice Cream with Wildflower Honey and Black Walnuts
- **277** Stroopwafel S'mores
- **281** Smoker Strawberry Pie
- **283** Pawpaw Semifreddo
- **287** Sumac Curd with Whipped Cream and Shortbread Crumbs
- **288** Dutch Oven Charcoal-Cooked Cherry Crumble
- **291** Pawpaw Colada
- **292** Beet'tle Juice
- **295** Wild Ginger Dark and Stormy
- **296** Sumac and Sotol Margarita
- **299** Nocino (Black Walnut Liqueur)
- **301** Mead

Introduction

Fire. We started eating animals more than two million years ago. Cooking with fire came more recently, maybe a million years ago. That's a lot of time for trial and error.

It probably started with error.

Cooking over live fire connects us with our earliest ancestors. A piece of meat turning on an open grill is like a work of art. People just stand and look at it. And talk about it. And anticipate it. With an oven, you put in your roast, you close the door, and . . . you lose something. But when there's a piece of meat hanging over a fire or sizzling on the grill, you see the browning process. You see and smell the smoke. You hear the hiss of fat as it hits the coals. You see the caramelization. And then, you taste.

Nothing matches that taste. Not just the flavour but the distinct textures: the caramelized exterior, the juicy, tender interior, the smoke.

A lot has happened in a million years of trial and error. People started marinating their meat in wine or vinegar to enhance its flavour, or to mask the spoiled taste (from lack of refrigeration). Others wrapped it in banana leaves. The firepit evolved from simply cooking on coals on the ground or burying meat and cooking it in the ground. Then came the tiny perfect hibachi of Japan, the Argentinian asado—a tilted rack on which an entire animal is cooked—along with offset smokers, barrel smokers, and cold smokers. In the 1950s, when George Stephen developed the kettle grill for the Weber company, barbecuing blasted off. In fact, that first kettle grill was nicknamed "Sputnik."

But cooking with live fire doesn't have to be rocket science. You don't need a fancy barbecue. You can use something as simple as a couple of cinder blocks, with a metal grate to bridge between them and a firepit below. The rest is a mixture of patience, persistence, and instinct (and maybe a probe thermometer). Wait for those coals to be just right. If you're not happy, keep trying till you get the result you want. Soon, you'll be like our ancestors, using your senses to know when it's time to chow down. In short, live fire makes meals taste better.

Wild ingredients are so special to me because they taste nothing like their store-bought counterparts, and sometimes they don't even exist in stores. In culinary school we were taught that a recipe is an equation. If you start with the very best ingredients, you get an amazing result, with minimal manipulation. Great in equals great out. Shit in, shit out. You get the idea. And for me, wild ingredients are great ingredients.

My yearly calendar is mapped out with ingredients and the time of year they're at their best for harvesting. In my family, we have got to the point where we rarely buy meat or fish from the store. The winter is for ice fishing. Spring is for tapping maple trees and producing maple syrup, and it's also wild turkey and black bear season, as well as the best time for morels, wild leeks, watercress, stinging nettle, pheasant back mushrooms, wild trout, and walleye. Summer is full-time fishing. Come fall, I hunt a lot of Canada geese, as there is a daily bag limit but no possession limit, meaning I could have over a hundred in my freezer if I wanted to. And I want to! Duck is a family favourite, but they can be quite small, and most species have possession limits under twenty. (Check your local regulations.) Another staple in our house that I hunt in the fall is deer. A large white-tailed buck will last about six months in my house, and I usually shoot two per season. Then there's the occasional big trip I take to hunt elk, moose, wild boar, or mule deer.

This book has been inspired by my many travels, from the east coast of Newfoundland hunting moose through to Ontario chasing turkeys, hunting white-tailed deer in Manitoba, muskox in Nunavut, waterfowl in Saskatchewan, mule deer in Alberta, giant lake trout in the Northwest Territories, incredible seafood in northern British Columbia and the Haida Gwaii territory and down to the westernmost tip of Vancouver Island, to pronghorn antelope and elk in Colorado, wild hogs in Mississippi and Texas, and tundra swan in North Carolina.

I hope this book inspires you to get outside and cook over the fire!

Fire Set-Ups

For a beginner, cooking over a fire can be intimidating, especially when there are so many products on the market. Here are some things to consider when you want to cook outside. Do you want to hang out around the fire and tend to coals, or are you a "set it and forget it" type of person? Live fire tends to be for the purist, someone who wants to master the flames and perfect their barbecue. If you consider yourself a purist, I recommend spit-roasting over a firepit, asado cooking, a live-fire grill, or an offset smoker fired with wood or charcoal. If you are into technology and like to set it and forget it, there are incredible technologically advanced grills and smokers on the market, such as digital pellet smokers, that provide incredible results while making the whole job very simple.

Spit Roasting

Spit roasting is a method of cooking in which meat, fish, vegetables, or fruit are skewered with a long, usually metal rod and slowly turned over an open flame or coals. The spit can be turned by hand, but most often today it is done with a small motor. The constant turning allows for even cooking and continual basting from the juices and fat of the meat. This technique is most often associated with outdoor cooking and festive gatherings, as the spit is the showpiece. It's a perfect technique for cooking whole animals or large pieces of meat. The results are crispy and flavourful on the outside and juicy and tender on the inside.

Asado

Asado is a Spanish word that does not have a direct translation in English but refers to a traditional barbecuing technique popular in the Latin American countries of Argentina, Uruguay, and Chile. But asado is not just a cooking technique; it is a deep culinary tradition that brings people together. An asado a la cruz resembles a cross that whole animals or large cuts of meat are tied to and hung over the fire on a slight angle. The cross is rotated and flipped from time to time to ensure even cooking. The meat is periodically basted with accumulated juices or marinade to keep it moist and flavourful, and the cross can be repositioned for direct or indirect heat for perfection.

Grilling

Live-fire grilling doesn't have to be complicated or expensive. There are many live-fire grills available on the market, like the classic round Weber-style charcoal barbecue that is lightweight and inexpensive, but you can simply place a metal grate over some rocks while camping. They will both give you the same result. Live fire is mostly used for direct heat to achieve those beautiful char marks on a steak with a smoky flavour, but it can also be used for indirect heat to slowly cook a roast or larger piece of meat or fish, or large vegetables like a whole cauliflower or squash.

Plancha

Plancha is Spanish for "griddle" and usually refers to a thick steel or iron plate set over a fire. Its origins can be traced back centuries to Spain. Today, commercial flat-top griddles can be electric or gas, but I still prefer to use live fire outside. Cooking a la plancha has a huge cultural significance in Spanish and Latin cuisine and is widely used in tapas restaurants and home kitchens. The plancha itself is heated over an open flame and can reach high temperatures. A quality plancha is thick and will distribute the heat evenly for even cooking. Seafood, meat, vegetables, and even some types of bread can be cooked on a plancha. When properly seasoned, a plancha is completely nonstick, and fish and meat sear beautifully, with a perfectly crispy caramelized exterior.

Smoking

Today we associate smoking with tasty BBQ like brisket, pulled pork, and ribs, but historically it was a means of survival and was used to preserve food before refrigeration and freezing were available. Smoking can be applied with direct heat, indirect heat, and even no heat, as in cold-smoking. Smoke contains antimicrobial properties that inhibit the growth of bacteria, mould, and other pathogens on the surface of food, all while dehydrating it, which also inhibits bacteria. A wide range of foods can be smoked. The most popular are meat and fish, but cheese and vegetables also benefit from flavour-enhancing smoke.

The type of wood you choose is important, as wood imparts distinctive flavours, ranging from mild and sweet to strong and pungent. Fruitwoods such as cherry, peach, apple, and pear are mild and sweet. Hickory and mesquite woods are a classic choice, offering a much bolder and more intense flavour that is very popular in the southern states barbecue culture. Oak produces a medium smoke flavour, so it is a versatile option. Maple wood is more delicately flavoured with a mild sweetness, making it a popular choice. Avoid softwoods such as pine and spruce for your main source of heat or smoke, as they have a high resin content that produces thick smoke with unpleasant flavours. However, a small amount of cedar chips can be added for a hint of flavour in some recipes, but it should be used sparingly and with caution. Green or unseasoned wood, which has not been dried and aged, produces excessive smoke, resulting in a bitter, acrid flavour. Be sure to never use wood from poisonous plants or any chemically treated wood.

Many different types of smokers are available for home use, and choosing one may feel daunting if you are new to smoking. They range from expensive and technical to quite basic and affordable.

Charcoal Smokers

Charcoal smokers use charcoal briquettes or lump charcoal as a heat and fuel source. I recommend using natural lump charcoal; I don't like briquettes because they leave a petroleum taste. Typically, charcoal smokers have a separate container for the charcoal below a chamber where the food is placed for cooking. Charcoal smokers offer great flavour but require a lot of attention: to maintain consistent heat, you'll need to manually add charcoal and open or close the dampers to control airflow.

Electric Smokers

Electric smokers are powered by an electric heating element that burns wood, charcoal, or both. Their simplicity is great if you're learning how to smoke or you're just looking for convenience, as they offer consistent heat and temperature control. They perfectly suit the "set it and forget it" person.

Propane and Gas Smokers

Propane and gas smokers use propane or gas as the fuel source, allowing you to burn wood and/or charcoal for cooking. They are convenient and easy to use as they offer temperature control. They are usually a cabinet-style shape, with the heat and smoke coming from the bottom and the food placed on multiple racks above the heat.

Pellet Smokers

Pellet smokers can be used for both grilling and smoking. They use compressed wood pellets as a smoke and fuel source. The wood pellets come in many different wood types, offering a wide range of flavours. The pellets are fed into a hopper with an electric element and a motorized auger. A fan pushes the heat and smoke into the chamber where the food is placed. Pellet smokers offer digital controls, and some can even be connected to an app on your phone for total remote control. Pellet smokers are extremely convenient and yield great results.

Offset Smokers

An offset smoker is a traditional style of smoker that is often prized by BBQ enthusiasts. It can use wood, charcoal, or both. It consists of two chambers: the smaller one is the firebox, and it's attached by a vent to a larger chamber where the food is cooked. The vent pulls the heat and smoke into the cooking chamber and out the top. These smokers cook and flavour the food via the indirect heat and smoke from the firebox as it travels through the chamber. This style of smoking offers a "hands-on" experience and requires a lot of attention, basic knowledge of smoking, and skilled operation of the smoker. For those who appreciate the science and art of barbecue, the effort is worth it!

Barrel or Drum Smokers

Barrel or drum smokers are most commonly homemade repurposed steel drums, but now commercial drum smokers are available to purchase ready to use or as parts kits so you can build your own (the most affordable option). They can be set up horizontally or vertically. They have a charcoal basket at the bottom and cooking racks above. Smaller pieces of wood or wood chips can be placed on top of the charcoal if you like. These smokers are known for simplicity and yield great results.

Ceramic-Style Barbecues

Ceramic barbecues, such as the Big Green Egg, are renowned for their superior heat retention and insulation, allowing for precise temperature control and efficient wood or charcoal usage. The thick ceramic walls maintain consistent heat and moisture. Their versatility enables a wide range of cooking styles, including grilling, smoking, roasting, and even baking. The design and functionality of ceramic barbecues make them a standout choice for both amateur and professional outdoor cooks.

Cast-Iron Skillets

Cast iron is inexpensive hardy cookware that when cared for will last multiple lifetimes. It's old-school and has stood the test of time. However, it's heavy and can rust if not dried after washing and reseasoned periodically. Cast-iron skillets are exceptional for cooking over a fire because of their superior heat retention and even heat distribution, ensuring consistent cooking results even in the unpredictable conditions of an open flame. They can withstand high temperatures without warping or other damage. Additionally, the nonstick surface that develops with proper seasoning means a wide variety of dishes to be prepared without sticking and ensures a crispy, perfectly cooked exterior. Cast iron's versatility and resilience make it a favourite among professional chefs and outdoor cooking enthusiasts.

Stainless Steel Frying Pans

Stainless steel is a good substitute for cast iron, as it also has great heat retention and heat distribution. Stainless steel frying pans are excellent cookware for outdoor use because of their durability, versatility, and resistance to the elements. These pans are highly resistant to rust and corrosion, making them ideal for use in all kinds of weather conditions. Stainless steel's sturdy construction ensures it can withstand rough handling and high temperatures, which are common in outdoor cooking, whether you're preparing a campfire breakfast or a gourmet meal on a portable stove. Their relatively light weight and ease of cleaning and maintenance makes them a reliable and practical choice for campers, hikers, and outdoor cooks.

Cast-Iron Dutch Ovens

Dutch traders introduced these revolutionary pots to Europe and the Americas in the seventeenth century. The thick-walled heavy cast-iron pot with a tight-fitting lid can withstand high temperatures in open-fire hearths and can be placed directly in the coals. My favourite feature is the top-down cooking achieved by placing coals or burning wood directly on the flat lid. Dutch ovens can be used for stews and braises but also function like a small oven for roasting meats, fish, and vegetables. They are even great for cooking pies for dessert.

Ponds, Streams, and Lakes

I grew up in the country about an hour and a half northwest of Canada's largest city, and our little farm had a pond. I spent hours almost every day at that pond trying to catch bass, trout, frogs, and crayfish. A family friend was a pro fly fisherman and fishing guide, and he taught me how to tie flies and cast a fly rod. I unknowingly developed a connection with my food, from water to grill wrapped in foil with butter and lemon. These ingrained memories have made me who I am today. I distinctly remember that burnt caramelized lemon flavour and how the fish would be so perfectly steamed you could just slide the meat off the bones. Looking back, I probably didn't catch as many fish as I think I did, but the experience taught me a lasting lesson that I've taken with me into my career as a chef, which is simplicity. You really don't need much to make something so fresh taste wonderful.

Fishing can be a very affordable hobby, and in Canada and the United States we are truly blessed with clean freshwater lakes, ponds, rivers, and streams. Recreational fishing licences are inexpensive, and so is basic equipment. For new and eager fishing enthusiasts, find a mentor who can teach you or hire a fishing guide to show you the ropes in your area. The types of freshwater fishing that I love are spin casting, fly-fishing, downrigging, trolling, ice fishing, and bowfishing.

Spin casting is often considered the easiest and most beginner-friendly fishing technique simply because of its simplicity, and it is one of the most popular types of freshwater fishing. A rod with a spin-casting reel or "close-faced reel" is used.

Fly-fishing is more of a challenge because of its casting technique and many types of hand-tied flies. Pre-tied flies can be purchased, but the true art and challenge is tying your own. Fly fishermen will tie their own flies based on what the fish are seen feeding on.

Downrigging is done in deep lakes or in the ocean, where a heavy weight assists your line and lure to reach specific depths, ranging from just below the boat to hundreds of feet below. The downrigger has a display that shows the lure's exact depth and a motorized puller to retrieve the weight.

Trolling is done in some types of boat, canoes, or kayaks. Your lure is pulled behind you and moves with the motion of your boat, which makes the lure or bait look like a wounded or maimed fish.

Ice fishing is one of my most favourite winter pastimes. It is so much fun and a great social activity, and is especially great for folks who don't have a boat. You can walk out or snowmobile miles onto the ice and fish in spots that are usually inaccessible. Pop-up tents or fish shacks are erected and secured to the ice, a large auger is used to drill a hole through the ice, you drop down a line, and that's it! Heaters, stoves, and cookouts are recommended, and your beer always stays cold.

Bowfishing is a cross between archery and fishing. A reel is attached to a bow, and string is attached to the rear of a specialized arrow. Unfortunately, catch-and-release isn't possible with bowfishing, so make sure you properly identify your target species and follow local regulations. Where I live, carp are so abundant there is no limit. Despite popular belief, carp are delicious, and I hope I can encourage you to try my smoked carp recipe on page 30.

Cooking fish over the fire can be as simple or technical as you like. Once you catch your fish, remove the guts as quickly as possible, then remove the scales and get the fish on ice in a cooler. Prepare your fire and season the fish with salt. There are endless ways to cook from here. Placing the whole fish directly on an oiled grill will give you a smoky flavour with nice char marks. Cooking in an aluminum foil or parchment paper package with indirect heat will steam the fish. Or you can use a stick or metal skewer and roast a whole fish directly over the fire. You can cut off the fillets, use pliers to remove the pin bones, and sear on a plancha for a crispier skin. A more technical approach could be baking in rock salt for a briny-flavoured, beautifully steamed fish like on page 70.

North America is home to abundant freshwater species that are delicious to eat, such as bass, trout, catfish, panfish, pike, walleye, and salmon. Each species has its characteristic habitat and behaviour, giving anglers a wide range of fishing experiences. Time on the water by yourself secluded in nature is meditative, or it can be a wonderful way to spend time with family and friends. Whether you are casting a line in a quiet stream or having adrenaline-pumping battles with trophy-size fish, it is a pastime that fosters a deep connection with nature and your food.

How to Cook a Whole Fish

Cooking a whole fish may seem like a daunting task, but it's the easiest method and requires very little prep. There are a number of ways to cook a whole fish: over the fire; on a grill with direct heat; tied with string or wire and hung near the fire's indirect heat; in a grill basket; baked in salt; or wrapped in parchment paper or foil. In the next pages I will demonstrate these cooking methods. It's hard to give exact cooking times per pound because every scenario is slightly different: Wood versus charcoal versus gas? Is it in a wood oven or over a fire? Is it windy? You just have to do it.

Like meat, fish cooked whole on the bone tastes better. The fish meat around the bones has a sticky texture and depth of flavour that's lost once a fish is filleted and boned. The most flavourful part is the head, specifically the cheek meat, eyes, and tongue. Trust me. It's something you really need to experience for yourself.

Fire cooking can't be rushed. Give yourself time. Use your senses. Look at the eyes, the skin, the head, and gills of the fish. The eyes will turn white, the jaw and cheekbones will curl, and the skin will crisp and pull back. A probe thermometer is very helpful. An internal temperature of 130°F (55°C) indicates medium doneness, and after resting, the fish should be wonderfully flaky.

Whole Fish

1 whole fish, gutted and scaled

Olive oil, for brushing

Kosher salt and black pepper

Cook the Fish

Prepare a wood fire in an outdoor grill or firepit and let the wood burn down until red embers are visible. Set a grate over the fire.

If your fish has been stored in the fridge, bring it to room temperature for at least 30 minutes before cooking. Cooking fish (or meat) from room temperature will ensure more even cooking.

If you caught the fish, you need to remove the guts and scales. Cut along the belly of the fish, from behind the jaw all the way to the anal fin, and pull all the contents out. (Reserve the roe if desired and follow the recipe for cured salmon roe on page 55.) Using a scaling tool or the back of a knife, rub the skin of the fish from the tail towards the head. If you're indoors, I recommend scaling the fish in the sink under cold running water to avoid making a mess. Once scaled, pat the fish dry with paper towel.

Brush both sides of the fish with olive oil to help crisp the skin and prevent it from sticking to the grill grate. Season both sides of the fish with a big pinch each of salt and pepper. Gently lay the fish on the grill grate and cook, without moving it, until the skin is crispy, easily lifts away from the grate, and has grill marks. This should take at least 5 to 8 minutes, depending on the size of the fish. A small trout might require 5 minutes per side, whereas a 15-pound (6.8 kg) salmon might require 10 minutes per side. Fish skin is incredibly sticky until it's cooked, at which point it will release from the grill. Test by gently lifting the fish with metal tongs or a metal fish spatula. If the skin is still sticking to the grate, leave it to cook longer. If the skin is charred and easily lifts, carefully turn the fish and cook on the other side until the fish appears cooked, and a probe thermometer inserted into the thickest part of the fish reaches 130°F (55°C). The skin will look roasted and crispy. Serve the fish with a shower of chopped fresh herbs, fresh lemon for squeezing, and your favourite sides.

Grilled Brook Trout

Brook trout is a beautiful fish known for its vibrant colours, especially the reddish-pink spots on its side and its green-and-brown marbled side and back. They vary in size depending on their age and can be quite exciting to catch, particularly on a fly rod. Brook trout like to hide in the cover of rocks, logs, and banks of freshwater streams, rivers, lakes, and ponds. They are prized by anglers and cooks for their rich, flavourful flesh that's tender and flaky. Grilled whole and served with chili aioli is a simple and tasty meal. Make the aioli ahead of time, then this can be prepared on the riverbank for a shore lunch.

Note: If your fish is stored in the fridge, bring to room temperature for at least 30 minutes before cooking. Cooking fish (or meat) from room temperature will ensure more even cooking. (Ensure your fish is scaled. If not, you can rub the skin with the back of a knife or fish scaler, rubbing back and forth along the skin to remove the scales. I like to do this in the sink under cold running water. After scaling, pat dry the fish with paper towel.)

SERVES **4**

Make the Chili Aioli

To a food processor, add the egg, garlic, mustard, and salt. Process until blended. With the processor running, slowly stream in the vegetable oil and blend until emulsified. The mixture should be thick and creamy. Add the lemon juice and chili paste and blend until incorporated. Taste and adjust seasoning with more salt, lemon, or chili paste, if desired. Store in an airtight container in the fridge for up to 1 week.

Grill the Fish

Prepare a charcoal or wood fire in an outdoor grill or firepit and set a grate over it. Allow 15 to 20 minutes for the charcoal to burn down to a bed of red coals. Wood takes longer, depending on the size of logs you are using. You want to cook over red coals, not flames.

Drizzle both sides of the fish with vegetable oil and generously season with salt. You can stuff the belly with herbs and lemon slices, if desired. Brush the hot grill grate, then wipe it with an oiled paper towel.

Chili Aioli

1 large egg

2 cloves garlic, crushed

1 tablespoon (15 mL) Dijon mustard

1 teaspoon (5 mL) kosher salt

2 cups (500 mL) vegetable oil

Juice of 2 lemons

2 tablespoons (30 mL) roasted red chili paste

Grilled Brook Trout

2 whole brook trout (2 to 3 pounds/900 g to 1.35 kg each, ranging from 12 to 18 inches/ 30 to 45 cm), gutted and scaled

Vegetable oil

Kosher salt

Fresh herb sprigs and lemon slices (optional)

recipe continues

Place the trout on the grill grate and cook, without moving it, until the skin on the bottom is crispy with dark grill marks, at least 5 minutes. Using a metal fish spatula or metal tongs, gently turn the fish and cook until the other side is crispy to the touch. The fish is perfectly cooked when the internal temperature reaches 130° to 135°F (55° to 57°C) on a probe thermometer.

Using a sharp knife, cut along the back of the fish just to cut through the skin. Gently remove the fillet with a spoon or pull off with your hands. When the fish is perfectly cooked, the flesh will easily pull away from the bones, which will be left on the spine. Carefully pull away the spine to reveal the second fillet. Serve immediately with your favourite sides.

Fire-Roasted Kelp-Planked Steelhead Trout

Steelhead are in the rainbow trout family but behave like salmon: unlike rainbows, which live in fresh water their whole lives, steelhead trout migrate to the ocean, change colour, and get much larger than a rainbow. This dish is fun to make and a real showpiece perfect for a party or family gathering. You will need a cedar plank and some large pieces of kelp, a few nails or tie wire to affix the fish to the wood, and of course fire. A probe thermometer is a great tool to check the doneness as the trout slowly smokes by the fire.

All kelp is edible—unlike mushrooms where some species are toxic—but some kelp is more nutritious and tastier than others. For this dish I use giant kelp, which is sightly salty and earthy and has its own subtle fishy essence. The moist kelp also helps to keep the cedar plank from burning. The smoke from the wood fire and the salinity from the kelp combined with the sweetness of char-grilled lemon on a beach makes for a truly epic meal.

SERVES 4 to 6

Prepare a wood fire in an outdoor firepit and let the wood slightly burn down until red embers are visible, 20 to 30 minutes. I recommend using wood instead of charcoal as heat is needed from wood's flames.

Season the fish with salt and pepper. Lay some kelp (if using) on the cedar plank. Place the fish on the kelp, then nail the fillet at the top and bottom, and once in the middle to firmly affix it to the wood.

Prop the plank with the fish near the fire so that it gets some smoke as well as indirect warm heat. Cook to medium-rare to medium doneness, until a probe thermometer inserted into the thickest part of the fillet reaches 125° to 135°F (52° to 57°C), 30 to 60 minutes, depending on the thickness of the fish and proximity to the heat. Once cooked, gently remove the nails if you can or pull the fillet from the board. Slice the fish and serve with fresh or grilled lemon halves.

Special Equipment

1 cedar plank slightly larger than your fillet

Nails or tie wire

---

1 large skin-on steelhead trout fillet (about 4 pounds/1.8 kg)

Sea salt and black pepper

Large pieces of giant kelp (optional)

Lemon halves, fresh or grilled, for serving

Smoked Carp

A friend of mine took me bowfishing for these giant freshwater fish that can grow to lengths over 3 feet (1 m) and weigh over 100 pounds (45 kg). I have heard that these giants are considered delicacies in Europe and Asia, but in North America they are regarded as less than desirable. I love a culinary challenge, so I opted to keep one and experiment. Carp have thick skin and tough scales. They have Y-bones much like a pike, but if you cut the bones out properly, making fillets isn't a problem. This fish is incredibly fatty and meaty in texture, and to my surprise it was delicious when brined and smoked. The meat flakes apart but it's more like pulled pork in texture. In Portugal you can buy canned carp packed in oil, and it is delicious.

SERVES 4 to 6 AS AN APPETIZER

---

4 cups (1 L) water

1½ cups (375 mL) Diamond Crystal kosher salt

½ cup (125 mL) granulated sugar

2 pounds (900 g) skinless carp fillet

For serving

Pickled wild leeks

Pickled green beans

Pickled jalapeño peppers

Dijon mustard

Fresh baguette or your favourite crusty bread or crackers

In a large bowl, whisk together the water, salt, and sugar until dissolved. Add the carp to the brine, cover, and refrigerate for 24 hours.

If using a digital pellet smoker, preheat your smoker at 225°F (110°C). If using a live-fire offset smoker, prepare a fire and let the flames die down, then partially close the air vent and flue vents to maintain the heat at 225°F (110°C).

Remove the fish from the brine and pat it dry. Discard the brine. Place the carp in the smoker and maintain the heat at 225°F (110°C) so the fish smokes but doesn't overcook. Check the internal temperature after 30 minutes. The fish is done when a probe thermometer inserted into the thickest part reaches 165°F (75°C). The fish will be golden in colour and will have slightly shrunk in size because of losing moisture. Remove the fish from the smoker and let cool. The smoked carp can be vacuum-sealed tightly and stored in the fridge for up to 1 month or in the freezer for up to 6 months.

Serve the smoked carp with pickled wild leeks, pickled green beans, pickled jalapeños, mustard, and bread or crackers.

Grilled Baitfish

This is one of my favourite snacks when I'm craving fish. The recipe is so simple, and the star is the fish. Baitfish are packed with flavour, and grilling them whole boosts that flavour. In North America, people somehow lost the taste for whole fish on the bone and the preference changed to eating boneless fillets. It's pleasant to eat a fillet, but the compromise is flavour. These tiny fish are deliciously oily and salty, and the bones are so thin I don't notice them when eating.

SERVES 2 AS AN APPETIZER

Prepare a charcoal or wood fire in an outdoor grill or firepit and let the flames die down with red embers visible. Set a grate over the fire. Alternatively, preheat a gas grill to at least 500°F (260°C).

Thread each fish on 2 skewers, inserting the first skewer about ½ inch (1 cm) from one end of the fish and the second skewer about 1 inch (2.5 cm) farther along the body of the fish. You should get 10 or so fish on each pair of skewers. Brush the fish with olive oil and season with salt.

Brush the grill grate with olive oil so the fish don't stick. Lay the skewers on the grill along with the lemon halves cut sides down. Grill the fish until grill marks are visible, 2 to 3 minutes. Using a metal spatula, gently turn the skewers and continue to grill until cooked with grill marks visible, another 2 to 3 minutes. Remove from the heat.

To serve, squeeze the grilled lemon over the fish skewers and garnish with the parsley.

Special Equipment

Large wooden skewers

1 pound (450 g) baitfish

Olive oil, for brushing

2 teaspoons (10 mL) sea salt

1 lemon, cut in half

2 tablespoons (30 mL) chopped fresh flat-leaf parsley

Grilled Lake Erie Whitefish

Whitefish is an underrated culinary gem that is native to the Great Lakes of Canada and the United States. I am proud to feature local wild-caught fish at our restaurant and don't understand why so many restaurants import fish like Mediterranean sea bass and sea bream when we have very similar white-fleshed fish right here at home. Not only is whitefish local, but its fishery on Lake Erie is abundant and sustainable. This fish is great for grilling and pan-searing for a crispy skin, and its roe is delicious cured and served with the crispy fillets. This species is also fun to catch on open "hardwater" in the cold of winter ice fishing. Whitefish roe or "caviar" are small yellow translucent pearls with a briny and elegant flavour that enhances the flavour of this dish.

SERVES 4

4 skin-on whitefish fillets (6 ounces/170 g each)

Sea salt

Olive oil, for frying and drizzling

2 tablespoons (30 mL) unsalted butter

2 lemon wedges, for squeezing

½ pound (225 g) garlic scapes

¼ cup (125 mL) sour cream

4 ounces (115 g) cured whitefish roe

1 tablespoon (15 mL) chopped fresh flat-leaf parsley

Prepare a charcoal or wood fire in an outdoor grill or firepit and let the flames die down with red embers visible. Set a grate over the fire. Alternatively, preheat a gas grill to 500°F (260°C). Preheat a large, heavy cast-iron skillet or plancha.

Season the fish with a big pinch of salt on both sides.

Add 1 tablespoon (15 mL) of olive oil to the hot pan. Place the whitefish skin side down in the pan and sear until crispy on the bottom, 2 to 3 minutes. Gently test the corner with a metal fish spatula to see whether it will lift easily (if you flip the fish before the bottom is crisp, the skin will stick). When the skin is golden and crispy, push the spatula down towards the pan, push under the skin, and turn the fish. Add the butter and squeeze some lemon into the pan beside the fish (not directly on the crispy skin) and let the butter and lemon reduce for another 1 to 2 minutes. Remove the fish from the pan.

In the same pan (no need to wipe it), add the garlic scapes with a splash of olive oil and more lemon juice, and sauté until tender, about 3 minutes.

Transfer the garlic scapes to plates and serve the fish on top. Place 1 tablespoon (15 mL) of sour cream on top of each serving of fish, then top each with 1 tablespoon (15 mL) of the whitefish roe. Sprinkle with the parsley and drizzle with olive oil. Serve immediately.

Fried Perch with Gribiche Sauce

I love ice-fishing for perch in the dead of winter. When the perch bite is on, it's a heck of a good time in the ice hut with friends. The beer stays cold outside, there's always a pot of chili on to warm everyone up, and the fish-fryer is working overtime. Perch is the perfect size for fast-frying appetizers, as they cook quickly and end up perfectly crispy. My favourite accompaniment for fried crispy perch is creamy rich gribiche sauce, a homemade tartar sauce with chopped hard-boiled eggs.

Note: For safety purposes, deep-frying outside is safer than indoors when using a pot. Always use a deep-frying thermometer attached to the pot to monitor the temperature. Cooking with a propane burner or live fire needs to be done with care.

SERVES 10 AS AN APPETIZER

Make the Gribiche Sauce

To a blender, add the raw egg, mustard, kosher salt, and black pepper and blend until smooth. With the blender running, slowly stream in the vegetable oil and blend until incorporated. Add the lemon juice and blend again. Transfer to a medium bowl. Fold in the parsley, capers, cornichon, hard-boiled egg and shallot. Reserve, covered, in the fridge until ready to use.

Bread and Fry the Perch

Heat the vegetable oil in a large pot on a propane burner until it reaches 350°F (175°C) on a deep-frying thermometer. Alternatively, prepare a charcoal or wood fire in an outdoor grill or firepit, set a grate over the fire, and heat the pot of oil.

Meanwhile, in a large bowl, stir together the flour, cornmeal, sea salt, paprika, and cayenne pepper. Add the perch fillets, 5 at a time, and press down into the seasoned flour to coat. Turn and coat the other side. Remove the fish from the breading and lay on a baking sheet. Set aside the bowl of breading.

When the oil is nearing 350°F (175°C), dredge the perch in the flour mixture a second time. Carefully drop half the fillets into the hot oil and deep-fry until crispy and dark golden brown, 4 to 5 minutes. Using a wire strainer, remove the fried fish from the oil, shake off the oil, and place on a baking sheet lined with paper towel to absorb excess oil. Season with sea salt. Repeat to deep-fry the remaining fish.

Garnish each fillet with a spoonful of the gribiche sauce and some parsley. Serve immediately.

Gribiche Sauce

1 large egg

2 teaspoons (10 mL) Dijon mustard

1 teaspoon (5 mL) kosher salt

½ teaspoon (2 mL) freshly ground black pepper

1 cup (250 mL) vegetable oil

Juice of 1 lemon

2 tablespoons (30 mL) finely chopped fresh flat-leaf parsley, plus more for garnish

2 teaspoons (10 mL) finely chopped drained capers

2 teaspoons (10 mL) finely chopped cornichon

1 large hard-boiled egg, finely chopped

1 small shallot, finely diced

Fried Perch

4 quarts (4 L) vegetable oil, for frying

2 cups (500 mL) all-purpose flour

1 cup (250 mL) cornmeal

2 tablespoons (30 mL) sea salt, plus more for seasoning

2 tablespoons (30 mL) sweet paprika

1 teaspoon (5 mL) cayenne pepper

20 perch fillets

Arctic Char Torched with Soy and Honey

Arctic char is a cold-water species that is a prized catch, partly because you have to travel to the Arctic to harvest them. Closely related to salmon and trout, it inhabits the frigid temperatures of the Far North's oceans and rivers. The pristine water conditions and the fish's diet contribute to its incredible flavour and stunning appearance. Char is pink to vibrant orangey-red with colourful spots along its silvery skin. Females appear silver, while the males have a darker complexion on their backs and fiery-red belly and mouth. Char can be enjoyed raw, smoked, grilled, pan-seared, or poached, making it an incredible fish to work with. Locally, a favourite way to eat it is sashimi-style raw dipped in soy sauce, which is the inspiration for this dish.

This dish can be made under a broiler, in a very hot pizza oven, or by simply holding a blazing hot coal above the fish with tongs. I like to blow-torch a piece of charcoal just above the fish to give it a hint of charcoal flavour. If you're not outside, make sure your hood fan is turned to high!

SERVES 4

Special Equipment

1 long piece of charcoal
Kitchen torch

½ cup (125 mL) pure liquid honey

⅓ cup (75 mL) soy sauce

4 skinless Arctic char fillets (6 ounces/170 g each)

1 tablespoon (15 mL) unsalted butter

1 tablespoon (15 mL) olive oil

1 bunch black kale, chopped

2 cloves garlic, crushed

Pinch of red chili flakes

Kosher salt and freshly cracked black pepper

Kosher salt

Juice of 1 lemon

In a small saucepan, combine the honey and soy sauce. Bring to a boil and cook, without stirring, until reduced to about ¾ cup (175 mL). Remove from the heat and let cool to room temperature.

Place the Arctic char on a baking sheet. Brush the cooled glaze over the fish and let sit for 5 minutes.

Melt the butter with the olive oil in a large stainless steel frying pan over high heat. Add the kale, garlic, chili flakes, and salt and black pepper to taste. Sauté until the kale is tender and wilted, 3 to 4 minutes. Sprinkle over the lemon juice and stir to combine.

Working outdoors and using metal tongs, hold a piece of charcoal over the fish and torch the charcoal. The torch flames will heat up the coal and the flames will rebound off the coal, picking up some smoke and cooking the fish. The glaze will sizzle, reduce, and stick to the fish. For a thicker glaze, you can brush the fish with more glaze a couple of times during this process. Cook the fish to desired doneness. (Alternatively, cook the fish under a broiler or in a 700°F/370°C pizza oven.) I prefer to eat char fairly rare, but it is still very enjoyable cooked medium or medium-well, if preferred.

Serve the fish on top of the sautéed kale.

Blackened Catfish with Creole Sauce

This dish has iconic roots in Louisiana and Cajun cuisine, and its creation is attributed to Chef Paul Prudhomme in the 1970s. The technique of blackening involves coating food with a spice blend and searing it in a hot skillet until the spices create a dark, flavourful crust. The intense flavours helped put Cajun and Creole cuisine on the culinary map, inspiring chefs around the world to experiment with the bold seasoning and innovative technique.

I was introduced to "jugging" for catfish—a popular method to hook these tasty fish—on the Tombigbee River in Mississippi. The method involves tying a piece of fishing line with a weight and baited hook to a floating jug. The jug is laid flat on the water, and when a catfish takes the bait the jug flips up, letting you know a fish is on. Multiple jugs are tossed out along the river. You park your boat up on a sandbar, light a fire for the upcoming catfish haul, and drink beer. It is the best time, outdoors with friends cooking on the river. And the catfish tastes incredible.

SERVES **4**

Creole Sauce

1 tablespoon (15 mL) vegetable oil

1 tablespoon (15 mL) unsalted butter

1 medium yellow onion, diced

2 stalks celery, diced

1 green bell pepper, diced

4 cloves garlic, minced

1 tablespoon (15 mL) sweet paprika

1 teaspoon (5 mL) cayenne pepper

1 teaspoon (5 mL) chopped fresh thyme

1 teaspoon (5 mL) chopped fresh oregano

1 cup (250 mL) dark chicken stock

1 can (28 ounces/796 mL) diced tomatoes

3 bay leaves

1 teaspoon (5 mL) kosher salt

Pinch of freshly ground black pepper

Blackened Catfish

¼ cup (60 mL) sweet or hot paprika

1 tablespoon (15 mL) dried thyme

1 teaspoon (5 mL) dried oregano

1 teaspoon (5 mL) onion powder

1 teaspoon (5 mL) garlic powder

1 teaspoon (5 mL) cayenne pepper

1 teaspoon (5 mL) freshly ground black pepper

1 teaspoon (5 mL) kosher salt

4 skinless catfish fillets (6 ounces/170 g each)

1 tablespoon (15 mL) vegetable oil

1 tablespoon (15 mL) unsalted butter

1 lemon, cut in half, for squeezing

Steamed Rice

1 cup (250 mL) white rice

1½ cups (375 mL) water

Sautéed Okra

1 tablespoon (15 mL) vegetable oil

1 cup (250 mL) sliced okra

recipe continues

Prepare a charcoal or wood fire in an outdoor grill or firepit and let the flames die down with red embers visible. Set a grate over the fire. Alternatively, preheat a gas grill to 500°F (260°C).

Make the Creole Sauce

Heat a medium pot over high heat for 2 to 3 minutes. Add the vegetable oil, butter, and the onion and cook, stirring occasionally, for 2 minutes. Add the celery and bell pepper and continue cooking, stirring occasionally, until the vegetables soften, 3 to 4 minutes. Add the garlic and stir to combine. Add the paprika, cayenne pepper, thyme, and oregano. Give it a stir, then add the stock, diced tomatoes, bay leaves, salt, and black pepper. Stir to combine, then reduce the heat to medium and cook, uncovered, stirring occasionally, until the sauce has reduced slightly and is thick like tomato sauce, 10 to 15 minutes. Discard the bay leaves.

Prepare the Catfish

In a medium bowl, stir together the paprika, thyme, oregano, onion powder, garlic powder, cayenne pepper, black pepper, and salt.

Place the catfish on a baking sheet and generously season both sides with the spice mixture. Let sit to marinate while you make the rice.

Make the Steamed Rice

In a medium pot, combine the rice and water and bring to a boil over high heat. Once boiling, cover with a lid, reduce the heat to low, and cook until the water has been absorbed and the rice is tender, 10 to 12 minutes. Remove from the heat but keep covered until ready to serve.

Fry the Catfish

Heat a large, heavy stainless steel frying pan or cast-iron skillet over high heat for at least 5 minutes. Add the vegetable oil. Using metal tongs to avoid splashing the oil, carefully place the fish in the hot pan. Fry, without moving the fish, until visibly dark around the edges and blackened on the bottom, 3 to 4 minutes. Turn the fillets, then add the butter to the pan and continue cooking until the fish is tender, flaky, and cooked through, another 3 to 4 minutes. Add a squeeze of lemon juice to finish. Remove the fish from the pan. Wipe the pan clean with paper towel.

Sauté the Okra and Serve

Return the pan to high heat. Add the vegetable oil and okra and sauté for 2 to 3 minutes until tender.

Serve the blackened catfish on top of the rice. Spoon the Creole sauce over the fish and top with the sautéed okra.

Brown Trout with Sweet Pea Risotto

Brown trout are a coveted freshwater sport-fishing species that are equally sought-after for the dinner table. There are several subspecies, and their appearance can vary depending on their habitat, though they generally range from yellowish-brown to olive-coloured sides to sometimes golden in colour. Brown trout is highly regarded for its fatty, firm, yet flaky texture and its delicate, mild taste. The best time to catch these beauties is in the spring and early summer.

I find bright green produce is best to pair with this fish. I wanted to play with the sweetness of the peas from my garden mixed with a creamy, rich risotto and a beautiful piece of crispy-skin trout on top. It's simple but so big on flavour.

SERVES **4**

Prepare a charcoal or wood fire in an outdoor grill or firepit and let the flames die down with red embers visible. Set a grate over the fire. Alternatively, preheat a gas grill to 500°F (260°C).

Start the Sweet Pea Risotto

Fill a medium bowl with ice water. Bring a medium pot of salted water to a boil over high heat. Add 1 cup (250 mL) of the peas to the boiling water and cook for 2 minutes or until tender. Drain the peas and plunge them into the ice water to stop the cooking. Drain the peas again. Transfer to a blender and purée until smooth. Set aside.

To the same medium pot over medium-high heat, add the rice and vegetable oil and cook while stirring to toast the rice, 2 to 3 minutes. When you see the first sign of colour on the rice, add the shallot and 1 tablespoon (15 mL) of the butter and cook, stirring occasionally, for 1 to 2 minutes, until the shallot is softened. Add the garlic, give it a stir, then pour in the white wine. Once the wine has been absorbed, slowly add the vegetable stock in 2 additions, stirring frequently until each addition is absorbed before adding more. (Stirring frequently will ensure the rice doesn't stick and will give the risotto a creamy texture.) Once all the liquid has been absorbed, remove from the heat, cover, and set aside while you make the beurre blanc and cook the fish.

Make the Beurre Blanc

In a small saucepan, combine the white wine, cream, and bay leaves. Bring to a boil over high heat, without stirring, and boil until the mixture is reduced and the cream begins to thicken, about 5 minutes. Discard the bay leaves. Reduce the heat to low and whisk in the butter, 1 or 2 cubes at a time, whisking until incorporated before adding more. Finish the sauce with a squeeze of lemon and a pinch of salt. Remove from the heat and keep warm.

Sweet Pea Risotto

1¼ cups (300 mL) shelled fresh peas, divided

1 cup (250 mL) arborio rice

1 tablespoon (15 mL) vegetable oil

1 small shallot, minced

4 tablespoons (60 mL) unsalted butter, divided

2 cloves garlic, minced

½ cup (125 mL) dry white wine

1 cup (250 mL) vegetable stock

4 ounces (115 g) grated Parmesan cheese

Beurre Blanc

½ cup (125 mL) dry white wine

¼ cup (60 mL) heavy (35%) cream

2 bay leaves

½ pound (225 g/1 cup/250 mL) unsalted butter, cut into cubes

½ lemon, for squeezing

Pinch of kosher salt

Pan-Fried Brown Trout

4 skin-on brown trout fillets (6 ounces/170 g each)

Sea salt

2 tablespoons (30 mL) olive oil

2 tablespoons (30 mL) unsalted butter, divided

2 sprigs fresh thyme

Juice of ½ lemon

recipe continues

Pan-Fry the Brown Trout

Season both sides of the trout fillets with salt. Heat a large cast-iron skillet or plancha over the fire. Add the olive oil to the pan. Place the fillets skin side down in the hot pan. Add 1 tablespoon (15 mL) of the butter and the thyme and cook until the skin is crispy, 3 to 4 minutes. Gently turn the fillets. Add the remaining 1 tablespoon (15 mL) butter and the lemon juice and continue cooking for another minute. Remove from the heat.

Finish the Risotto and Serve

Return the risotto to medium heat. Stirring constantly, add the pea purée and the remaining ¼ cup (60 mL) peas. Once the risotto is hot, stir in the remaining 3 tablespoons (45 mL) butter and the Parmesan until combined.

To serve, spoon the risotto into shallow bowls or rimmed plates. Place the fish crispy skin side up on top of the risotto. Spoon the butter sauce around the fish and risotto.

Saltwater Fish

Saltwater Fishing

I grew up in rural Ontario, in Canada, an extremely long way from any salt water. However, my father lived in California, and I vividly remember fishing off the coast of Long Beach in his friend's little centre-console Boston Whaler. I can recall the rolling waves and the excitement of being on the vast open ocean. The flying fish were jumping, and I had never seen anything like that before in my life. One fish landed right in our boat. We caught a lot of barracuda, a couple of smaller tuna, and a small shark. It truly is incredible how experiences in the outdoors can stay with you for a lifetime. I certainly don't remember the movies I went to see with friends and family over the years, but I can tell you exactly what fish we caught on every fishing trip I've ever been on. I probably am a little foggy on size—they always seem bigger in my memory!

Cooking these fish over a fire really is delicious. Some require a lot less cooking than freshwater fish. Tuna and swordfish, for example, tend to dry out if cooked too much and benefit from a very light sear so they're served blue-rare. Naturally, marine fish have higher levels of sodium in their bodies, and that can be tasted while eating. Subtle sweetness and salinity with a hint of charcoal smoke is a beautiful combination. It's often recommended that you freeze saltwater fish before consuming rare or raw, but the risk of parasites in saltwater fish is much lower than in freshwater fish.

Some of my best fishing memories have been fishing in the Pacific Ocean off the coast of Alaska and British Columbia. Here is a great place to use a downrigger to troll for salmon and ling cod. Halibut is also caught with the aid of a downrigger, but the boat is stationary, as jigging is used for halibut. Halibut tend to hang out on the ocean floor, so big, heavy hooks are baited with fish trimmings, scraps, or guts and dropped down to the bottom of the ocean. I have been warned many times that halibut are not fun to catch, and that's something you can't truly understand until you catch one for yourself. Landing a halibut is like pulling up a mattress from the bottom of the ocean. There isn't much excitement with jumping out of the water or fighting back—it's just deadweight. The beauty, however, is in the meal. Their delicate white tender fillets make a magnificent meal, perfect for the grill.

Salmon have proved to be the most exciting to catch. King (or chinook) salmon are the largest of the species and will put your fishing skills to the test. Landing a king salmon is an exhilarating experience, given the fish's size, strength, and acrobatic leaps. The initial strike when they take the bait is forceful, followed by a long, fast run—the reel screams as the fish takes the line at an incredible speed to hundreds of feet away from the boat. Reeling the fish back requires constant tension of the line to avoid the fish spitting or shaking off the hook.

A give-and-take battle can last upwards of thirty minutes to reel in a fish over 30 pounds (13.6 kg). It is truly a memorable and rewarding experience that showcases the thrill of sport fishing. Salmon is a versatile fish, and there are many ways to cook it with fire. It can be cured and cold-smoked, sweet-cured, or hot-smoked for salmon candy (see Coho Salmon Candy, page 69) or simply grilled to perfection and served a little on the rare to medium side to showcase its succulent fatty texture.

Downrigging isn't the only way to fish the ocean. Striped bass, native to the Atlantic coast, are catchable on the top water and in the shallows close to rocky shores or under bridges. Anglers use a variety of tackle and techniques to catch these fish, such as live bait or lures and either baitcasting, jigging, or trolling. Striped bass are known for their aggressive strikes, and fishing them can be exciting and challenging.

Grilling or cooking over an open fire allows for versatile seasoning, from the simplest preparation with just salt and pepper to more complex marinades and spice rubs. Visually appealing grill marks, and seeing the coals and flames, stimulates the appetite and heightens the whole dining experience.

Grilled King Salmon with Roasted Garlic Compound Butter and Sautéed Sweet Peas

The Pacific Ocean is home to the remarkable king (or chinook) salmon, which can grow to be anywhere between 10 and 80 pounds (4.5 to 36 kg). Catching one is the experience of a lifetime: they are a feisty, aggressive fish to reel in. Some fishing clubs and guides prohibit keeping king salmon over 30 pounds (13.6 kg), called tyee, meaning "chief," because they are typically the adult breeding size. The king's life cycle is usually three to five years, and they return only once to fresh water to spawn in the rivers where they themselves were conceived.

King salmon is a perfect fish for grilling because of its rich fat content. (Leaner species such as coho and pink salmon lend themselves better to curing and cold-smoking rather than cooking.) King salmon skin is delicious; I like salty crispy fish skin, so I'm generous with the salt. This recipe uses a compound butter as the "sauce" for the dish. These flavoured butters are made ahead of time and can be kept in the fridge or the freezer until needed. When placed on fish at the very end of cooking, the butter melts, adding its wonderful rich flavour to your fish.

SERVES 4 to 6

Make the Compound Butter

Cut a 12-inch (30 cm) square of foil and plastic wrap or wax paper. Place the plastic wrap or wax paper on top of the foil.

Preheat the oven to 400°F (200°C).

Trim about ¼ inch (5 mm) off the top of the heads of garlic to expose the cloves, keeping the head intact. Drizzle the olive oil over the exposed cloves. Wrap in the foil and roast until the garlic is golden and soft, about 45 minutes. Using a small spoon, extract the garlic cloves and squeeze the skin to pop out the roasted garlic.

In a medium bowl, combine the roasted garlic cloves, butter, parsley, salt, cayenne pepper, and lemon zest and juice. Lightly mash the roasted garlic cloves with a spatula against the side of the bowl; the garlic should be chunky. Stir to combine. Scoop the butter mixture onto the reserved lined foil and shape into a 1-inch (2.5 cm) thick log lengthwise across the foil. Roll the butter log inside the wrap and twist the ends of the foil to tighten the butter and squeeze out any air pockets. Transfer to the fridge and chill for at least 1 hour to firm up the butter. The compound butter can be stored in the fridge for up to 1 week or in the freezer for up to 3 months. (The butter can be sliced frozen.)

Compound Butter

2 heads garlic

1 tablespoon (15 mL) olive oil

½ pound (225 g/1 cup/250 mL) unsalted butter, at room temperature

2 tablespoons (30 mL) chopped fresh flat-leaf parsley

1 teaspoon (5 mL) sea salt

Pinch of cayenne pepper

Zest and juice of 1 lemon

Grilled King Salmon

2½ pounds (1.125 kg) skin-on king salmon fillet

Olive oil, for brushing

Kosher or sea salt and black pepper

Sautéed Sweet Peas

1 tablespoon (15 mL) olive oil

3 cups (750 mL) shelled sweet peas

Pinch of sea salt

Pinch of freshly ground black pepper

1 bunch red radishes, thinly sliced, for garnish

recipe continues

Grill the Salmon

Prepare a charcoal or wood fire in an outdoor grill or firepit and let the flames die down with red embers visible. Set a grate over the fire. Alternatively, preheat a gas grill to 500°F (260°C).

Brush both sides of the salmon with olive oil and season evenly with salt and pepper. Brush the hot grill grate, then wipe it with an oiled paper towel.

Place the salmon skin side up diagonally on the grill grate and sear, without moving the fish, for 3 to 4 minutes. Using a metal spatula, gently lift a corner of the fillet to check whether there are dark grill marks and whether the fish is sticking. If it is sticking, allow more cooking time; the fish will easily come off the grill once it has seared properly. Using a metal spatula and tongs, rotate the fillet 90 degrees for a diamond grill pattern. Cook for another 3 to 4 minutes, until dark grill marks form.

Meanwhile, remove the compound butter from the fridge and cut crosswise into ¼-inch (5 mm) thick slices.

Using a metal spatula and tongs, gently turn the fish skin side down and cook for another 5 minutes or until the skin is crispy and golden. Salmon is a perfect fish eaten at medium doneness (130°F/55°C), but you can cook it to your liking. Place the sliced butter on top of the salmon for the last 1 minute of cooking. (Alternatively, top the fish with the butter immediately after serving.)

Meanwhile, Sauté the Sweet Peas

While the salmon is cooking, preheat a large cast-iron skillet for 2 minutes on the grill next to the fish or on a separate burner. Once the skillet is hot, add the olive oil, peas, and salt and pepper. Cook, stirring or shaking the pan frequently, until the peas are tender, 3 to 4 minutes. Transfer the peas to a serving platter and keep warm.

Serve the fish on top of the sautéed peas and garnish with the radishes.

How to Cure Salmon Roe

Salmon roe is often discarded or used as fishing bait, but it's considered a delicacy in many parts of the world. If you catch salmon, you will more than likely find eggs in a few of them. Do not discard this incredible nutrient-rich and flavourful secret ingredient. Salmon roe can be used in a multitude of culinary ways. When you clean your fish and slice open the belly, the orange-reddish roe sac will be noticeable. Remove the sac and keep on ice until you get home.

Cured Salmon Roe

8 cups (2 L) warm water (100° to 110°F/38° to 43°C)

1½ cups (375 mL) Diamond Crystal kosher salt

1 salmon roe sac (about 1 pound/450 g)

Cure the Salmon Roe

Combine the warm water and salt in a large stainless steel or glass bowl; stir to dissolve the salt. Add the roe sac and let soak for 5 minutes. This will loosen the eggs from the white membrane. Remove the roe sac from the brine. Reserve the brine.

Set a wire baking rack over a large stainless steel or glass bowl of cold water. Gently rub the roe sac back and forth over the rack to gently push the eggs through the wires. This action will remove the eggs from the membrane and they will fall into the water below. Discard the membrane. Carefully drain the roe through a fine-mesh sieve.

Place the eggs back in the brine. The salt will cure the outer skin of the fish eggs, and the texture is determined by the time in the brine. If you want a fresh, soft texture, soak in the brine for about 1 minute, then scoop out an egg, give it a bite, and taste. Does it have texture to the outside? If you want more of a crisp texture to the roe, continue to cure until the roe tastes seasoned and has the texture you prefer. I wouldn't cure the roe for longer than 20 minutes, though, because the eggs will be completely cured and hard. (Fully curing the fish eggs to a hard state is how roe is prepared for fishing bait, so if you do accidently overdo the curing, freeze them for your next fishing trip.)

Cured roe can be stored in an airtight container in the fridge for about 1 month or in the freezer for up to 6 months. Freezing does affect the quality, so the roe is best eaten freshly cured from the fridge.

Pacific Albacore Tuna Donburi

Donburi is a popular and flavourful Japanese rice-bowl dish consisting of steamed seasoned rice and raw fish accompanied by cured fish roe. There are many variations, but this was my favourite take when I was visiting Japan. One taste of this dish transports me back to the fish market where I first tried it. I like to use albacore tuna because it is plentiful off the coast of British Columbia and Alaska, and I love the fatty flavour of albacore compared to yellowfin or bluefin tuna.

Donburi has a lot of flavours going on. Kewpie mayonnaise is a common garnish in Japan; it is a rich mayonnaise that is thicker than North American brands. Tonkatsu sauce is also drizzled all over the dish, adding a barbecue sauce flavour. Furikake is a crispy salty umami seasoning made with nori and sesame seeds. Bonito flakes add a rich smoky flavour, and pickled ginger brings a refreshing crispy sweetness. Maximum flavour with minimal effort!

SERVES 4

Rice
1 cup (250 mL) sushi rice
1¼ cups (300 mL) cold water
⅓ cup (75 mL) mirin
1 tablespoon (15 mL) granulated sugar
1 teaspoon (5 mL) sea salt

Seared Tuna
1 wild albacore tuna loin (about 2.2 pounds/1 kg)
2 teaspoons (10 mL) shichimi togarashi, more to taste
1 teaspoon (5 mL) sea salt

For assembly
2 ounces (60 g) Cured Salmon Roe (page 55)
2 ounces (60 g) fresh sea urchin roe
Shredded nori flakes
Bonito flakes
Kewpie mayonnaise
Tonkatsu sauce
Furikake seasoning
Pickled ginger
Fresh shiso leaves

Prepare a charcoal or wood fire in an outdoor grill or firepit and let the flames die down with red embers visible. Set a grate over the fire. You want to sear the tuna on very high heat for a short period of time. Alternatively, preheat a gas grill to at least 500°F (260°C).

Prepare the Rice

Rinse the sushi rice in a fine-mesh sieve under cold running water until the water runs clear, then place the sieve over a bowl to drain for 3 minutes.

Transfer the drained rice to a small pot and cover with the cold water. Cover with a lid and bring to a boil over high heat. Once the rice starts to boil, reduce the heat to low and simmer until the water is absorbed; check after 5 minutes and every minute thereafter. Remove from the heat.

Meanwhile, in a small bowl, stir together the mirin, sugar, and salt until dissolved.

Stir the mirin mixture into the cooked rice and mix to coat. The rice will appear wet, but it will absorb the liquid while you prepare the fish.

Sear the Tuna

Season both sides of the tuna with the shichimi togarashi and salt. (For a spicier flavour, double the amount of shichimi togarashi.)

Brush the grill grate with a little vegetable oil. Place the fish on the grill and sear for 30 to 60 seconds per side, just to leave char marks and add flavour. Be careful not to cook the fish; it should be raw on the inside, similar to a black-and-blue steak. Once charred, remove from the heat and thinly slice.

Assemble

Divide the rice among shallow bowls. Arrange the sliced tuna on top of the rice and top with the salmon roe, sea urchin roe, nori flakes, bonito flakes, mayonnaise, tonkatsu sauce, furikake, pickled ginger, and shiso leaves.

Rockfish with Caper Butter Sauce and Pickled Shallots

There are more than a hundred species of rockfish worldwide, and around seventy of those make their homes in the Pacific Ocean off the coast of North America. They are commonly overlooked as table fare. Some people, like a fishing guide I had in British Columbia, will tell you they aren't good to eat. (I later found out my guide simply didn't want to clean them while we were targeting salmon!) But let me tell you, rockfish are delicious. They have a mild, subtle sweet flavour, making them suitable for a wide range of recipes. This dish is best prepared on a cast-iron plancha or in a large cast-iron skillet over fire.

Pictured on the opposite page is a black rockfish I caught off the coast of Langara Island, which is just south of the southern tip of Alaska.

SERVES **2**

Prepare a charcoal or wood fire in a firepit or a wood fire in an outdoor wood pizza oven. Allow the flames to die down with red embers visible. Preheat a cast-iron plancha or large skillet over the fire. If cooking indoors, preheat the oven to 500°F (260°C); preheat the pan.

Meanwhile, Make the Pickled Shallots

In a small bowl, stir together the water, red wine vinegar, and salt. Add the sliced shallots and stir. Cover and set aside on the counter for at least 10 minutes. Store in an airtight container in the fridge for up to 1 month.

Roast the Turnips

Cut a large piece of foil. Place the turnips on the foil. Drizzle with the olive oil and season with the salt. Wrap the turnips tightly in the foil. Place the wrapped turnips near the coals under the plancha or in the wood oven and roast until tender, about 15 minutes.

Start the Caper Butter Sauce

In a small saucepan, boil the white wine over high heat until reduced by half. Add the cream, bring to a simmer, and simmer for 2 minutes. Reduce the heat to low and whisk in the butter, a cube at a time. As the first cube of butter is melting, add another cube, whisking constantly and adding more cubes until all the butter has been added and melted. The sauce should be pale yellow and creamy. If the mixture gets too hot, the butter will separate; lift the pan if necessary to cool things down. (If it does split, you can try to emulsify it with a hand blender and use it right away.) Squeeze the lemon half into the sauce, then add the salt and stir. Cover and keep warm until ready to serve.

Pickled Shallots

¼ cup (60 mL) water

¼ cup (60 mL) red wine vinegar

Pinch of kosher salt

1 shallot, thinly sliced

Roasted Turnips

2 small white turnips

1 tablespoon (15 mL) olive oil

Pinch of kosher salt

Caper Butter Sauce

½ cup (125 mL) dry white wine

¼ cup (60 mL) whipping (35%) cream

½ pound (225 g/1 cup/250 mL) cold unsalted butter, cubed

½ lemon, for squeezing

Pinch of kosher salt

3 tablespoons (45 mL) drained capers

1 tablespoon (15 mL) chopped fresh flat-leaf parsley

Seared Rockfish

2 skin-on rockfish fillets (7 ounces/200 g each)

Kosher salt

2 tablespoons (30 mL) vegetable oil

recipe continues

Sear the Fish and Finish the Sauce

Season both sides of the fillets with salt. Add the vegetable oil to the hot plancha or skillet. Place the fish skin side down on the hot plancha and sear until the skin is crispy to the touch, 2 to 3 minutes. Using a metal spatula, gently turn the fish and cook for another 2 to 3 minutes, depending on the thickness of the fillets. The skin should be crispy and the fish flaky and moist.

Remove the turnips from the fire and slice. Place the fish on top of the turnips.

To finish the caper butter sauce, add the capers and parsley and stir. Spoon the sauce over the fish. Garnish with the pickled shallots and serve.

Halibut with Cucumber Kohlrabi Slaw and White Wine Cream Sauce with Herb Oil

Halibut is one of my favourite fish to eat because of its rich, buttery texture and flavour. But I never understood why people complained about catching them until I tried it myself. I heard the phrases "pulling up a mattress" or "sheet of plywood" thrown around, and that is exactly what it's like. They are a flat fish and are difficult to reel up by hand. The first fish is exciting, but if it doesn't meet the proper size or if you are trying for a larger one, it can be daunting because these fish live at the bottom of the ocean, over 300 feet (90 m) down, and you must literally drag them up. Halibut can be found in the northern Pacific Ocean off the coast of British Columbia and Alaska and in the northern Atlantic Ocean. They are also found off parts of Australia, but those ones are much smaller.

Halibut is a very delicate fish and does not hold up very well when cooked directly on a grill. It is great to cook on a cast-iron plancha or in a cast-iron skillet in a wood oven or in a cast-iron skillet on a charcoal grill. It is best eaten at medium to medium-well doneness. It can be very dry if overcooked.

SERVES 4

Cucumber Kohlrabi Slaw

1 small kohlrabi, peeled and thinly sliced on a mandoline

2 medium mini or pickling cucumbers, thinly sliced

1 Anaheim chili or other mild or medium-heat chili, chopped (if you like heat, leave the seeds in, or for less heat, slice the chilies in half and remove the seeds)

1 small shallot, thinly sliced

¼ cup (60 mL) rice vinegar

Sea salt and black pepper

White Wine Cream Sauce with Herb Oil

½ cup (125 mL) dry white wine

1 bay leaf

2 sprigs fresh thyme

2 cups (500 mL) heavy (35%) cream

1 cup (250 mL) packed mixed fresh soft green herbs (parsley, basil, oregano, chives, fennel fronds)

½ cup (125 mL) canola or grapeseed oil

Halibut

1½ pounds (675 g) skinless fresh halibut fillet, cut into 4 pieces

2 teaspoons (10 mL) kosher salt

1 tablespoon (15 mL) unsalted butter

1 tablespoon (15 mL) canola or grapeseed oil

1 lemon, for squeezing

For garnish

Fresh fennel fronds (optional)

1 tablespoon (15 mL) chopped fresh flat-leaf parsley

recipe continues

Prepare a charcoal or wood fire in an outdoor grill or build a wood fire in an outdoor wood pizza oven. Let the flames die down with red embers visible. If using a grill, preheat a cast-iron skillet; if using a wood pizza oven, preheat a large cast-iron plancha or skillet.

Meanwhile, Make the Cucumber Kohlrabi Slaw

In a medium bowl, combine the kohlrabi, cucumbers, chili, and shallot. Add the rice vinegar and mix, then season to taste with salt and pepper. Set aside.

Start the White Wine Cream Sauce

In a medium saucepan, combine the white wine, bay leaf, and thyme. Bring to a boil over high heat and boil until reduced by half. Add the cream; bring back to a boil, and reduce by a third. Remove from the heat and cover to keep warm.

Fill a medium bowl with ice water. In a large saucepan, bring 2 cups (500 mL) of water to a boil over high heat. Place the fresh herbs in the boiling water and cook for 15 to 20 seconds. Using a wire strainer, transfer the blanched herbs to the ice water to stop the cooking. Once cool, transfer the herbs to a kitchen towel and squeeze out the water. Transfer the herbs to a small blender. With the blender running, slowly stream in the canola oil and blend until the oil is incorporated and the herbs are well blended. Strain the herb oil through a coffee filter or thin kitchen towel into a container and set aside.

Sear the Halibut

Season both sides of the halibut with the salt. Melt the butter with the canola oil in the hot pan. Carefully place the fish in the pan and sear until it has a caramelized golden crust but is still tender, 2 to 3 minutes per side. If your fillet is quite thick, move it into indirect heat to continue cooking until done to your liking. Finish the halibut with a squeeze of lemon while in the pan. The juice will reduce and caramelize on the fish.

Finish the Sauce and Serve

Remove the bay leaf and thyme sprigs from the cream sauce and discard. Whisk in the reserved herb oil. The oil will not emulsify but will give a beautiful broken colour contrast and flavour to the sauce.

Divide the cucumber kohlrabi slaw among plates. Place the halibut on the slaw. Pour the sauce over the fish and garnish with the fennel fronds (if using) and parsley.

Ling Cod with Red Pepper Butter Sauce and Grilled Tomatoes

Ling cod has a face only a mother could love. They are by far the scariest-looking fish I have ever caught. They have a massive mouth, big sharp teeth, and big buggy eyes. What they lack in appearance is made up for in flavour, as these are one of the tastiest fish in the ocean. Sweet, delicate flavour and super-fatty oily meat that just flakes apart and is so supple when properly cooked. It really is a treat. These fish can live close to a hundred years and weigh about a hundred pounds.

SERVES **4**

Prepare a charcoal or wood fire in an outdoor grill or firepit and let the flames die down with red embers visible. Set a grate over the fire. Alternatively, preheat a gas grill to at least 500°F (260°C).

Make the Red Pepper Butter Sauce

Place the bell peppers on the grill grate. Blister the peppers, turning frequently, until the skin is black and charred on all sides, about 10 minutes total. Transfer the charred peppers to a small bowl and cover tightly with plastic wrap. Let steam until cool enough to handle. (The heat from the peppers will create steam between the pepper and its skin, helping to loosen the skin. Do not rinse the peppers with water to remove the skin. This will wash off the subtle sweet flavour that has developed from roasting.) Using your fingers, peel away as much of the charred black skin as you can. Pull away the seeds as well.

In a medium saucepan, combine the white wine, shallot, and bay leaf. Bring to a boil and boil until reduced by half. Remove the bay leaf, then reduce the heat to low and gradually whisk in the butter, a cube at a time. When the first cube is halfway melted, add another cube, then repeat until all the butter has been added and melted. Add the lemon juice and whisk to incorporate, then remove from the heat. Cover with a lid and keep warm.

Place the peeled roasted peppers in a blender and purée on high speed. Slowly pour in the melted butter mixture and blend until incorporated. Add the sherry vinegar, then season with the salt. Pour the sauce back into the pot, cover with a lid, and keep warm.

Red Pepper Butter Sauce

2 red bell peppers

½ cup (125 mL) dry white wine

1 small shallot, minced

1 bay leaf

½ pound (225 g/1 cup/250 mL) unsalted butter, cut into cubes

Juice of 1 lemon

1 teaspoon (5 mL) sherry vinegar

½ teaspoon (2 mL) kosher salt

Ling Cod

4 skin-on ling cod fillets (6 ounces/170 g each)

1 teaspoon (5 mL) kosher salt

2 tablespoons (30 mL) olive oil

Grilled Cherry Tomatoes

1 pound (450 g) cherry tomatoes on the vine

1 tablespoon (15 mL) olive oil

Kosher salt and black pepper

For garnish

4 sprigs fresh dill

4 sprigs fresh basil

recipe continues

Sear the Ling Cod

Heat a cast-iron plancha or skillet big enough to fit the 4 fillets on the grill grate.

Season both sides of the ling cod with the salt. Add the olive oil to the hot pan. Place the fish skin side down in the pan and cook for 2 to 3 minutes to let the skin properly cook and caramelize. Once the skin is crispy, turn the fish and cook for another 2 to 3 minutes. Ling cod should be eaten at medium to medium-well doneness (135° to 145°F/57° to 63°C).

Meanwhile, Grill the Cherry Tomatoes

While the fish is cooking, brush the tomatoes (on the vine) with the olive oil and season with salt and pepper. Gently place the tomatoes on the grill grate and cook until you can see grill marks or slight blistering.

To serve, pour the red pepper butter sauce into large shallow bowls and place a fish fillet on top. Add the grilled cherry tomatoes. Garnish with sprigs of dill and basil.

Coho Salmon Candy

Salmon candy is an awesome treat and super-nutritious snack with Indigenous origins. Coho is known for being a bit on the lean side and not the very best type of salmon for cooking, especially when compared with its super-fatty relative the king salmon. However, coho is great for curing or eating raw, as it has a beautiful flavour. This on-the-go snack is incredibly simple to make. Pack this with you on fishing, hunting, or hiking trips as a delicious and good-for-you treat.

Note: For this recipe I used a cold smoker and a food dehydrator. If you don't have a smoker, you can use just a dehydrator for the same texture but you will miss the smoky flavour.

SERVES **4** AS A SNACK

Prepare your smoker to cook on low heat at 150°F (65°C) and add your insert of ice (see Note). Line a baking sheet with parchment paper.

Starting at the thick end of the fillet and cutting away from the tail end, slice the salmon into ⅛- to ¼-inch (3 to 5 mm) strips on a 45-degree angle. Arrange the slices in one layer on the prepared baking sheet. Brush the salmon with a little of the maple syrup. Evenly sprinkle the brown sugar over the fish and finish with the salt. Transfer the sheet to your smoker on the lowest rack above the ice tray and smoke the fish for 30 minutes.

Meanwhile, set a dehydrator to 130°F (55°C). Line a dehydrator tray with parchment paper.

After 30 minutes, lay the smoked salmon in a single layer on the prepared dehydrator tray and brush with more maple syrup. Dehydrate for about 3 hours, checking the salmon every 30 to 45 minutes and continuing to brush with maple syrup, until the candy is semi-dry with a soft, chewy texture. Overdrying will result in a brittle texture. The salmon candy can be stored in an airtight container in the fridge for up to 2 weeks or vacuum-sealed and stored in the freezer for up to 6 months.

Special Equipment

Food dehydrator

1 skin-on side coho salmon, pin bones removed (about 2 pounds/900 g)

½ cup (125 mL) pure maple syrup

¼ cup (60 mL) packed brown sugar

2 tablespoons (30 mL) Diamond Crystal kosher or sea salt

Baked Salt-Crusted Trout

Salt-baking fish is a culinary technique that uses a paste of salt, water, and egg white to seal in the moisture of the fish so it steams itself. When baked, the paste hardens, sealing all the flavours inside while imparting a subtle salinity to the fish. The result is incredibly delicious and perfectly flaky moist fish. The drama of cracking open the salt crust in front of your friends and family adds to the anticipation for the meal to come.

SERVES **4**

4½ pounds (2 kg) Diamond Crystal kosher salt

2 cups (500 mL) egg whites (from 8 to 12 large eggs)

1 cup (250 mL) water

1 whole head-on sea trout (5 pounds/2.25 kg), gutted and cleaned

1 bunch fresh flat-leaf parsley

1 lemon, thinly sliced

2 leaves black kale

1 batch Caper Butter Sauce (page 59)

Lemon wedges, for garnish

Prepare a wood fire in an outdoor wood pizza oven and allow it to reach 500°F (260°C). If cooking indoors, preheat the oven to 500°F (260°C).

In a large bowl, mix together the salt, egg whites, and water to form a paste. The mixture will feel like wet sand.

Stuff the cavity of the trout with the parsley and lemon slices.

Scoop half the salt mixture onto the middle of a baking sheet and pat it flat in the shape of the fish, about ½ inch (1 cm) thick. Lay a kale leaf over the salt, then place the fish on top. Place the second kale leaf on the fish, then cover with the remaining salt mixture. Pat the salt mixture to form a smooth outer layer of salt. Bake the fish until a probe thermometer inserted in the thickest part reaches 130°F (55°C), about 30 minutes. When the fish is done, remove from the oven and let rest on the sheet for 15 minutes.

Using a serrated knife, gently cut the sides of the baked salt crust and pull off the outer layer to reveal a perfectly steamed and succulent trout. The fish fillet should gently pull away from the bones with a metal spatula and a spoon. Serve with caper butter sauce and lemon wedges.

Grilled Swordfish with Roasted Tomatoes and Olive Tapenade

Swordfish is a majestic and powerful marine fish that is as equally appealing to eat as it is to catch. Like white tuna, it's best eaten rare, as it tends to dry out when fully cooked. The fish is meaty with a mild salinity and sweet undertone. It's perfect for grilling paired with Mediterranean flavours. Swordfish are caught all over the world but specifically on the west and east coasts of Canada and the United States. Swordfish are typically caught longlining, but they can also be shot with spear guns under the moonlight when they are near the surface of the ocean.

SERVES 4

Prepare a charcoal or wood fire in an outdoor grill or firepit and let the flames die down with red embers visible. Set a grate over the fire. Alternatively, preheat a gas grill to 500°F (260°C). If roasting the tomatoes indoors, preheat the oven to 400°F (200°C).

Meanwhile, Make the Olive Tapenade

In a blender, combine the olives, capers, lemon zest and juice, and honey. Mash the garlic with the salt with the side of a fork, then add to the blender (this softens the garlic taste). Blend until the mixture is chopped and loosely comes together. Do not purée. Reserve.

Roast the Tomatoes

Place the field tomatoes and cherry tomatoes in a large bowl. Drizzle with olive oil. Add the garlic, thyme, and a pinch each of salt and pepper. Mix to coat. Evenly spread the tomato mixture on a baking sheet or in a large cast-iron skillet. Roast on the top rack of your barbecue, or away from the fire on indirect heat (or in your indoor oven) until the tomatoes have lost a considerable amount of liquid and are roasted, about 15 minutes. Remove from the heat and keep warm.

Grill the Swordfish and Sauté the Green Beans

Brush the swordfish on both sides with olive oil and season with salt and pepper. Place the fish on the hot grill grate and char for 1 to 2 minutes per side, depending on the thickness of your fish. You only want the fish lightly grilled with a warm centre. The fish is done when a probe thermometer inserted into the thickest part reaches 125°F (52°C). Remove from the heat.

At the same time, heat a sauté pan on the grill grate. Add the olive oil and green beans to the hot pan and sauté for 2 minutes. Remove from the heat.

To serve, slice the swordfish and arrange on plates with the roasted tomatoes, sautéed green beans, and fresh cherry tomatoes. Garnish with the capers and caper berries. Squeeze the lemon over the fish and top with a dollop of the olive tapenade.

Olive Tapenade

1 cup (250 mL) pitted Kalamata olives

1 tablespoon (15 mL) drained capers

Zest and juice of 1 lemon

1 tablespoon (15 mL) pure liquid honey

2 cloves garlic

Pinch of kosher salt

Roasted Tomatoes

3 field tomatoes, quartered

1 cup (250 mL) red cherry tomatoes, cut in half

Olive oil, for drizzling

2 cloves garlic, sliced

2 sprigs fresh thyme

Kosher salt and freshly cracked black pepper

Grilled Swordfish

4 swordfish steaks (6 ounces/170 g each)

Olive oil, for brushing

Sea salt and black pepper

Sautéed Green Beans

1 tablespoon (15 mL) olive oil

4 ounces (115 g) green beans, trimmed

For garnish

1 cup (250 mL) mix of red and yellow cherry tomatoes, cut in half

2 tablespoons (30 mL) drained capers

8 caper berries in brine, drained

1 lemon, for squeezing

Seafood by Fire

Shellfish, molluscs, cephalopods, and crustaceans are some of the many gifts from the sea. Sea urchins are depleting the ocean's kelp forests because it is their main diet. These spiny creatures are filled with delicious roe-like gonads that are similar to the texture of foie gras and just as rich. Harvesting and eating urchin is beneficial to the ecosystem while also providing incredibly mouthwatering food for us.

Crabs, lobster, and shrimp fall under the crustacean family and are packed with tender, sweet, and briny meat. Cooking crustaceans over a fire is one of the simplest and most rewarding ways to cook them. All their juices are trapped in their outer shell, steaming the meat during the cooking. Molluscs such as mussels, oysters, and clams can be placed directly on the grill in their closed shells. The heat forces them to pop open to reveal their sweet, juicy interior. These delicacies of the sea need little manipulation since they are so tasty on their own, but a little butter, cheese, and breadcrumbs makes a fantastic grilled oyster topping (see page 99).

Seafood and shellfish are well suited for the open fire because of their fast cooking time and ability to absorb flavours from the smoke and fire. When cooking over a fire, make sure your seafood is fresh and properly cleaned. Mussels and oysters sometimes need to be scrubbed with a brush to remove mud and grit from the shells. Clams should be purged in fresh salted water. Make sure to remove the brown outer skin of squid before cooking.

Caramelization is often talked about with meat, but the high heat of live fire also has a wonderful effect on fish and seafood. Fish skin becomes brown and crispy, locking in the moisture and adding depth of flavour. The caramelization process enhances the natural sweetness of fish and seafood, creating a delicious contrast of textures and flavours.

Cooking seafood over open fire or on the grill infuses it with a special flavour that is hard to achieve with other cooking methods. The smoky aromas and caramelizing flavours from direct heat combined with the natural sweetness of fresh seafood is truly exceptional. From the thrill of the catch to the satisfaction of a perfectly grilled meal, cooking seafood over fire is not only a culinary treat; it is also a celebration of the great outdoors and gathering around the flames with friends and family.

Uni—Foie Gras of the Sea

The edible part of the sea urchin, known as uni in Japanese and often called sea urchin roe, is highly nutritious and incredibly tasty. These little gonads are beneath the spiky surface of the hard shell. Uni are high in protein and omega-3 fatty acids, and they have a beautiful creamy texture and savoury, briny, umami-rich flavour that is unlike anything I can describe. One of my favourite ways to eat them is raw, but fire and smoke add great flavour to this beautiful ingredient. Because of their creamy texture, uni don't require much cooking to warm them up. Uni can be puréed into aiolis and other sauces such as hollandaise to accompany meat or seafood dishes, or blended into a compound butter to be served with a steak (see page 81).

To eat the uni raw, simply cut a large circle around the beak of the sea urchin with heavy-duty kitchen shears, tip it over, and drain the liquid. Gently rinse out the inside of the urchin with cold running water to remove the brown mushy seaweed and kelp that it has been eating. Using a spoon, gently scoop out the uni and eat! The roe can be added to sushi dishes, raw tuna appetizers, raw meat tartares, or simply eaten with rice. When buying uni, they should have a sweet smell with a hint of the sea. Avoid uni that smells fishy or has a muddy, metallic taste, signs that it is not fresh. When processed for sale, it is often sold on little wood trays with a clear plastic lid. Look for bright yellowy-orange colours and avoid darker brown colours.

Smoked Uni Butter and Bison Tenderloin

This is my take on wild game and ocean-harvested surf and turf. The sweet, irony flavour of the uni has a salinity to it that complements the earthy grass-fed bison tenderloin. The rich, tender bison paired with the umami of sea urchin is a lavish treat.

SERVES 4

Make the Smoked Uni Butter

Using heavy-duty kitchen shears, cut a large circle around the beak of the sea urchins, tip them over, and drain the liquid. Gently rinse out the inside of the urchin with cold running water to remove the brown mushy seaweed and kelp. Be careful not to disturb the uni (roe) inside. Leave the uni in the shell and place in a cold smoker, or in a covered container if you have a smoking gun. (If you don't have a smoker set up for cold-smoking, you can place the uni in a tray of ice and smoke on the lowest setting for 5 to 10 minutes, then turn the smoker off and let the uni sit in the smoke chamber for 20 minutes. You want to smoke the uni enough to impart the smoky flavour but not cook it.)

Using a spoon, remove the uni from the shell and place it in a medium bowl. Add the butter, lemon zest and juice, parsley, and salt. Mix to combine, breaking up the roe but leaving it chunky.

Lay a piece of plastic wrap or a sheet of parchment paper about 12 inches (30 cm) in length on a work surface with a long side facing you. Scoop the butter mixture onto the plastic wrap in a 2-inch (5 cm) thick line. Starting at the long edge closest to you, roll up the butter into a log inside the wrap, then twist the ends to tighten the butter mixture inside to form a smooth log. Place the wrapped butter in the fridge for at least 1 hour to harden. The compound butter can be stored in the fridge for up to 3 days or frozen for up to 1 month. (The butter can be sliced frozen.)

Make the Mashed Potatoes

Place the skin-on potatoes in a large pot, cover with water, and add the salt. Boil until soft, 20 to 30 minutes. Drain the potatoes. Add the milk and butter to the pot and mash the potatoes. Season with more salt, if needed. Cover with a lid and keep warm.

Special Equipment

Heavy-duty kitchen shears

Smoked Uni Butter

4 large fresh sea urchins

½ pound (225 g/1 cup/250 mL) unsalted butter, at room temperature

Zest and juice of 1 lemon

2 tablespoons (30 mL) chopped fresh flat-leaf parsley

1 tablespoon (15 mL) kosher or sea salt

Mashed Potatoes

4 to 5 large unpeeled yellow potatoes

1 tablespoon (15 mL) kosher or sea salt, plus more for seasoning

½ cup (125 mL) whole milk

8 tablespoons (125 mL) unsalted butter

Grilled Bison Tenderloin

4 bison tenderloin steaks (5 ounces/140 g each)

Sea salt and black pepper

Olive oil, for brushing

Grilled Asparagus

1 bunch asparagus, trimmed

recipe continues

Grill the Bison and Asparagus

Prepare a charcoal or wood fire in an outdoor grill or firepit and let the flames die down with red embers visible. Set a grate over the fire. Alternatively, preheat a gas grill on high to 600°F (315°C).

Season both sides of the bison with salt and pepper. Brush the grill grate with a little olive oil. Place the steaks on the grill and sear for 2 to 3 minutes per side for medium-rare doneness. Remove from the grill and let rest on a wire rack for at least 5 minutes while you grill the asparagus.

Grill the asparagus for 2 to 3 minutes per side until tender.

To finish, cut four ¼-inch (5 mm) thick slices of the uni butter. Place a disc of butter on each steak. The warmth of the meat will start to melt the butter, but for added effect you can torch the butter for a quicker melt. Serve with the mashed potatoes and grilled asparagus.

Lobster Rolls on Squid Ink Buns

The lobster roll is a mouthwatering sandwich that hails from New England. It's a culinary delicacy of succulent lobster claw and tail meat fresh from the ocean, usually mixed with a mayonnaise-based creamy dressing with lemon juice and stuffed into a New England–style toasted and buttered hot dog bun. The combination of sweet, briny lobster in a crispy, buttery roll is a beautiful experience and the essence of coastal dining.

I like to add squid ink to my bun recipe for an added visual pop and flavour. Weighing the ingredients for making the squid ink buns is recommended for best results.

Note: You can boil the lobster outdoors in a charcoal or wood fire in an outdoor grill or firepit. If so, prepare your fire when you preheat your oven.

MAKES **18** APPETIZER-SIZE LOBSTER ROLLS

Special Equipment

Kitchen shears

Squid Ink Buns

2 large eggs, beaten

2 tablespoons (30 mL/25 g) granulated sugar

¼ teaspoon (1 mL) ascorbic acid powder

Water, at room temperature

2 tablespoons (30 mL/35 g) squid ink

8 cups (2 L/1 kg) all-purpose flour

2 tablespoons (30 mL/18 g) instant yeast

1 tablespoon + 1 teaspoon (20 mL/15 g) kosher salt

Egg Wash

1 egg

6 tablespoons + 2 teaspoons (100 mL) whole milk

Lobster Filling

4 cooked whole lobsters (about 1 pound/450 g each; see page 86)

1 cup (250 mL) mayonnaise or aioli

1 small shallot, minced

Zest and juice of 1 lemon

Leaves from 1 bunch fresh tarragon, chopped

Pinch of cayenne pepper

Pinch of sea salt

Soft butter, for toasting the buns

2 tablespoons (30 mL) sliced fresh chives, for garnish

Make the Squid Ink Buns

Place the bowl of a stand mixer on a digital scale and set to 0 g. Add the eggs, sugar, and ascorbic acid to the bowl. Gradually pour the water into the bowl just until the scale registers 700 g. Then add the squid ink. Remove the bowl from the scale. Add the flour, yeast, and salt. Attach the dough hook and mix on low speed for 6 minutes. The dough should come together with a smooth, soft consistency that can easily be handled and formed into a ball. (Alternatively, you can knead the dough by hand. Be sure to wear plastic gloves to avoid staining your hands black from the squid ink.)

Transfer the dough to a lightly floured work surface. Using a dough knife, cut the dough into 18 equal portions (3 ounces/90 g each). Working with one portion of dough at a time, use the palm of your hand to press down on the dough in a circular motion and shape into a ball. Cover the buns with a plastic bag or a damp kitchen towel and let sit for 5 minutes.

recipe continues

Spray a hot dog bun pan(s) or a baking sheet lined with plastic wrap with oil or cooking spray.

Working with one portion of dough at a time, use the palm of your hand to flatten the ball into a flat disc. Fold the bottom third up to the middle, then fold the top down to the middle. Gently roll each portion of dough into the shape of a small hot dog bun and place on the prepared hot dog bun pan or evenly spaced on the baking sheet. The sides of the buns should be almost touching. The buns will touch when proofed and baked. Once baked, they will be pull-apart buns.

Egg Wash the Buns and Bake

In a small bowl, whisk together the egg and milk. Gently brush the tops of the buns with the egg wash. Place the bun pan or baking sheet inside a larger container or a large plastic bag with enough air inside to allow the buns to rise without touching the bag. Let proof in a warm draft-free place until the dough has doubled in size, 45 to 60 minutes.

Preheat the oven to 400°F (200°C).

Once the buns have risen, bake until the buns sound hollow when tapped and have a firm crust, 12 to 15 minutes. Transfer to a rack to cool for at least 45 minutes before pulling apart.

Make the Lobster Filling

Using kitchen shears, remove the lobster meat from the tail and claws. Use a knife to chop the lobster meat into bite-size pieces. Place the lobster meat in a medium bowl. Add the mayonnaise, shallot, lemon zest and juice, tarragon, cayenne pepper, and salt. Mix well. Set aside.

Toast the Buns and Assemble

Prepare a charcoal or wood fire in an outdoor grill or firepit and let the flames die down with red embers visible. Set a grate over the fire. Alternatively, preheat a gas grill to 500°F (260°C).

Heat a large cast-iron skillet or griddle pan until hot. (If cooking indoors, heat a large skillet over high heat.)

Pull apart the cooled buns and brush the sides with butter. Toast the buns on their sides until crispy on both sides. Slice an opening down the centre of the buns. Spoon the lobster mixture into the buns. Serve on a large platter and garnish with the chives.

Lobster Boil

Lobster is an indulgent ingredient that has a beautiful briny and sweet taste. Rich, succulent, sweet, and incredibly flavourful would be a good way to describe a lobster boil, a traditional cooking method in the coastal towns along the shores of the northeastern United States and Canada. Something magical happens when boiling lobster with sausage, corn, and a medley of spices that I simply cannot explain.

The boil can be prepared in a large pot over a propane rocket burner, but it is more fun over open flame because everything over a smoky fire just tastes better.

SERVES 4 to 6

---

3 gallons (12 L) water

1 cup (250 mL) Diamond Crystal kosher salt or sea salt

¼ cup (60 mL) black peppercorns

6 bay leaves

1 head garlic, cloves separated and peeled

1 bunch fresh thyme

4 to 5 fresh hot red chilies (optional)

6 live lobsters (1 to 1½ pounds/ 450 to 675 g each)

2 pounds (900 g) mini potatoes

4 sweet corn cobs, husked and cut into 2-inch (5 cm) rounds

1 pound (450 g) andouille sausage (cured smoked pork sausage)

2 lemons, cut in half

8 tablespoons (125 mL) butter, melted

For garnish

Flaky sea salt

Fresh flat-leaf parsley, chopped

Lemon wedges

In a very large stockpot (40 to 50 quarts/38 to 47 L) over high heat, bring the water to a rolling boil. Add the salt, peppercorns, bay leaves, garlic, thyme, and chilies (if using). Reduce the heat and simmer for 8 to 10 minutes to infuse the flavour into the water.

Carefully add the live lobsters, potatoes, corn, sausage, and lemon halves to the pot. Cover with a lid and return to a boil. Remove the lid and cook the lobsters for 8 to 12 minutes (about 8 minutes per pound/450 g), until bright red. Using metal tongs, remove the lobsters from the boiling stock. If the potatoes are still firm, continue cooking while cutting the lobsters. Once the potatoes are cooked, drain the pot.

The fun classic way to serve this epic feast is to dump all the ingredients onto a picnic table covered with butcher paper and dig in with your hands. For a more refined approach, crack open the lobster shells and carefully remove the claw and tail meat. Arrange it on a platter with the potatoes, corn, and sausage. Drizzle with the melted butter. Garnish with a sprinkle of flaky sea salt and parsley. Serve with the lemon wedges for squeezing.

Pizza Oven Baked Clams

North America is home to over a dozen edible varieties of clams—quahog, Manila, Pacific razor, Atlantic razor, cockles, and geoduck, to name just a few. Clams are prized by seafood lovers across the globe for their slightly sweet, briny flavour, and mildly chewy texture. The secret to cooking clams is to keep things simple. Butter, wine, and a little seasoning are all you need to let the natural taste of the clam shine. Baked clams are a personal favourite, as their sweet, salty natural juices flavour the sauce, which is best soaked up with a chunk of buttered fresh-baked bread. The trick with any seafood is to not overcook it, or the texture turns rubbery, but for the most part baking clams is simple. In this recipe, a wood-fired pizza oven adds a smoky touch to an already rich and beautiful dish.

When digging for clams, be sure to check local regulations and beware of red tide or other algal blooms that can release toxins into the water and make wild clams unsafe during certain times of the year.

SERVES 4 to 6 AS AN APPETIZER

Prepare a wood fire in an outdoor wood pizza oven and let it burn for 45 to 60 minutes, until the temperature reaches at least 500°F (260°C). Alternatively, if cooking indoors, preheat the oven to 500°F (260°C).

Meanwhile, prepare the clams by rinsing them under cold running water and removing any "beards" where the two shells meet. Add ⅓ cup (75 mL) of sea salt to 1 gallon (4 L) of water and soak the clams for 30 minutes to an hour, agitating or stirring the clams periodically. This will purge them of any sand inside that you don't want released into your cooking.

Break apart the sausage with your hands or chop with a knife into bite-size pieces. Set aside.

Preheat a large stainless steel frying pan or cast-iron skillet with a tight-fitting lid in the pizza oven (or indoor oven) for 3 to 4 minutes.

Remove the hot pan from the oven. Melt the butter with the olive oil in the hot pan. Add the shallot and stir for a minute or so, then add the garlic, chili flakes, sausage, and clams. Shake the pan and toss the clams to coat with the olive oil and butter, then season with salt. Add the white wine and bay leaves. Cover with a lid, transfer to the pizza oven (or indoor oven), and cook for 5 to 10 minutes, depending on temperature. After 3 or so minutes give the clams a stir and check whether they are starting to open. Once the clams have started to open, remove the lid and finish cooking in the oven, stirring occasionally to coat the clams with the natural juices they have released with the oil and butter. Remove from the oven. Discard any unopened clams and the bay leaves. Garnish with the parsley.

Place a trivet on your table and serve family-style into bowls.

- 4 pounds (1.8 kg) live Manila clams
- 8 ounces (225 g) cured chorizo sausage (casing removed if possible)
- 4 tablespoons (60 mL) unsalted butter, divided
- 1 tablespoon (15 mL) olive oil
- 1 small shallot, minced
- 2 cloves garlic, crushed
- Pinch of red chili flakes
- Sea salt
- 2 cups (500 mL) dry white wine
- 3 bay leaves
- 4 sprigs flat-leaf parsley, chopped

How to Harvest and Prepare Geoduck

Harvesting Geoduck

Geoduck (pronounced "gooey duck") is a goofy-looking specimen. It is considered the largest burrowing clam in the world and is found all along the Pacific coast, from as far north as Alaska all the way to Baja California. They grow to 1 to 3 pounds (450 g to 1.25 kg) in weight and measure 6 to 8 inches (15 to 20 cm) in length. In the culinary world they are considered a delicacy and come at a very high price, so it's pretty cool that you can go to the beach and simply dig these creatures up during low tide. Commercial harvesters use specialized high-pressure water jets to loosen the dirt and mud around the shells, but recreational harvesters are usually limited to hand-harvesting. Be sure to acquire the proper licences and ensure it is safe to harvest in your area. You'll need a shovel, and a length of plastic PVC pipe can be a good tool as well. Look for dollar-coin-size holes in the sandy mulch and start digging.

Preparing Geoduck

This phallic-looking clam can be simply prepared in a few ways, as sashimi eaten raw, grilled, pan-cooked, or simmered in seasoned water. Follow these step-by-step instructions to prepare your geoduck.

STEP 1

Set up a work surface with the geoduck and a sharp knife.

STEP 2

Remove the clam from the shell: Using a sharp knife, gently cut along the inside of the shell on one side, pulling the shell back as you continue to slice, hugging the shell with the tip of your knife until you reach the base of the first side. Flip and repeat on the second shell.

STEP 3

Pull the shell off the remaining meat. Keep the shells for presentation or discard.

STEP 4

Pull or cut off and discard the sac-shaped stomach at the back/bottom of the shell. Keep the collar, which looks like a tongue at the top and is attached to the long neck of the clam.

STEP 5

Fill a large bowl with ice water. Bring a large pot of salted water to a boil. Place the clam in the simmering water and cook for 30 to 60 seconds.

STEP 6

Using metal tongs, remove the blanched clam from the water and plunge into the ice water. This will stop it cooking. The clam will still be raw inside, but blanching makes it easier to pull off the skin in one long piece.

STEP 7

Once cooled, remove the clam from the ice water. Using your fingers, pull the skin off the clam and discard.

STEP 8

Thinly slice the clam tongue and neck on a slight diagonal into oval-shaped pieces as outlined in recipes; see Sashimi-Style Geoduck (page 95) and Grilled Geoduck (page 96).

Sashimi-Style Geoduck

Follow the instructions on pages 90–94 to prepare the geoduck (remove the shell, blanch, and shock).

Thinly slice the neck and tongue on a slight diagonal into oval-shaped pieces—the thinner the better. Arrange the raw pieces in their shell with the chili slices. Drizzle with olive oil and a squeeze of lemon juice. Sprinkle with the flaky sea salt, green onion, and fennel fronds.

1 geoduck clam neck and tongue (the tongue is the part that was inside the shell and looks like a tongue; the neck is the piece outside the shell)

Olive oil, for drizzling

1 lemon, for squeezing

1 Anaheim chili, thinly sliced (if you like heat, leave the seeds in, or for less heat, slice the chilies in half and remove the seeds)

Flaky sea salt

Green onion, thinly sliced

Fresh fennel fronds, for garnish

Grilled Geoduck

1 geoduck clam neck and tongue (the tongue is the part that was inside the shell and looks like a tongue; the neck is the piece outside the shell)

2 jalapeño peppers, thinly sliced

1 cucumber, thinly sliced

2 tablespoons (30 mL) soy sauce

2 teaspoons (10 mL) chili oil

Flaky sea salt

1 tablespoon (15 mL) chopped fresh cilantro

Follow the instructions on pages 90–94 to prepare the geoduck (remove the shell, blanch, and shock).

Prepare a charcoal or wood fire in an outdoor grill or firepit and let the flames die down with red embers visible. Set a grate over the fire. Alternatively, preheat a gas grill to 500°F (260°C).

Grill the clam on the very hot grill grate very quickly, just enough to develop char marks and impart some smoky flavour, 1 to 2 minutes per side. The inside should still be raw. Thinly slice the neck and the tongue crosswise. In the middle of a serving plate, arrange the slices of tongue with the jalapeño. Arrange alternating slices of clam neck and cucumber around the pieces of sliced tongue. Drizzle with the soy sauce and chili oil. Sprinkle with the flaky sea salt and cilantro.

Grilled Oysters Rockefeller

North America is blessed with oysters on the east, west, and southern Gulf coasts where each coast boasts oysters with unique flavour and texture. West Coast oysters tend to be quite meaty in texture with a creamy, sweet fishy taste, whereas East Coast oysters are a little more delicate, brinier, and much less fishy in flavour. Gulf Coast oysters are usually brinier than those from the east and west coasts, with more of a minerality from the minerals and salts found in the Gulf of Mexico. They also tend to be larger. I personally love all three kinds, but regardless of where they come from, cooking them over a fire and roasting them is a real treat. They can be popped ahead of time and stuffed with butter and cheese or grilled live where the heat will open them on its own. This is my favourite grilled oyster recipe.

MAKES 2 dozen OYSTERS

Preheat an outdoor wood pizza oven or grill to 500°F (260°C). If cooking indoors, position a rack 6 inches (15 cm) under the broiler; set the broiler on low.

Scrub the oysters under cold running water to remove any mud and grit.

To shuck the oysters, position an oyster with the flat part facing up and the cup part facing down. Shielding your hand with a kitchen towel or a shucking glove, insert an oyster knife into the hinge at the back of the shell and apply pressure while twisting the blade to pop the oyster open. Inside the shell there is a small white muscle connecting the two shells. Gently scrape the top of the shell to cut the muscle, being careful not to damage the oyster. Remove the top shell. Scoop the knife under the oyster meat to cut the bottom muscle and free the oyster. Pour the liquid and oyster into a medium container. Repeat until all the oysters are shucked, then store in the fridge until ready to use. Reserve the bottom shells and keep in the fridge until ready to use.

When ready to cook, using a spoon, carefully remove the oysters one at a time from their liquid and transfer to a clean container. Strain the oyster liquid through a fine-mesh sieve back into the oysters to remove any shell or grit.

Preheat a large cast-iron skillet in the pizza oven or over high heat for 2 to 3 minutes. (Alternatively, you can use a burner on your stovetop.) Add the 1 tablespoon (15 mL) butter to the hot pan. Add the spinach and season with salt. Cover with a lid and steam just until the spinach is wilted, 2 to 3 minutes. Add the green onions, garlic, and half the oyster liquid. Sauté for 2 to 3 minutes, reducing the oyster liquid until the pan is almost dry. Remove from the heat and let cool.

24 fresh oysters

1 tablespoon (15 mL) unsalted butter

3 cups (750 mL) chopped fresh spinach

½ cup (125 mL) chopped green onions

4 cloves garlic, minced

¾ cup (175 mL) freshly grated Parmesan cheese

½ cup (125 mL) dried breadcrumbs

½ cup (125 mL) chopped fresh flat-leaf parsley

8 tablespoons (125 mL) unsalted butter, melted

Pinch of sea salt, plus more for seasoning

Pinch of black pepper

Pinch of sweet paprika

Pinch of cayenne pepper

For serving

Lemon wedges

Hot sauce

recipe continues

In a medium bowl, combine the Parmesan, breadcrumbs, parsley, the 8 tablespoons (125 mL) melted butter, salt, black pepper, paprika, and cayenne pepper. Mix well. The mixture should resemble crumbly pie dough.

Sprinkle 1 tablespoon (15 mL) of kosher salt or rock salt on a baking sheet to stabilize the shells. Place the bottom shells on the baking sheet. Using a spoon, place an oyster in each shell. Place 1 tablespoon (15 mL) of the spinach mixture on top of each oyster, then top with some of the Parmesan crumbs to cover the oysters. Bake in the pizza oven, or outdoor grill with the lid closed, or indoor oven, until the top is melted, golden brown, and bubbling around the edges, 2 to 3 minutes. Serve immediately with the lemon wedges and hot sauce on the side.

Grilled Octopus with Romesco Sauce and Salsa Verde

The beauty of octopus is how succulent and tender its meat is. Octopus has a slightly sweet seafood flavour and a firm texture similar to lobster or chicken. Undercooked octopus is tough and chewy, so the length of cooking time is important, though very dependent on the size of octopus and the temperature of the braising. By simply checking the doneness after the initial 45 minutes, cooking it to perfection is easy to master. I like to braise the octopus first before grilling to ensure a perfect texture.

The tentacles can be quite sticky, so it's important to clean your grilling surface diligently to avoid grit sticking to the octopus. Romesco sauce is a classic pairing with its robust and tangy profile that complements the mild sweetness of the octopus, creating a harmonious and delicious dish.

SERVES **4**

Grilled Octopus

- 2 fresh baby octopus (about 2 pounds/900 g total)
- 4 cups (1 L) vegetable or fish stock
- 2 cups (500 mL) dry white wine
- Juice of 2 lemons
- 2 tablespoons (30 mL) kosher or sea salt
- 1 teaspoon (5 mL) black peppercorns
- 4 cloves garlic
- 4 bay leaves
- 4 sprigs fresh flat-leaf parsley

Romesco Sauce

- 3 field tomatoes (about 1 pound/450 g total), cut into quarters
- 3 Anaheim chilies (2 ounces/60 g total; if you like heat, leave the seeds in, or for less heat, slice the chilies in half and remove the seeds)
- 1 head unpeeled garlic, sliced in half horizontally
- 2 tablespoons (30 mL) olive oil, plus more if needed
- Salt and black pepper
- 2 slices baguette or white bread (about 2 ounces/60 g total)
- 1 cup (250 mL) slivered almonds, toasted
- 2 tablespoons (30 mL) sherry vinegar

Salsa Verde

- 1 cup (250 mL) chopped fresh flat-leaf parsley
- ½ cup (125 mL) chopped fresh cilantro
- 4 cloves garlic, minced
- 1 tablespoon (15 mL) drained capers
- 2 anchovy fillets, minced (optional)
- 1 tablespoon (15 mL) red wine vinegar or sherry vinegar
- Pinch each of kosher salt and black pepper

Braise the Octopus

Place the octopus in a large pot. Add the stock, white wine, lemon juice, salt, peppercorns, garlic, bay leaves, and parsley. Bring to a simmer over high heat, then reduce the heat to low, cover with the lid slightly ajar, and simmer until the octopus is tender, about 45 minutes. Using a wire strainer and tongs, gently remove the octopus from the liquid. Let cool at room temperature for 5 minutes, then cover and refrigerate while you prepare the sauces. Discard the cooking liquid.

recipe continues

Make the Romesco Sauce

Preheat the oven to 400°F (200°C). Line a baking sheet with parchment paper.

Place the tomatoes, the chilies, and the garlic cut side up on the prepared baking sheet. Drizzle with the olive oil and season with salt and pepper. Roast until the tomatoes are visibly blistered and have lost liquid, 10 to 15 minutes. This concentrates the flavour as moisture is lost and natural sugars caramelize. The garlic should be soft and creamy in texture and the peppers soft and slightly blistered.

Meanwhile, toast the bread in a toaster or in the oven with the vegetables until golden brown, 2 to 3 minutes. Break up the toasted bread into crouton-size pieces and transfer to a food processor or blender.

Squeeze the roasted garlic cloves from the skins and add to the blender. Add the roasted tomatoes and chilies, almonds, sherry vinegar, 2 tablespoons (30 mL) olive oil, and season with salt and pepper. Blend until smooth. Adjust the consistency with more olive oil, if needed. If you want more acid, add another 1 teaspoon (5 mL) of sherry vinegar. Adjust the salt and pepper to taste. Transfer the sauce to a container and reserve at room temperature. Rinse the blender jar.

Make the Salsa Verde

In the blender, combine the parsley, cilantro, garlic, capers, anchovies (if using), red wine vinegar, salt and pepper. Purée until smooth. Adjust seasoning as needed. Set aside.

Grill the Octopus

Prepare a charcoal or wood fire in an outdoor grill or firepit and let the flames die down with red embers visible. Set a grate over the fire. Alternatively, preheat a gas grill to 500°F (260°C).

Scrape and brush the hot grill grate well to clean, then wipe it with an oiled paper towel. Octopus is very sticky and needs a very clean and well-oiled grill.

Place the octopus on the hot grill and cook for 3 to 4 minutes, until grill marks are visible and it no longer sticks to the grill. If it's sticking, cook for a couple of minutes more. Gently turn and cook for another 3 minutes. Remove from the grill and cut each octopus in half lengthwise, leaving the tentacles whole.

To serve, spread a scoop of the romesco sauce on plates. Place the octopus on the plates and drizzle with the salsa verde.

Grilled Squid with Peperonata

Many types of squid inhabit the oceans all over the world. They range from tiny little ones that are smaller than your thumb to giant squid that are larger than you. I've eaten many types and find that they all taste quite similar, but the texture differs with their size. The flesh of the giant Humboldt squid is almost an inch thick and very dense, whereas that of tiny baby squid is much thinner and delicate. Squid has a mild briny sweet flavour that really benefits from a light charring on a grill. I must admit deep-fried is one of my favourite ways to cook squid, but I recommend grilling it. Deep-fried squid is usually well done and tastes more like the seasoned flour coating and the aioli it is dipped in. When it is grilled, you can taste more of its special natural and delicate flavour. Squid is ideally eaten medium doneness, which is best determined by sight and feel.

Purchased squid is usually white in colour because the brown skin has been removed. If the squid is brown, you can ask the fishmonger to remove the skin or you need to remove it before cooking, which can be a bit laborious.

SERVES **4** AS AN APPETIZER OR **2** AS A MAIN

Pull the tentacles from the body of the squid (this will also remove the innards). Cut off the innards from behind the tentacles and discard. Check for a thin clear piece of cartilage (skeleton) from inside the squid and discard. Cut away the wings at the narrow end of the body and discard. Locate the beak, a ball located in the middle of the tentacles, and squeeze it to pop it out; discard. Cut the body into ¼-inch (5 mm) rings, leaving attached ¼ inch (5 mm) from the top. (Be careful not to completely cut off the rings; you want them intact.) Place the sliced squid body and the tentacles in a large bowl. Drizzle with some olive oil, season with the kosher salt, and mix to coat. Set aside to marinate while the grill heats.

Prepare a charcoal or wood fire in an outdoor grill or firepit and let the flames die down with red embers visible. Set a grate over the fire. Alternatively, preheat a gas grill to 500°F (260°C.)

Heat 3 tablespoons (45 mL) olive oil in a medium saucepan over high heat. Add the onion and cook, stirring occasionally, for 2 minutes. Add the bell peppers and thyme and continue cooking, stirring occasionally, for another 2 minutes. Add the garlic and stir to incorporate. Add the sugar, a pinch each of sea salt and black pepper, and red wine vinegar and cook until the vinegar has evaporated. The peperonata should be soft and tender and appear stewed. Remove from the heat and keep warm.

Using metal tongs, place the squid (body and tentacles) on the hot grill. The squid will cook in 2 to 3 minutes per side with defined char marks.

Spoon the peperonata onto plates. Place the squid and tentacles on top. Garnish with the oregano and a drizzle of olive oil.

2 fresh squid (6 ounces/170 g each)

3 tablespoons (45 mL) olive oil, plus more for drizzling

½ teaspoon (2 mL) kosher salt

1 small white onion, sliced lengthwise into ⅛-inch (3 mm) strips

1 red bell pepper, sliced into ⅛-inch (3 mm) strips

1 yellow bell pepper, sliced into ⅛-inch (3 mm) strips

Leaves from 2 sprigs fresh thyme, chopped

4 cloves garlic, sliced

1 tablespoon (5 mL) granulated sugar

Sea salt and black pepper

1 tablespoon (5 mL) red wine vinegar

Leaves from 2 sprigs fresh oregano, for garnish

Seafood and Rabbit Paella

Paella is a cherished dish in Spanish cuisine, known for its vibrant colours and deep richness of flavour. Historically from the region of Valencia, it has developed and taken many forms over centuries to become the famous dish we know so well today.

Paella was made with what people had around them, using ingredients like rabbit, snails, and seafood, depending on proximity to the coast. Rabbit with seafood is my favourite combination, and I love to make it for family and friends. Bomba rice is traditionally used, but any short-grain rice will work if you can't find bomba. One of my favourite aspects of paella is the outer crispy edges similar to a lasagna.

SERVES 4 to 6

- 4 cups (1 L) chicken stock or game broth
- 1 teaspoon (5 mL) saffron threads
- 2 tablespoons (30 mL) olive oil
- 2 cups (500 mL) bomba or other short-grain rice
- 2 shallots, minced
- 2 teaspoons (10 mL) sea salt, divided
- 1 whole rabbit, quartered
- 4 cloves garlic, minced
- 2 jalapeño peppers, minced (leave in seeds if you prefer more heat)
- ½ cup (125 mL) dry white wine
- 2 pounds (900 g) live mussels, washed and beards removed
- 2 pounds (900 g) fresh head-on prawns
- 2 medium tomatoes, diced
- ¼ cup (60 mL) fresh flat-leaf parsley, chopped
- ¼ cup (60 mL) fresh cilantro, chopped
- Lemon wedges, for garnish

Prepare a charcoal or wood fire in an outdoor grill or firepit and let the flames die down with red embers visible. Set a grate over the fire. Alternatively, preheat a gas grill to 500°F (260°C).

Heat the stock in a small saucepan until scalding hot. Add the saffron and let steep and flavour the stock for 5 minutes.

Heat a large shallow paella pan (or thin steel pan) over the fire. Once hot, add the olive oil, then add the rice, stir, and cook for 2 minutes. Add the shallots, 1 teaspoon (5 mL) of the salt, the rabbit, garlic, and jalapeños. Stir to combine, then cook, stirring occasionally, for 2 to 3 minutes, until the rabbit is lightly browned. Add the white wine and cook for another 2 to 3 minutes, until evaporated. Pour in the saffron stock and cook until the liquid is reduced by half. Add the mussels and prawns. At this point stop stirring. One of paella's signature features is the crispy rice at the bottom and sides of the pan. Arrange the tomatoes on top and continue to cook until the liquid is absorbed, the mussels have opened, and the bottom rice is getting sticky and crispy around the edges, 4 to 6 minutes. Discard any mussels that did not open.

Top with the parsley and cilantro and sprinkle with the remaining 1 teaspoon (5 mL) salt. Serve with lemon wedges.

Gooseneck Barnacles

Gooseneck barnacles, also called percebes, are a delicacy in Spanish and Portuguese cultures, and they are slowly making their way to North American tables. These bizarre-looking creatures don't even look like they could be consumed, but they are incredibly tasty little bites and can be harvested off rocky shorelines on the Pacific coast. They taste very similar to clams but are a bit meatier in texture. Naturally sweet and briny seafood doesn't need a lot of help to bring out its flavour, and I keep the preparation simple. If you are a seafood lover, these are a must-try and a voyage for the senses.

SERVES **4**

Prepare a charcoal or wood fire in an outdoor grill or firepit and let the flames die down with red embers visible. Set a grate over the fire. Alternatively, preheat a gas grill to 500°F (260°C).

Meanwhile, soak the barnacles in a large bowl of cold salted water (1 tablespoon/15 mL kosher salt per 4 cups/1 L water) for 10 minutes. Drain the barnacles. Scrub the outside of the hard shell with a brush or green scrubbing pad to remove any seaweed or grit. Once cleaned, rinse and drain well.

Heat a large pot or mussel pot on the grill. Once hot, add the olive oil, shallots, salt, chili flakes, and the barnacles. Pour in the white wine and cover with a lid. Let the wine and natural juices steam the barnacles until hot, 3 to 4 minutes. Check that all the barnacles are hot, gently stir, and return to the heat if needed. Once cooked, remove from the heat.

Serve the barnacles immediately with a squeeze of fresh lemon juice and the parsley sprinkled on top. To eat, I trim the bottom of the barnacle with scissors and cut the tough black skin lengthwise from the bottom towards the hard shell and then peel off the skin. Then I bite off the succulent meat and toss the hard shell.

2 pounds (900 g) fresh gooseneck barnacles

1 tablespoon (15 mL) olive oil

1 shallot, minced

½ teaspoon (2 mL) kosher salt

Pinch of red chili flakes

1 cup (250 mL) dry white wine

1 lemon, for squeezing

1 tablespoon (15 mL) minced fresh flat-leaf parsley

Mussels in White Wine Cream Sauce with Grilled Baguette

Mussels can be found on many coastlines of the United States and Canada, and they come in various sizes with various flavour profiles. The best-known regions are the Atlantic shores of Canada and the northeastern States, but Pacific and Gulf Coast oysters are showing up more and more on menus across the country. I find Atlantic oysters to be delicate and briny and Pacific oysters to be meatier and earthy, while those from the warmer waters of the southern coasts have a characteristic slight sweetness to them. Regardless of where mussels are from, though, they are delicious, with a velvety texture and oceanic brininess quite unlike anything else.

Mussels can be cooked in various ways: in a cast-iron Dutch oven over a fire, in a pot on a grill, or in a wood-fired pizza oven. The main thing you must do to cook mussels properly is heat the pan on high for several minutes before adding any of the ingredients. Mussels are a delicate seafood and can overcook very quickly. The trick is to cook with intense steam from the white wine and cream so the mussels open quickly. At that point they are done.

This dish, inspired by the French classic moules à la crème, elevates the humble mussel's salinity with a rich cream sauce. A buttered and crunchy grilled baguette to soak up the sauce is key to fully enjoying the experience.

SERVES 2 to 4

Grilled Baguette

1 baguette

2 tablespoons (30 mL) unsalted butter, softened

2 cloves garlic, cut in half

Mussels in White Wine Cream Sauce

2 pounds (900 g) live mussels, washed and beards removed

1 shallot, minced

2 cloves garlic

1 sprig fresh thyme

Pinch of kosher salt

Pinch of freshly cracked black pepper

Pinch of red chili flakes

½ cup (125 mL) dry white wine

½ cup (125 mL) heavy (35%) cream

1 tablespoon (15 mL) chopped fresh flat-leaf parsley

1 tablespoon (15 mL) chopped fresh tarragon

Grill the Baguette

Prepare a charcoal or wood fire in an outdoor grill or firepit and let the flames die down with red embers visible. Set a grate over the fire. Alternatively, preheat a gas grill to 500°F (260°C).

Cut the bread in half lengthwise (and cut in half crosswise if very long). Butter the cut surfaces. Grill cut side down until toasted with char marks. Remove from the heat and rub the buttered sides with the garlic halves.

recipe continues

Prepare the Mussels in White Wine Cream Sauce

Preheat a large pot (if using a grill) or cast-iron Dutch oven (if cooking over a firepit) on high heat for at least 5 minutes. To test whether the pot is hot enough, flick a drop of water into the pot: it should sizzle. Once the pot is very hot, add the mussels, shallot, garlic, thyme, salt, pepper, and chili flakes. Shake the pot or stir to mix, then add the white wine and cream. Cover with a lid (the liquid should instantly steam) and cook for 2 minutes, then check to see whether all the mussels have opened. If not, give the mussels a stir, cover with the lid, and continue cooking for another 3 minutes. Remove the pot from the heat and discard any mussels that did not open. Top the mussels with the parsley and tarragon.

Spoon the mussels into warmed serving bowls, evenly distributing the broth. Serve with the grilled baguette.

Fowl and Small Game

Hunting Fowl and Game

Hunting small game is a great way to introduce newcomers and kids to hunting. It usually has more action than a deer hunt and is more social. You might find yourself walking fields with friends hunting upland birds with working dogs or sharing a duck blind with a group. Small-game hunters generally have more opportunities to harvest an animal than those who go hiking a mountain for a week in search of the mature bull elk.

Small game includes squirrels, rabbits, pheasants, quail, wild turkey, goose, and duck species, to name just a few. What these little critters lack in size they make up for in taste. For comparison, I like to explain my first reaction to harvesting and eating a wild turkey, because we have all seen and tasted farmed turkey. Wild turkey's skin and fat are yellow in colour and the breast meat is darker than that of a farmed bird. The leg meat is almost purple, like a duck breast. And the flavour of the cooked bird is far superior to farmed turkey, so much so that my mother exclaimed, "This doesn't even taste like turkey!" Then a family friend who'd taken me hunting for the first time corrected her, saying, "No, that shit in the grocery store doesn't taste like turkey. This is what turkey is *supposed* to taste like." It must be the natural diet of a wild turkey that is responsible for the drastic difference.

Those who hunt have a deep sense of satisfaction knowing where their food comes from. Small game and fowl are a lean and nutritious food source that is free from antibiotics, hormones, and other food additives unfortunately found in much store-bought meat.

When cooking with game, I try to think of recipes using conventional meat that I can substitute with game. Chicken is quite similar to rabbit, squirrel, grouse, and pheasant, so I adapt chicken recipes for those meats. Game is leaner and a little tougher than chicken, so you must think about solving that. You can brine the game in a salt solution with spices and herbs to tenderize it, marinate it, or in some cases pound the meat with a mallet to physically break up the tissues. From there you can stew or braise or cook slower with indirect heat—low and slow is the best approach. The darker small game meats such as ducks, geese, and spruce grouse lend themselves to being cooked to medium-rare to medium doneness.

My first time moose hunting was also the first time I hunted grouse. In northern Ontario the grouse are abundant. It was common to see groups of ten or more. They were coming to the roads to eat gravel for their gizzards. Birds swallow small pebbles that are stored in their gizzard to help grind their food for digestion. I would walk the old logging roads and flush them, shooting them with a small .410-gauge shotgun. I was fairly new to hunting and when I got back to camp, I had several spruce grouse and ruffed grouse in my vest. Some of the guys laughed and said, "You can't eat spruce grouse—they're awful." I thought I would give it a try anyway. I plucked my birds and noticed the meat of the spruce grouse was dark like a duck's while the ruffed grouse was more the colour of chicken. I built a fire and drizzled the birds with a little oil and seasoned them with some salt and pepper. I simply grilled them and instinctually (as a chef) grilled the darker grouse like I would duck, a little on the medium-rare side. To my surprise it was delicious. All my friends were shocked. They had grown up eating grouse that was overcooked, which brings out an unpleasant spruce and liver flavour from their diet of spruce needles. Now I love and welcome the challenge when someone tells me, "Oh, you can't eat that" or "Those are too tough," like my Pulled Goose Leg Barbecue (page 176).

Snacking Sticks

Snacking sticks, or pepperettes, are everyone's favourite snack on the go (they're essential fare in the hunt blind) and are a great gift for friends to share your game. Making them at home is easier than you might think and a fun way to spend an afternoon with friends and family.

The spices here are the classic pepperoni spices. Feel free to play around with your own spice blends and flavours, like honey garlic, hot pepperoni, and so on, but stick to the recipe's per-pound ratios for salt and curing salt.

Note: You can find curing salt (sodium nitrate) at your local butcher shop or online. I use Prague Powder #1.

MAKES ENOUGH STICKS FOR **4 to 6**

Prepare your smoker at 200°F (93°C).

Wearing gloves, put the venison and pork in a very large bowl. Add the black pepper, fennel seeds, paprika, garlic powder, cayenne pepper, kosher salt, and curing salt. Add the ice water and vigorously mix with gloved hands until well incorporated and sticky. The meat should stick to your hands when raised out of the bowl. (Alternatively, you can mix using a sausage meat mixer.)

Transfer the meat mixture to a sausage stuffer fitted with the fine or "breakfast" size stuffing horn. Slip the casing onto the horn and tie off the end. Push the meat into the casing, creating a firm pack. Do not overstuff the casing or it will break when you're twisting off the links. Once all the meat has been stuffed into the casing, measure the size of sausage you want to make and pinch the meat in the casing with your fingertips. Then twist off the links to separate into the desired size.

Hang the sausage with butcher twine in your smoker and smoke until the internal temperature reaches 165°F (75°C) on a probe thermometer, about 3 hours. Remove from the smoker and let cool to room temperature. Transfer to the fridge and let sit overnight.

Vacuum-seal and store in the fridge for up to 1 month. Snacking sticks do not freeze well, losing their snappy texture.

Special Equipment

Butcher twine

---

4 pounds (1.8 kg) ground venison

1 pound (450 g) ground fatty pork

1 tablespoon (15 mL) black pepper

2 teaspoons (10 mL) fennel seeds

2 teaspoons (10 mL) sweet paprika

1 teaspoon (5 mL) garlic powder

1 teaspoon (5 mL) cayenne pepper (use another 1 teaspoon/5 mL if you like it spicier)

2 tablespoons + 1 teaspoon (35 mL) Diamond Crystal kosher salt

1 teaspoon (5 mL) curing salt (Prague Powder #1)

1 cup (250 mL) ice water

Lamb, goat, or 22 mm collagen sausage casing (10 feet/3 m in length)

Goose Jerky

Canada goose jerky is a staple for me while adventuring outdoors. This high-protein nutritious snack keeps very well vacuum-sealed in the fridge or freezer, so I make big batches to last all year. I take this on hunting trips, camping trips, and long car trips with my family. Feel free to double this recipe if you are up for it and you shoot a lot of birds like I do. I'm so fortunate to live in a great migratory zone where at certain times of the year we can shoot ten of these birds per day, as they are an overabundant species.

This recipe involves smoking to dry the meat, but it can also be made in a dehydrator or home oven on the lowest setting with a convection fan on. You can use this recipe as a base guideline and tweak with your own favourite spices in the initial marinade.

SERVES 6 to 8

- 1½ cups (375 mL) soy sauce
- ½ cup (125 mL) pure maple syrup, plus more for brushing
- ¼ cup (60 mL) apple cider vinegar
- ½ cup (125 mL) packed brown sugar
- Pinch of red chili flakes
- 1 tablespoon (15 mL) sea salt
- 1 teaspoon (5 mL) freshly ground black pepper
- 10 skinless, boneless Canada goose breasts (about 5 pounds/ 2.25 kg total), sliced horizontally about ⅛ inch (3 mm) thick

Marinate the Meat

In a large bowl, whisk together the soy sauce, maple syrup, cider vinegar, brown sugar, chili flakes, salt, and pepper until the sugar is dissolved. Add the goose meat and mix to coat in the marinade. Transfer to a large container fitted with a lid or cover with plastic wrap and marinate in the fridge for at least 24 hours.

Smoke the Goose

Prepare your smoker at 165°F (75°C). You can use an offset smoker, pellet smoker, or barrel smoker. Light your wood fire and allow the flames to die down with red embers visible.

Lay the slices of goose meat in a single layer on a wire rack or baking sheet (discard the marinade). Smoke for 3 hours. Brush the meat with more maple syrup if you prefer a sweeter candied flavour. Continue to smoke for another 1 to 2 hours for a chewier jerky. If you like it dried more, smoke for another 30 minutes to 1 hour.

Remove from the smoker and let cool completely. Vacuum-seal the cooled jerky and store in the fridge for up to 1 month or in the freezer for up to 6 months.

Crane Steak au Poivre

Sandhill crane is famed for being the "ribeye in the sky" for its remarkable tasty resemblance to beef. However, it is not anywhere near as fatty and marbled as a beef ribeye, though it is quite tender, and the beef flavour is a shock for first-time tasters. I think a more appropriate name would be "flat-iron in the sky," but it doesn't quite have the same ring to it. If you don't have crane meat, you can use goose or duck breast.

This recipe is inspired by classical French cuisine's famous peppercorn sauce, usually served with beef steak. This rich, creamy sauce is fortified with cognac and reduced veal stock, known as demiglace. Alongside black peppercorns I use green peppercorns, which are unripe black peppercorns that are brined, resulting in a more tender, milder peppercorn than the dried version you find in the spice aisle.

SERVES 4

Roasted Stuffed Potatoes

4 medium baking potatoes, scrubbed

Olive oil, for brushing

Kosher salt and freshly ground black pepper

4 tablespoons (60 mL) unsalted butter, softened

2 tablespoons (30 mL) sour cream

Thinly sliced fresh chives, for garnish

Crane Steak au Poivre

2 skinless, boneless sandhill crane breasts (about 12 ounces/340 g each)

Salt and freshly ground black pepper (use a peppermill or mortar and pestle)

1 tablespoon (15 mL) olive oil

3 teaspoons (15 mL) unsalted butter, divided

1 small shallot, finely minced

2 cloves garlic, minced

2 tablespoons (30 mL) cognac, brandy, or dry sherry

½ cup (125 mL) heavy (35%) cream

¼ cup (60 mL) veal demiglace

2 tablespoons (30 mL) green peppercorns in brine, drained and patted dry

1 tablespoon (15 mL) black peppercorns, cracked (use a peppermill or mortar and pestle)

2 sprigs fresh thyme

1 bunch rapini, sautéed (optional)

Roast the Potatoes

Prepare a charcoal or wood fire in an outdoor grill or firepit and let the flames die down with red embers visible. Set a grate over the fire. Alternatively, preheat a gas grill to 500°F (260°C).

Brush the potatoes with some olive oil and season with salt and pepper. Individually wrap the potatoes in foil. Place the wrapped potatoes around the fire or on the top rack of your grill. Roast the potatoes until they are soft and can easily be pierced all the way through with a metal skewer, about 1 hour.

recipe continues

Make the Crane Steak au Poivre

Season the crane breasts all over with salt and a generous amount of freshly ground black pepper.

Preheat a large cast-iron skillet on the grill or directly on the fire. Add the olive oil and 1½ teaspoons (7 mL) of the butter to the hot pan. Place the breasts in the pan and sear over high heat for 1 to 2 minutes per side, until visibly caramelized and a crust has developed with the pepper. Transfer the pan to a wire rack or grill above the fire or to the top rack of the grill for indirect heat. Cook for another 6 to 8 minutes or until the internal temperature reaches 125°F (52°C) on a probe thermometer for medium-rare doneness. Remove the breasts from the pan and let rest for 5 minutes.

Meanwhile, melt the remaining 1½ teaspoons (7 mL) butter in a small saucepan. Add the shallot and sauté over high heat for 2 minutes. Add the garlic, then deglaze the pan with the cognac and cook, stirring, for another minute. Add the cream, demiglace, green peppercorns, cracked black peppercorns, and thyme and cook, stirring occasionally, until the sauce is reduced to a slightly thick consistency, 4 to 5 minutes.

Stuff the Potatoes

When the potatoes are soft, remove them from the foil. Lay the potatoes horizontally on a work surface and cut an oval opening in the top of each. Scoop out half of the potato flesh and add to a medium bowl. Add the butter and sour cream and season with a pinch each of salt and pepper. Mash the mixture with a spoon or fork to combine well. Generously stuff the hollowed potatoes.

Slice the crane breasts and arrange on plates. Spoon the pepper sauce over top. Place a stuffed potato on each plate and top with a sprinkle of chives. Serve with sautéed rapini, if desired.

Buffalo-Fried Quail

Quail is such a fun little bird to hunt, as being so incredibly fast and small, they are challenging to shoot. Unfortunately, their size means there isn't a lot of meat on the bones and they're very laborious to debone. Luckily, they are easy to pluck, as their feathers come off quite easily when pulled and rubbed. That said, this recipe is easy and fun to prepare, and both the awesome vinegar-based hot sauce that rhymes with Hanks and the homemade blue cheese dipping sauce will ruin store-bought stuff forever for you.

Buffalo wings are traditionally not breaded, but I like to lightly dust the quail with flour.

Note: For safety purposes, deep-frying outside is safer than indoors when using a pot. Always use a deep-frying thermometer attached to the pot to monitor the temperature. Cooking with a propane burner or live fire needs to be done with care.

SERVES 2 to 4

Red Hot Sauce

10 fresh cayenne peppers, ends and stems removed, chopped into ½-inch (1 cm) pieces (remove seeds for less heat)

1 cup (250 mL) white vinegar

4 cloves garlic

1 teaspoon (5 mL) kosher salt

Blue Cheese Dipping Sauce

¼ cup (60 mL) sour cream

¼ cup (60 mL) mayonnaise

Juice of ½ lemon

½ teaspoon (2 mL) kosher salt

Pinch of freshly ground black pepper

½ cup (125 mL) crumbled blue cheese

Buffalo-Fried Quail

6 whole quail, gutted and plucked

1 tablespoon (15 mL) kosher or sea salt

2 teaspoons (10 mL) freshly ground black pepper

¼ cup (60 mL) all-purpose flour

8 cups (2 L) vegetable oil, peanut oil, or lard, for deep-frying

Finely chopped fresh flat-leaf parsley, for garnish

For serving (optional)

Sliced heirloom carrots

Celery spears

Sliced radishes

Sliced Anaheim chilies (if you like heat, leave the seeds in, or for less heat, slice the chilies in half and remove the seeds)

Make the Red Hot Sauce

In a medium saucepan, combine the cayenne peppers, vinegar, garlic, and salt. Bring to a boil over high heat, then reduce the heat and simmer until the peppers and garlic are soft, 6 to 8 minutes.

Carefully pour the hot mixture into a blender and purée until smooth. Strain the puréed sauce through a fine-mesh sieve into a container and let cool. The cooled hot sauce can be stored in an airtight container in the fridge for up to 1 month.

recipe continues

Make the Blue Cheese Dipping Sauce

In a medium bowl, whisk together the sour cream, mayonnaise, lemon juice, salt, and pepper. Stir in the blue cheese; the sauce should be chunky. Store in the fridge until ready to use or in an airtight container in the fridge for up to 1 week.

Prepare and Fry the Quail

Cut each quail in half by cutting through the breastbone and backbone. Season all over with the salt and pepper. Place the quail in a large bowl. Dust with the flour and toss to evenly coat.

Prepare a charcoal or wood fire in an outdoor grill or firepit and let the flames die down with red embers visible. Set a grate over the fire. Alternatively, preheat a gas grill to 500°F (260°C).

If you are cooking over a fire, heat the vegetable oil in a large pot fitted with a deep-frying thermometer on the grill in a low indirect heat area. If you are using a propane burner, slowly heat the oil in a large pot fitted with a deep-frying thermometer. Heat to 375°F (190°C) and adjust the heat as needed to maintain this temperature.

Carefully lower the quail into the hot oil and fry until they are crispy and golden, 4 to 6 minutes, turning the quail halfway through cooking. Using metal tongs, remove the quail from the hot oil, shake off the excess oil in a wire basket strainer, and place them in a large bowl. Toss with the red hot sauce.

Garnish the quail with a sprinkle of parsley. Serve with sliced vegetables, if desired, and the blue cheese dipping sauce.

Smoked Pintail Duck

The northern pintail duck is a beautiful waterfowl species named for its striking long, pointed "pin" tail feathers stretching 4 to 5 inches (10 to 13 cm) behind them. They have pretty chocolate-coloured feathered heads and striking grey, white, and black markings on their body. The birds migrate primarily along the central, Mississippi, and Pacific flyways. I shot some in Saskatchewan in the largest flocks of ducks I have ever seen. Thousands of birds flew in intricate unison, circling the field before decoying into our spread—a truly spectacular experience. The meat reminds me of a slightly smaller mallard and is just as tasty. This is a great duck to pluck and smoke whole.

SERVES **4**

Air-Dry the Ducks

Rinse the cavity of each duck with cold running water. Pat dry with paper towel. Brush the ducks with olive oil and season with a big pinch each of salt and pepper. Stuff the cavities with the rosemary and thyme. Place the ducks on a wire rack set over a baking sheet and refrigerate, uncovered, overnight to air-dry. This helps the skin to crisp while cooking.

Smoke the Ducks

The next day, prepare a charcoal or wood fire in an outdoor grill or firepit and let the flames die down with red embers visible. Set a grate over the fire. Alternatively, prepare a digital or offset smoker set at 200°F (93°C).

Place the ducks on a wire rack or grill above the smoke and flames for indirect heat. If using a smoker, cook at 200°F (93°C). Slowly smoke the duck until the internal temperature reaches 130°F (55°C) on a probe thermometer. For crispy skin, move the ducks closer to the flames for 1 to 2 minutes. The skin will cook quickly, so be careful not to burn it. Remove from the grill or smoker and let rest for 10 minutes.

Carve the meat into thin slices. Garnish with sliced jalapeños and chilies along with your favourite sides.

2 whole pintail ducks, gutted and plucked

Olive oil, for brushing

Kosher salt and freshly ground black pepper

1 bunch fresh rosemary

1 bunch fresh thyme

For garnish

2 jalapeño peppers, thinly sliced

2 Anaheim chilies, thinly sliced (if you like heat, leave the seeds in, or for less heat, slice the chilies in half and remove the seeds)

Crispy-Skin Snow Goose

I have been working on mastering this dish for years. Wild birds are completely different from farmed birds. Farmed birds are usually slaughtered under a year old, so their meat is naturally tender, whereas wild birds can live to over twenty years of age. That's a long time to develop strong muscles, tendons, and tough sinews in the meat which take much longer to become tender in cooking. As well, farmed birds have luscious fatty skin that easily renders and gets crispy during cooking, whereas wild birds have thinner skin that can become rubbery. I've finally figured out how to achieve crispy skin while not overcooking the meat! The secret lies in the following method.

For this recipe, it is best to use a juvenile snow goose. When hunting, these birds will appear smaller and lighter in weight; they usually have a grey plumage and their feet and bills are a dark olive colour. After their first winter, the birds' feathers are replaced by white ones, and by their second year they are a beautiful snow-white colour.

SERVES 4

Pluck, Gut, and Dry-Age the Goose

After hunting, remove the feathers, wing tips, and feet from the goose. Cut the belly open and remove the innards, saving the heart and liver to freeze for later use. Remove the neck, cutting it about 2 inches (5 cm) up from the breast. This will leave the skin intact because there will be some shrinkage when cooking. Rinse out the cavity of the bird with water and pat dry with a kitchen towel.

This next step is a little tricky and is based on the technique for Peking duck in Chinese cuisine. The goal is to leave the skin on the bird but to separate it from the meat so its fat can render from the top (outside) and bottom (inside). If your results are not perfect, that's okay, and this step can even be skipped, but it does help crisp the skin. Starting from the cut at the belly and working around the sides to the back, gently pull the skin away from the meat, being careful not to tear it. You can gently use a small paring knife if it doesn't come away easily. Leave the wings, as it's very difficult to lift the skin at the joints. Season the goose with salt and rub it into the skin, set the bird on a wire rack in a small baking sheet, and let it dry-age in the fridge for 2 days.

Roast the Goose

After 2 days, remove the goose from the fridge.

Prepare a charcoal or wood fire in a heavy ceramic grill (Big Green Egg style) or build a wood fire in an outdoor wood pizza oven. Let the flames die down with red embers visible. The ideal cooking temperature is 700°F (370°C).

Special Equipment

Butcher twine

---

1 whole young wild snow goose

1 tablespoon (15 mL) kosher or sea salt

1 teaspoon (5 mL) freshly ground black pepper

1 bunch fresh thyme

1 bunch fresh rosemary

recipe continues

Boil a kettle full of water. Place the goose on a wire rack in the sink and slowly pour boiling water all over the skin. The bird's skin will shrink and tighten up, which is what you want. Rinse with cold water and pat dry. Season with salt and pepper, then stuff the cavity with the thyme and rosemary.

To truss the bird, place it on a cutting board breast side up with the legs pointing at you. Cut a piece of butcher twine about 3 feet (1 m) long. Holding each end of the twine, place the middle of the twine at the neck end of the bird. Pull the twine towards you, wrap it around the wings once, and pull it towards the legs. Crisscross the twine around the legs, pull tight, and tie tightly. This pulls all the meat tightly together and promotes more even cooking.

Place the trussed bird in a roasting pan and cook for about 20 minutes. (If using a pizza oven, rotate the pan every 5 minutes.) The goose is done when the internal temperature reaches 125° to 130°F (52° to 55°C) on a probe thermometer. The skin should be dark amber in colour and crisp. Remove the goose from the oven and let rest, uncovered, for at least 15 minutes before slicing. (Covering the bird with foil can cause condensation on the inside of the foil and ruin the hard work of crisping the skin.)

Thinly slice the bird and serve with your favourite sides.

Whole Roasted Woodcock

When I say whole roasted, I mean it! In France this little bird is traditionally cooked with the entrails still inside; they are then used to make a pâté-like sauce. This odd-looking little bird has an enormously long beak for eating earthworms and other invertebrates. The woodcock is a migratory game bird, breeding in northeastern Canada and the United States and migrating south to Florida, Texas, Louisiana, and parts of Mexico in the winter. Pointing dogs are used to hunt this tasty upland bird because they are so well camouflaged that they are near impossible to hunt and retrieve without a dog.

SERVES 4 AS AN APPETIZER

Prepare a charcoal or wood fire in an outdoor grill or firepit and let the flames die down with red embers visible. Set a grate over the fire. Alternatively, preheat a gas grill to 500°F (260°C). Heat a large, heavy cast-iron skillet over the fire.

Season the woodcock with salt and pepper.

Add the olive oil to the hot pan. Place the woodcock in the pan and sear until golden brown all over, 2 to 3 minutes per side. Add the butter and the rosemary to the pan, then baste the butter and pan drippings over the birds with a spoon. Continue cooking until the birds are golden and the internal temperature reaches 130°F (55°C) on a probe thermometer. Remove the birds from the pan and let rest while you cook the shallots.

To the same pan (no need to wipe it), add the shallots, then move the pan to indirect heat and cook over medium heat, stirring occasionally, until the shallots have softened and begin to caramelize, 2 to 3 minutes.

Using scissors or a knife, cut the skin of the bird under the breastbone, scoop out the insides with a spoon, and add them to the sautéing shallots. Add the thyme and brandy, stir to combine, and cook until the alcohol has evaporated, 1 to 2 minutes. Season with a pinch each of salt and pepper. Break up the liver and heart with the back of the spoon to make a chunky purée (or remove from the pan and chop with a knife, then return to the pan). Add the parsley and stir to combine. It should resemble a chunky pâté. Remove from the heat.

Brush one side of the baguette slices with olive oil. Toast or grill oiled side down until lightly golden.

To serve, spread the pâté over the baguette. Cut each woodcock in half lengthwise, following the breastbone and cutting into the cavity through the breastbone and backbone. Place the woodcock halves on the toasted baguette and pâté. Cut the head in half and present the beak on the plate. The beak is used to help scoop out the brain and eat it. Spread the grape jelly on the plate as a garnish.

2 whole woodcock, gutted and plucked

Kosher salt and black pepper

1 tablespoon (15 mL) olive oil, plus more for brushing the baguette

1 tablespoon (15 mL) unsalted butter

1 sprig fresh rosemary

1 shallot, minced

Leaves from 1 sprig fresh thyme, chopped

2 tablespoons (30 mL) brandy or cognac

Leaves from 1 sprig fresh flat-leaf parsley, chopped

1 demi baguette, cut crosswise on a diagonal into ½-inch (1 cm) thick slices

¼ cup (60 mL) grape jelly, for garnish

Smoked Duck Wings with Maple Hot Sauce

SERVES 4 to 6

This is one of my favourite recipes to enjoy with friends, whether for a special football game or just a fun night together, because it's such a crowd-pleaser. Chicken wings are no comparison to these meaty smoked duck wings. Farmed duck wings tend to be larger than wild duck wings but similar to wild goose wings. Both farmed and wild are much tougher than chicken wings and must be smoked for a lengthy period to break down, but it is worth it, I promise.

Smoked Duck Wings

½ cup (125 mL) sweet paprika

¼ cup (60 mL) packed brown sugar

2 tablespoons (30 mL) Diamond Crystal kosher salt

1 tablespoon (15 mL) garlic powder

1 tablespoon (15 mL) onion powder

1 teaspoon (5 mL) black pepper

1 teaspoon (5 mL) cayenne pepper (or 2 teaspoons/10 mL for spicy, or 1 tablespoon/15 mL for hot)

4 pounds (1.8 kg) duck wings, separated into drumettes and flats

Maple Hot Sauce

½ cup (125 mL) vegetable oil, divided

1 cup (250 mL) chopped Anaheim chilies (if you like heat, leave the seeds in, or for less heat, slice the chilies in half and remove the seeds)

4 cloves garlic

2 bay leaves

2 sprigs fresh thyme

1 teaspoon (5 mL) kosher salt

1 cup (250 mL) pure maple syrup

Prepare the Duck Wings

In a large bowl, stir together the paprika, brown sugar, salt, garlic powder, onion powder, black pepper, and cayenne pepper. Add the duck wings and mix to completely coat in the dry rub. Cover and refrigerate overnight.

Make the Maple Hot Sauce

Heat a medium saucepan over high heat. Add 1 tablespoon (15 mL) of the vegetable oil, the chilies, garlic, bay leaves, and thyme. Sauté until the chilies are soft, about 5 minutes. Add the remaining vegetable oil, reduce the heat to low, and gently cook the chilies and garlic, without letting them simmer in the oil, until very soft, about 30 minutes. Remove from the heat. Discard the bay leaves and thyme sprigs.

Purée the sauce with a hand blender or transfer the sauce to a blender and purée until smooth. Season with the salt, then add the maple syrup and stir. Strain the sauce through a fine-mesh sieve into a container. Reserve if you are using right away or store in an airtight container in the fridge for up to 2 weeks. Bring to room temperature before using.

Smoke the Duck Wings

Remove the wings from the fridge.

Prepare your smoker at 225°F (110°C). Place the wings directly on the grill of the smoker and smoke for 1½ hours. Transfer the wings to a baking sheet and wrap the tray tightly with foil. Return to the smoker and smoke for another 1 to 1½ hours, until the wings are tender and can be pulled apart. (Avoid cooking until the wings fall apart or they will be difficult to handle and eat.)

Toss the wings in the maple hot sauce and serve.

Grilled Quail with Honey-Lime Glaze and Corn Salsa

Wild quail can be found in a variety of habitats in every continent except Antarctica. Their homes include grasslands, open woodlands, agricultural fields, and brushy areas. Wild quail require a mix of cover, such as dense vegetation or shrubs, and open areas for foraging. They are easily one of the most fun and challenging game birds to pursue, and for good reason. They are incredibly tasty.

This recipe uses a sweet-and-sour glaze to complement the grilled flavour of the quail. The quail can be served as an appetizer or served with your favourite side dish for a main course.

SERVES 4 to 6 AS AN APPETIZER

Prepare a charcoal or wood fire in an outdoor grill or firepit and let the flames die down with red embers visible. Set a grate over the fire. Alternatively, preheat a gas grill to 500°F (260°C).

Prepare the Quail and Make the Honey-Lime Glaze

To spatchcock the quail, cut each quail along one side of the backbone, then cut along the other side of the backbone to remove it from the quail. Discard the backbone or save for making stock. Spread the quail flat.

In a small bowl, combine the honey, lime zest and juice, and salt and pepper to taste. Mix well with a spoon. Drizzle half of the glaze over the quail, then brush it on both sides. Reserve the remaining glaze.

Make the Corn Salsa

Brush or wipe the grill grate with a little oil. Put the corn on the grill and cook until lightly charred on all sides, 2 minutes per side (about 8 minutes total). Remove from the grill and let sit until cool enough to handle. Cut the corn kernels off the cobs into a large bowl. Add the serrano chili, shallot, cilantro, and a squeeze of lime juice. Season to taste with salt and pepper. Set aside.

Grill the Quail

Place the quail on the grill and cook for 2 to 3 minutes per side until char marks are visible. Then brush the remaining glaze on each side of the quail. This will caramelize on the bird from the heat. Cook until the quail is firm and the skin is crispy and charred.

Serve immediately with the corn salsa.

Grilled Quail with Honey-Lime Glaze

8 whole quail, gutted and plucked

¼ cup (60 mL) pure liquid honey

Zest and juice of 2 limes

Kosher salt and black pepper

Corn Salsa

2 sweet corn cobs, husked

1 small serrano chili or jalapeño pepper, minced

1 small shallot, minced

Leaves from 6 sprigs fresh cilantro leaves, for garnish

1 lime, for squeezing

Kosher salt and black pepper

Barbecued Pheasant with Alabama White Sauce

White sauce is an underdog in the BBQ game, and it really is a shame. The vinegar in the marinade tenderizes and brines the meat, producing an incredible juicy bird. Horseradish and vinegar give this sauce a zip, while the mayonnaise provides a rich, creamy depth. It's quite delicious and worthy of a spot in your BBQ repertoire.

SERVES **2**

Prepare the White Sauce and the Pheasant

In a large bowl, whisk together the mayonnaise, white wine vinegar, horseradish, mustard, lemon juice, salt, black pepper, and cayenne pepper. Pour about half of the white sauce into a container fitted with a lid and reserve in the fridge until ready to use (you'll toss the grilled bird in it).

To spatchcock the pheasant, cut out the backbone, then turn the bird over and press down on the breastbone to flatten the bird. Add the pheasant to the bowl with the remaining sauce and toss or brush to thoroughly coat both sides. Cover with plastic wrap and marinate in the fridge for at least 3 to 4 hours or overnight.

Make the Potato Salad

Place the baby potatoes in a large pot, cover with water, and boil over high heat until tender, about 10 minutes. Drain.

While the potatoes are boiling, sauté the bacon in a large skillet over high heat to render the fat, 3 to 4 minutes. Reduce the heat to medium and continue cooking until the bacon is golden brown and crispy. Transfer the bacon to paper towel to drain.

Strain the warm fat and transfer ¼ cup (60 mL) to a medium bowl. Add the olive oil, cider vinegar, and mustard. Season with salt and pepper. Whisk to combine.

Cut the drained potatoes in half or quarters if large. Add the potatoes to the warm dressing and toss to combine. Set aside.

Make the Broccoli Salad

Cut the broccoli florets off the stem. Cut the florets into bite-size pieces. Cut off and discard the tough outer green skin of the stem. Chop the inner white part into bite-size pieces.

Barbecued Pheasant

1½ cups (375 mL) mayonnaise

½ cup (125 mL) white wine vinegar

3 tablespoons (45 mL) hot prepared horseradish

1 tablespoon (15 mL) ballpark mustard

Juice of 1 lemon

1 teaspoon (5 mL) kosher salt

Pinch of black pepper

Pinch of cayenne pepper or garlic powder

1 whole pheasant, gutted and plucked

Potato Salad

8 ounces (225 g) baby potatoes

4 ounces (115 g) bacon, chopped

¼ cup (60 mL) olive oil

¼ cup (60 mL) apple cider vinegar

2 tablespoons (30 mL) Dijon mustard

Salt and pepper

1 small shallot, minced

1 green onion, thinly sliced

1 tablespoon (15 mL) chopped fresh flat-leaf parsley

Broccoli Salad

1 bunch broccoli

½ cup (125 mL) olive oil

¼ cup (60 mL) red wine vinegar

1 shallot, minced

2 tablespoons (30 mL) pumpkin seeds

2 tablespoons (30 mL) dried cranberries

recipe continues

In a large bowl, whisk together the olive oil, red wine vinegar, and shallot. Add the broccoli and toss to coat. Top the salad with the pumpkin seeds and dried cranberries. Set aside.

Grill the Pheasant

Prepare a charcoal or wood fire in an outdoor grill or firepit and let the flames die down with red embers visible. Set a grate over the fire. Alternatively, preheat a gas grill to 500°F (260°C).

Remove the reserved white sauce from the fridge and scrape it into a large bowl; set aside. Place the pheasant skin side down on the grill grate in an area with medium heat. Cook until deep char marks are visible and the skin no longer sticks to the grill, 5 to 7 minutes. Turn the bird 90 degrees and cook for another 5 to 7 minutes. Flip the bird and cook for another 5 to 7 minutes, until the skin is golden and crispy. Turn 90 degrees a final time and cook until the internal temperature reaches 155°F (70°C) on a probe thermometer, checking every 2 to 3 minutes. Remove from the grill. Toss the bird in the reserved white sauce (or brush it on just before serving).

Top the potatoes with the shallot, green onion, parsley, and reserved crispy bacon; toss to combine. Serve the pheasant with the potato salad and broccoli salad.

Hot Rabbit with Braised Collard Greens

Nashville hot chicken has become one of the most popular fried dishes in the United States, and for good reason: it is delicious. And I promise you it's even better made with wild rabbit. Now, if you don't have a wild rabbit, I am seeing farmed rabbit more readily available in major grocery stores. According to legend, a woman (whose name isn't recorded) was angry at her womanizing suitor, a Mr. Thornton Prince, and created the recipe to try to kill his palate with spice. Her plan backfired when Prince praised the dish, and he began perfecting the recipe to share with his family and friends. Today the legend lives on at Prince's Hot Chicken Shack in Nashville, Tennessee.

Note: I recommend frying the rabbit outside rather than indoors, which can be a fire hazard. Use a deep-frying thermometer attached to the pot to monitor the temperature. Cooking with a propane burner needs to be done with care.

SERVES 4

Rabbit and Marinade

4 skinless, bone-in rabbit legs (about 2 pounds/900 g total)

2 cups (500 mL) buttermilk

3 eggs

½ cup (125 mL) Maple Hot Sauce (page 138) or your favourite vinegar-based hot sauce

1 tablespoon (15 mL) +1 teaspoon (5 mL) kosher salt, divided

Black pepper

3 quarts (3 L) vegetable oil, for frying

4 cups (1 L) all-purpose flour

¼ cup (60 mL) sweet paprika

1 tablespoon (15 mL) garlic powder

2 teaspoons (10 mL) cayenne pepper

Braised Collard Greens

8 ounces (225 g) bacon or salt pork, cut crosswise into ¼- to ½-inch (5 mm to 1 cm) strips

1 small yellow onion, diced

1 large bunch collard greens, stems removed, and chopped into 1- to 2-inch (2.5 to 5 cm) pieces

4 cups (1 L) chicken stock

1 teaspoon (5 mL) red wine vinegar

2 bay leaves

Pinch of red chili flakes

Spiced Oil

1 tablespoon (15 mL) sweet paprika

1 teaspoon (5 mL) garlic powder

1 teaspoon (5 mL) cayenne pepper

1 teaspoon (5 mL) brown sugar

Pinch each of salt and black pepper

½ cup (125 mL) hot frying oil (from frying the rabbit; at left)

For serving

4 slices white bread

Bread-and-butter pickles

Coleslaw (optional)

Prepare and Marinate the Rabbit Legs

Using a boning knife, cut along the inside of each rabbit leg directly on top of the bone that runs in an L shape. Pull the meat back and cut close along each side of the bone until you can cut underneath the bone and fully remove it. Cover the meat with plastic wrap or wax paper and gently pound the rabbit meat to flatten it slightly and tenderize. Do not pound so hard that the meat breaks and separates.

recipe continues

In a container large enough to fit the rabbit, whisk together the buttermilk, eggs, hot sauce, 1 teaspoon (5 mL) of the salt, and a pinch of black pepper. Add the rabbit meat, turning to coat it well, and marinate, covered, in the fridge for at least 4 hours or overnight.

Make the Braised Collard Greens

Preheat a gas grill at high heat. If cooking the collard greens indoors, preheat the oven to 300°F (150°C).

In a large stainless steel frying pan on the grill, sauté the bacon, stirring occasionally, until brown and caramelized, 3 to 4 minutes. Add the onion and collard greens and continue sautéing for another 3 to 4 minutes, stirring occasionally, until both are softened. Add the stock, red wine vinegar, bay leaves, and chili flakes. Season with salt and pepper. Cover with a lid, reduce the heat to a simmer (or transfer to the oven), and braise the collard greens for about 2 hours or until the collards are very tender and most of the liquid has evaporated. Start cooking the rabbit at the halfway mark.

Prepare the Spiced Oil Seasoning

In a small metal or heat-resistant bowl, stir together the paprika, garlic powder, cayenne pepper, brown sugar, salt, and black pepper. Set aside.

Deep-Fry the Rabbit

Using a propane burner, slowly heat the vegetable oil in a medium pot fitted with a deep-frying thermometer. Heat to 375°F (190°C) and adjust the heat as needed to maintain this temperature.

In a large bowl, stir together the flour, paprika, garlic powder, cayenne pepper, and remaining 1 tablespoon (15 mL) salt. Using tongs, remove the rabbit legs from the buttermilk mixture and transfer to the seasoned flour, dredging both sides. Using the same tongs, return the rabbit to the buttermilk mixture and coat again. Return to the seasoned flour and toss to evenly coat the rabbit. Leave the rabbit meat in the seasoned flour until ready to fry.

Using metal tongs, gently lower the rabbit legs into the hot oil. Fry the rabbit for 6 to 8 minutes or until the flour crust is dark golden brown and the internal temperature of the meat reaches at least 165°F (75°C) on a probe thermometer. Using tongs or a wire strainer, remove the rabbit, shaking off the excess oil, and place in a large bowl.

Finish the Spiced Oil and Toss with the Fried Rabbit

Ladle ½ cup (125 mL) of the hot frying oil into the bowl of spice mixture. Mix well with a small whisk. Pour the hot spiced oil over the fried rabbit legs and toss to coat well. Serve the hot rabbit on top of the slices of bread, topped with pickles. Serve with the collard greens and your favourite coleslaw, if desired.

Large Game

Hunting Large Wild Game

My pursuit of large game is deeply primal and exhilarating. Chasing large game animals has been ingrained into human culture for millennia and captivates my imagination, fuelling my instinctual connection with the natural world. The more time I spend outdoors in nature, the less time I want to spend indoors. Cities have become bothersome—the traffic, congestion, concrete structures all weigh heavily on my mind. I'm always daydreaming of the next hunt and adventures I want to create. I regularly dream of what it was like to have to hunt for survival and live off the land.

The challenge of outsmarting elusive prey continually humbles me. Elk, deer, bear, muskox, and moose have scented me countless times, leaving me dumbfounded and amazed at their defence mechanisms. Hunting these animals is a true test of physical and mental prowess that is rewarding and demanding whether the animal is harvested or not. Some of my most memorable hunts have been my failures; the memory of the chase will last a lifetime.

Pursuing large game offers a profound opportunity for self-reliance, connecting us to nature and personal growth while we overcome the rugged elements of Mother Nature. My first elk hunt hiking a mountain in Colorado left me gasping for air because I wasn't used to the low oxygen levels at 9000 feet above sea level. Navigating rugged terrain while trying to predict animal behaviour instills the utmost appreciation and respect of the natural world and the delicate balance between life and death in their environment. The sound of a screaming bugle from an elk made me tremble so much I could barely keep my rifle steady. These animals are majestic and resilient and leave hunters to recognize our duty to look after these lands not only for the animals' well-being but to ensure the enjoyment for our children and the generations to come. Ethical hunting, fair chase, sustainable harvests, land management, and fees from hunting are paramount to ensure the long-term health of wild game.

Ultimately, hunting large game is far more than just the chase or the satisfaction of a successful kill. It's a deeply meaningful experience that connects us to the natural world. Whether you are hunting for sustenance or sport hunting, it is a timeless tradition that continues to inspire all who partake.

After all the physical and mental demands, after the shot is taken and the animal is down, the work is not over. Proper skinning, gutting, butchering, and cooling are all equally important cogs in the wheel of the hunt. When someone tells me that they found game meat to have offensive off-tastes, that's usually because of a problem with one or more of those cogs I just mentioned. Cloth game bags are a great tool to carry while hunting. Meat is deboned and stored in the bags, which breathe and can be hung from a tree branch to cool in the shade at camp. Meat can be stored outside for days in these bags if the temperature stays below 40°F (5°C). However, in warmer weather, it is imperative to get the meat into a fridge the same day if not within hours, depending on how warm it is outside.

Once the meat has been transported home, wrapping and storing begins. Freezer butcher paper is very easy to source online and comes in a giant roll. I have been able to freeze tightly wrapped meat without discoloration or any freezer burn for five years. It could last longer, but that's the longest storage to date at my home. I consider vacuum-sealing second-best, but the clear bags are convenient and make it easy to tell what's inside. Proper labelling is always important, noting the species, the specific cut, and the date. Countless times I didn't label meat properly and months later had to play a guessing game of what some package was. You don't want to mistake bear meat for elk, as bear needs to be thoroughly cooked to kill all potential parasites.

Large game is incredibly delicious when cooked properly. It's well suited for cooking over the fire, especially whole hindquarters or other large cuts, partly because of the visual show. Indirect heat slowly breaks down the tough cuts and the meat takes on the beautiful smoke flavour. Ribs, shoulders, and shanks are great to cook over the fire but need to be wrapped halfway through the cooking so the tough connective tissues can soften.

Overall, cooking large game over the fire is an excellent way to celebrate your harvest and enjoy the rich flavours of game meat with those close to you.

Boar Bacon Fig Poppers

This is a fun recipe I developed while visiting friends in Mississippi in the summer when the fig tree at their cabin was absolutely bursting with figs. We had a slab of boar bacon in the fridge and a chunk of goat cheese, and I instantly thought of a tasty appetizer to share around the campfire. The salty, fatty bacon wrapped around a sweet fig packed with tangy goat cheese is incredible.

For this recipe I use a double-smoked cured and cooked bacon. If you are using cured and cold-smoked raw bacon, precook the slices so that most of the fat renders but the bacon is still pliable enough to wrap around the figs.

SERVES 4 to 6 AS AN APPETIZER

Prepare a charcoal or wood fire in an outdoor grill or firepit and let the flames die down with red embers visible. Set a grate over the fire. Alternatively, preheat a gas grill to 500°F (260°C).

Partially cut the figs lengthwise, starting at the base and leaving the stem end intact. "Butterfly" the fig so it lies flat. Scoop 1 tablespoon (15 mL) of goat cheese and pack it in the middle of each fig. Press together the sides to partially close the fig, then wrap a slice of boar bacon around each stuffed fig. Skewer with a toothpick to hold everything in place.

Preheat a large cast-iron skillet on the grill or directly on the coals.

Place the stuffed figs on their sides in the hot skillet and heat, gently turning until the bacon is cooked and slightly crispy, 2 to 3 minutes per side.

Transfer the poppers to a serving dish and drizzle with the honey. Garnish with basil and mint, if using. Finish with a sprinkle each of flaky sea salt and pepper.

12 fresh ripe green or black figs (they should be soft)

8 ounces (225 g) soft goat cheese

1 pound (450 g) thickly sliced double-smoked wild boar bacon

2 tablespoons (30 mL) wildflower honey

For garnish

Chopped fresh basil (optional)

Chopped fresh mint (optional)

Flaky sea salt and freshly ground black pepper

LARGE GAME
156

Fire-Roasted Antelope Chops with Rosemary and Tzatziki

SERVES 4

I was completely surprised how incredible pronghorn antelope tastes. It's exceptionally tender and has a sweet, mild lamb-like flavour. These animals are the fastest creatures in North America and can only be outrun by the African cheetah in short distances, but the cheetah will be outrun in distance by the antelope. They are also the oldest living mammal in North America, once living here with giant mammoths. They can mainly be found in western and central parts of North America, including as far north as Alberta and Saskatchewan and down into Montana, Wyoming, Colorado, California, Nevada, Utah, Arizona, and New Mexico. This recipe features Mediterranean flavours that are perfect with smoky grilled and fire-roasted meat.

Special Equipment
Butcher twine

Tzatziki
1 cup (250 mL) plain full-fat Greek yogurt
Juice of 1 lemon
¼ cup (60 mL) grated cucumber
1 tablespoon (15 mL) minced shallot
2 cloves garlic, crushed
1 teaspoon (5 mL) chopped fresh dill
1 teaspoon (5 mL) kosher salt
Freshly cracked black pepper

Fire-Roasted Antelope
2 racks of antelope (about 3 pounds/1.35 kg total)
Kosher salt and freshly cracked black pepper
2 sprigs fresh rosemary
2 lemons, cut in half

For garnish
Fresh oregano leaves
Fresh mint leaves

Make the Tzatziki

In a medium bowl, combine the yogurt, lemon juice, cucumber, shallot, garlic, dill, salt, and pepper. Mix well. Store, covered, in the fridge until ready to use.

Fire-Roast the Antelope Racks

Prepare a charcoal or wood fire in an outdoor grill or firepit and let the flames die down with red embers visible. Set a grate over the fire. Alternatively, preheat a gas grill to 500°F (260°C).

For a clean presentation, scrape any fat and sinew off the antelope racks with the back of a boning knife (this is called French trimming or frenching). Truss the meat in between the bones with butcher twine for even cooking. Season the meat with a big pinch each of salt and pepper.

Grill the racks for 4 to 5 minutes per side to sear the meat and develop a charred flavour. Once grill marks appear, move the racks to indirect heat on the grill and place the rosemary on the meat. (Cooking over direct high heat for too long may burn and overcook the outside meat while leaving the inside undercooked.) The meat is done (medium-rare) when the internal temperature reaches 125°F (52°C) on a probe thermometer. Remove from the heat and let rest for 10 minutes before slicing.

While the meat rests, place the lemon halves cut side down on the grill over high heat. Grill until the surface is caramelized with dark char marks.

Remove the butcher twine from the racks and slice between the bones into chops.

To serve, spread the tzatziki on plates. Arrange the chops over the tzatziki. Garnish with the oregano and mint. Serve with the grilled lemons.

Sausage-Stuffed Grouse with Maple Candied Yams

Grouse is one of my favourite game birds to hunt. If you have a hunting dog it makes it even more enjoyable, not just to watch the dogs work but also to improve your success rate. However, in northern Ontario where I moose hunt, grouse are all over the trails searching for gravel to swallow, which fills their gizzard and grinds up their food. These small chicken-size birds freeze as a defence mechanism, so they are, unfortunately for them, very easy to shoot. We give them a sporting chance by flushing them up into the air before shooting, but it you are stranded and starving, they are an easy target.

Stuffing the bird helps crisp the outside while slowing down the cooking from the inside so the meat doesn't dry out before the skin is crisp. The result is a beautifully juicy bird.

SERVES **4**

Prepare a charcoal or wood fire in an outdoor grill or firepit and let the flames die down with red embers visible. Set a grate over the fire. Alternatively, preheat a gas grill to 500°F (260°C).

Stuff and Truss the Grouse

In a medium bowl, mix together the ground boar and pork back fat. Add the garlic, fennel seeds, paprika, salt, black pepper, and cayenne pepper and mix well. Stuff the meat mixture into the cavities of the grouse.

To truss the birds, place one bird at a time on a cutting board breast side up with the legs pointing at you. Cut 2 pieces of butcher twine each about 18 inches (45 cm) long. Holding each end of the twine, place the middle of the twine at the neck end of the bird. Pull the twine towards you, wrap it around the wings once, and pull it towards the legs. Crisscross the twine around the legs, pull tight, and tie tightly. This pulls all the meat tightly together and promotes more even cooking.

Roast the Maple Candied Yams and Grouse

Place the sliced yams in a roasting pan. Toss with the olive oil and season with salt and pepper. Cover with foil (or close the lid if using a barbecue). Place the roasting pan on the grill grate and roast at high heat between 400° and 500°F (200° to 260°C) for 10 to 15 minutes, until golden. Remove from the grill and remove the foil. Brush the sliced yams with 1 tablespoon (15 mL) of the maple syrup. Return to the grill to reduce the maple syrup.

Special Equipment

Butcher twine

Sausage-Stuffed Grouse

10 ounces (280 g) ground wild boar or pork

6 ounces (170 g) ground pork back fat or fatty pork

2 cloves garlic, crushed

1 teaspoon (5 mL) fennel seeds

1 teaspoon (5 mL) smoked paprika

1 teaspoon (5 mL) kosher or sea salt

½ teaspoon (2 mL) freshly ground black pepper

¼ teaspoon (1 mL) cayenne pepper

2 wild or farmed ruffed grouse, gutted and plucked (about 1 pound/450 g each)

Maple Candied Yams

4 small yams, thickly sliced (about 3 cups/750 mL)

2 tablespoons (30 mL) olive oil

Kosher salt and pepper

2 tablespoons (30 mL) pure maple syrup, divided

Sliced green onions, for garnish

recipe continues

Place the grouse breast side up in a separate roasting pan and place on the grill grate alongside the yams. Roast the yams and grouse until golden, 10 to 15 minutes. Remove the yams from the grill, brush with the remaining 1 tablespoon (15 mL) maple syrup, and continue cooking until tender and glazed, another 5 to 6 minutes; remove from the heat. Roast the grouse until the internal temperature reaches 145°F (63°C) on a probe thermometer. Remove from the heat and let rest for 10 minutes before cutting.

Slice the grouse in half by cutting lengthwise along the breastbone and through the stuffing and backbone. Serve with the maple candied yams, garnished with green onions.

Bison Tomahawk Steaks with Chimichurri

These bone-in ribeye steaks are the showpiece for any grilling occasion with their long, frenched (cleaned) rib bones and fatty, succulent meat. Ask your butcher to special order and cut these for you, since they are not always readily available. These steaks are naturally tender, as the location of the muscle along the spine ensures it never moves or works, whereas the leg and shoulder meat is in constant motion working and developing tough structure. Cooking on the bone intensifies the flavour and overall experience. Because of their huge size, these steaks need to be cooked on a grill rather than in a pan. The trick with bigger cuts of meat is to not overcook the outside before the inside is properly done. I prefer these steaks grilled over live coals for a smokier flavour.

Chimichurri is one of my favourite sauces for grilled meat. Hailing from Argentina, which is arguably the grilling capital of the world, it has a light, fresh, and tangy flavour that cuts through the fat on meat and is great for an outdoor experience.

SERVES 6 to 8

Make the Chimichurri

In a blender, combine the garlic, jalapeños, shallot, parsley, cilantro, oregano, olive oil, red wine vinegar, salt, and a pinch of pepper. Pulse until still a little chunky but not puréed. Reserve if using soon or store in an airtight container in the fridge for up to 3 days.

Grill the Steaks

These are thick steaks, so remove them from the fridge 30 minutes before cooking.

Prepare a charcoal or wood fire in an outdoor grill or firepit and let the flames die down with red embers visible. Set a grate over the fire. Alternatively, preheat a gas grill to 600°F (315°C).

Generously season the steaks on both sides with salt and pepper. Place the steaks on the hot grill grate and sear until char marks are visible, 2 to 3 minutes per side, then move the steaks farther away from the fire so they don't burn. Turn the steaks every 3 to 5 minutes until the internal temperature reaches 125°F (52°C) on a probe thermometer. Remove the steaks from the grill and let rest on a wire rack for 10 minutes before slicing.

Cut the steaks off the bone, then slice against the grain. Stir the chimichurri, spoon it over top, and serve.

Chimichurri

4 cloves garlic, crushed

2 jalapeño peppers, minced (leave seeds in for more heat)

1 shallot, minced

½ cup (125 mL) chopped fresh flat-leaf parsley

½ cup (125 mL) chopped fresh cilantro

1 teaspoon (5 mL) chopped fresh oregano

1 cup (250 mL) olive oil

¼ cup (60 mL) red wine vinegar

1 teaspoon (5 mL) kosher salt

Black pepper

Bison Tomahawk Steaks

4 (2-inch/5 cm thick) bone-in bison ribeye steaks (1½ pounds to 2 pounds/675 to 900 g each)

Salt and freshly ground black pepper

Mule Deer Tataki

Mule deer are bigger than white-tail but smaller than elk. They live west of the Missouri River to the Rocky Mountains, as far north as Alaska, and as far south as Baja California. One way to tell them apart is that the mule's antlers fork at the top of their main beam, whereas white-tails' come to a single point. Another trait is the way they run: mule deer hop like a giant rabbit, which made me laugh the first time I saw a herd of muleys bounding through a field. Much like white-tail, the taste of mule meat is a product of their environment, but it is very similar to white-tail, at least the one I shot in Alberta was. A muley in the sagebrush plains might be a little grassier and sage-tasting, but with proper handling and field dressing that shouldn't be an issue. Hunting these critters was certainly more challenging, as we were hunting in the foothills of the Rocky Mountains and were putting considerable miles on our boots.

The robust flavour of the mule deer's tender backstrap (striploin) is perfect for the classic Japanese preparation of tataki, in which marinated meat is seared, then served thinly sliced. Sesame and soy sauce pair very well with game, and it shows in this preparation.

SERVES 4

Mule Deer and Marinade

12 ounces (340 g) boneless mule deer loin

1 tablespoon (15 mL) mirin

1 tablespoon (15 mL) crushed garlic

1 tablespoon (15 mL) grated unpeeled fresh ginger

1 tablespoon (15 mL) sesame oil

1 teaspoon (5 mL) freshly ground black pepper

Sauce

½ cup (125 mL) soy sauce

¼ cup (60 mL) brown rice vinegar

1 (2-inch/5 cm) piece kombu (dried seaweed)

Garnishes

1 Anaheim chili, thinly sliced crosswise (if you like heat, leave the seeds in, or for less heat, slice the chilies in half and remove the seeds)

2 green onions, thinly sliced on the diagonal

Marinate the Meat

Place the deer loin in a medium glass dish or plastic container. In a small bowl, stir together the mirin, garlic, ginger, sesame oil, and pepper. Pour the marinade over the meat, cover, and refrigerate overnight.

Make the Sauce

In a small mason jar, stir together the soy sauce and brown rice vinegar. Add the kombu, screw on the lid, and let soak overnight on the counter.

Sear the Meat

The next day, prepare a charcoal or wood fire in an outdoor grill or firepit and let the flames die down with red embers visible. Set a grate over the fire. Alternatively, preheat a gas grill to 500°F (260°C).

Remove the deer meat from the container and pat dry with paper towel. Discard the marinade.

Heat a large, heavy cast-iron skillet or plancha. (The meat can also be seared over charcoal on a wire rack, but the coals must be very hot.) Quickly sear the meat on all sides just enough to lightly caramelize the very outer edges, 2 to 3 minutes total. Do not begin to cook the meat. Tataki is meant to be served very rare, almost raw. Remove from the heat and let rest for 5 minutes.

Thinly slice the meat across the grain. Arrange the slices on a plate and brush with the sauce, or serve the sauce in a small ramekin and dip the slices before eating. Garnish with the chili and green onion.

Wild Boar Peameal Bacon

A.k.a. Canadian bacon. A.k.a. back bacon. I can assure you that the thinly sliced griddled ham some restaurants are trying to sell in the United States is *not* peameal bacon. Real Canadian bacon hails from central Canada, specifically Toronto, Ontario, where I live. It was created in the mid-1850s as a preservation method in which a pork loin was cured in a saltwater brine and then rolled in ground yellow peas, which not only aided the preservation but also gave it a distinctive flavour. Today's peameal is commonly rolled in cornmeal, giving it a similar crunch and texture but also a bit of a different flavour. I recommend trying both to see which you like; however, you may have to mill your own dried yellow peas.

Now, I'm not saying peameal bacon is better than the classic smoked bacon from the belly of the pig, because it's just too different to even compare. It is its own thing, it's delicious, and it's worth adding to your wheelhouse of recipes as it's so easy to make. Pan-fry or griddle the bacon for eggs benedict or enjoy on a bun (see page 168).

SERVES 6 to 8

In an extra-large bowl, combine the water, salt, sugar, peppercorns, cloves, and bay leaves. Stir to dissolve the salt and sugar. Place the boar loin in a large glass or plastic rectangular container that will fit it. Submerge the boar loin in the brine, cover, and refrigerate for 5 days.

After 5 days, remove the cured loin from the brine. Dry the meat with a kitchen towel. Discard the brine.

Spread the cornmeal on a baking sheet. Roll the cured loin in the cornmeal to evenly coat. Place the coated boar on a wire rack set on a second baking sheet and air-dry in the fridge overnight. Your homemade peameal bacon is now ready to slice. Store, tightly wrapped, in the fridge for up to 1 week or in the freezer for up to 6 months.

- 1 gallon (4 L) water
- ½ cup (125 mL) Diamond Crystal kosher salt or sea salt
- ½ cup (125 mL) granulated sugar
- 1 tablespoon (15 mL) black peppercorns
- 1 teaspoon (5 mL) whole cloves
- 2 bay leaves
- 2 pounds (900 g) whole boneless wild boar loin
- 4 cups (1 L) cornmeal or ground dried yellow peas

Wild Boar Peameal on a Bun

SERVES 4

This sandwich is a famous staple at the St. Lawrence Market in Toronto, but the best place to get one is right here in this book made in your home with your family. However, if you are visiting Toronto, you must try one from the St. Lawrence Market.

2 tablespoons (30 mL) vegetable oil

1 pound (450 g) Wild Boar Peameal Bacon (page 167), sliced

4 sandwich buns

¼ cup (60 mL) mayonnaise

¼ cup (60 mL) grainy mustard

Toppings (optional)

Sliced onions

Sliced tomatoes

Sliced pickles

Lettuce

Prepare a charcoal or wood fire in an outdoor grill or firepit and let the flames die down with red embers visible. Set a grate over the fire. Alternatively, preheat a gas grill to 500°F (260°C) or cook indoors on the stovetop over high heat. I prefer to cook it outdoors over a fire.

Preheat a large griddle pan or large cast-iron skillet over direct high heat.

Add the vegetable oil to the hot pan. Place the peameal bacon in the pan and cook for 2 to 3 minutes per side or until golden around the crust.

Cut the buns in half horizontally. Grill cut side down until very light brown.

Spread the mayo and mustard on the bottom of each bun, then top each with grilled peameal bacon. Top with onions, tomatoes, pickles, and lettuce, as desired. Close with the bun tops. Serve with pickles, if desired.

Muskox in White Wine Cream Sauce with Orecchiette and Kale

Orecchiette, or "little ears," is a fun shape of pasta from the Puglia region of Italy. This pasta is great for holding sauce in its cup shape, and I love to serve it with a rich wine cream sauce. Muskox meat tastes very similar to bison. In this recipe the meat is quickly sautéed in the pan, then removed to keep it medium-rare. Then the sauce is made in the same pan in just a few minutes and tossed with the freshly boiled pasta. This is a flavourful and rich dish to impress your friends at home or at the hunt camp. Bonus points for cooking outside!

SERVES 4 to 6

Prepare a charcoal or wood fire in an outdoor grill or firepit and let the flames die down with red embers visible. Set a grate over the fire. Alternatively, preheat a gas grill to 500°F (260°C).

Bring a large pot of salted water to a boil over direct high heat.

Once the water is boiling, add the orecchiette and cook until al dente, 6 to 8 minutes. (If you are following the directions on the package, shorten the cooking time by a couple of minutes.) Drain the pasta and reserve.

Meanwhile, season the muskox meat all over with salt and pepper. Heat a large skillet or pot over high heat. Heat the olive oil in the pan, then add the meat and cook, without stirring, until caramelized, 2 to 3 minutes. Stir and turn the meat with a spoon or metal tongs and continue cooking for another 1 to 2 minutes, until caramelized on the other sides. Transfer the meat to a plate.

To the same skillet (no need to wipe it) over medium or indirect heat, add the shallot, kale, and ¼ cup (60 mL) of the butter and stir. Add the garlic, chili flakes, and thyme and cook, stirring occasionally, until the kale is wilted, 2 to 3 minutes. Deglaze the pan with the white wine and cook for another minute to evaporate it. Add the cream and continue cooking until the sauce thickens, another 2 to 3 minutes. Stir in the Parmesan and season to taste with salt and pepper. Add the muskox and the remaining 1 tablespoon (15 mL) butter to the sauce and stir. Add the cooked pasta and toss to coat. Serve in shallow bowls, topped with more Parmesan.

Ingredients

- 1 pound (450 g) dried orecchiette
- 1½ pounds (675 g) 1 inch (2.5 cm) cubed muskox
- Salt and black pepper
- 1 tablespoon (15 mL) olive oil
- 1 small shallot, minced
- 2 cups (500 mL) sliced black kale
- ¼ cup (60 mL) + 1 tablespoon (15 mL) unsalted butter, divided
- 4 cloves garlic, crushed
- 1 teaspoon (5 mL) red chili flakes
- Leaves from 2 sprigs fresh thyme
- ½ cup (125 mL) dry white wine
- 1 cup (250 mL) heavy (35%) cream
- ¼ cup (60 mL) freshly grated Parmesan cheese, plus more for serving

Muskox Sausage and Rapini Pizza

Muskox meat is incredibly tender and perfect for making sausage. Very similar in flavour to grass-fed bison and grass-fed beef, it lends itself well to the sweet taste of fennel seed in this sausage. This pizza is inspired by a Neapolitan-style called pizza carrettiera, referring to the cart drivers or rural labourers who would eat this. A hot wood oven is essential for making great pizza, and I like to cook it at around 700°F (370°C), whereas an indoor oven usually maxes out around 550°F (290°C). If you are using an indoor oven, place a pizza stone on the bottom rack and preheat to 550°F (290°C) for at least 45 minutes.

Pizza dough is most flavourful when made a day in advance and fermented in the fridge. It's also much easier to work with cold dough, as it's less sticky. I like my pizza dough a little higher in hydration, meaning a bit wetter, as they stretch thinner, giving you a crispier crust. No two flours are the same and they hold water slightly differently. You also have to factor in humidity when making dough. If your dough is a little too wet when mixing or kneading, add 3 ounces (90 g) additional 00 flour. Once the dough absorbs the flour and rests overnight it will feel less sticky.

MAKES six 12-inch (30 cm) PIZZAS

Tomato Sauce

3 pounds (1.35 kg) ripe in-season Roma tomatoes

1 tablespoon (15 mL) kosher salt

1 cup (250 mL) olive oil

6 cloves garlic

1 tablespoon (15 mL) red chili flakes

1 bunch fresh basil

Dough

2 teaspoons (10 mL) instant yeast

1 teaspoon (5 mL) granulated sugar

24.5 ounces (700 g) room-temperature water, reserving ½ cup (125 mL)

2.2 pounds (1 kg) 00 pizza flour, plus more for dusting (use bread flour if 00 flour is unavailable)

1 tablespoon (15 mL) kosher salt

¼ cup (60 mL) olive oil

Semolina and all-purpose flour, for dusting when handling and stretching the dough

Muskox Sausage

1 pound (450 g) ground muskox (can substitute bison or grass-fed beef)

2 cloves garlic, crushed

2 teaspoons (10 mL) fennel seeds, coarsely ground

2 teaspoons (10 mL) kosher or sea salt

1 teaspoon (5 mL) sweet or hot paprika

½ teaspoon (2 mL) red chili flakes

Pinch of black pepper

Toppings

1 pound (450 g) sliced smoked provolone cheese

1 pound (450 g) shredded mozzarella

2 bunches rapini, trimmed and blanched

Flaky sea salt

Olive oil, for drizzling

recipe continues

Make the Tomato Sauce

Fill a large bowl with ice water. Bring a large pot of salted water to a boil over high heat.

Using a small knife, remove the core of the tomatoes. Cut a shallow X into the bottom. Working in batches, drop the tomatoes into the boiling water and cook for 1 minute. Using a wire strainer or slotted spoon, transfer the blanched tomatoes to the ice water to stop the cooking. Once the tomatoes are cool enough to handle, pull off the skin, starting at the X on the bottom. It should easily peel away.

Using your hands, squeeze the tomatoes to squish out the seeds. Discard the seeds. Add the tomatoes and salt to a large pot and lightly squish with a potato masher. Bring to a rapid boil over high heat and cook the tomatoes, stirring often and mashing from time to time, for 30 minutes. (Rapidly reducing the natural liquid will give the sauce a fresh tomato flavour. Slowly stewing the tomatoes gives the sauce a deeper stewed flavour.)

In a small pot over medium heat, combine the olive oil, garlic, and chili flakes. Once it starts to simmer, remove from the heat. Add the basil and let steep for 15 minutes.

Once the tomatoes have softened and reduced in volume, strain the oil mixture into the sauce. Purée with a hand blender or transfer to a blender and purée until smooth. Cool the sauce to room temperature, then store in the fridge, covered, until ready to use. The sauce can be stored in an airtight container in the fridge for up to 1 week or in the freezer for up to 6 months.

Make the Dough

In a small bowl, stir together the yeast, sugar, and the reserved ½ cup (125 mL) water. Let sit for 10 minutes or until frothy. (If the yeast mixture does not foam, your yeast has expired. Start again with fresh yeast.)

This dough is easily mixed by hand in a large bowl or with a stand mixer fitted with the dough hook. To your bowl, add the flour, salt, the remaining water, and olive oil. Stir to just wet the flour, but don't mix yet. Cover with a kitchen towel and let sit until the yeast mixture is frothy. Add the yeast mixture to the dough and knead for 10 minutes by hand or on low speed until a smooth dough forms.

Lightly oil a large bowl with olive oil or cooking spray. Place the dough in the bowl. Cover the bowl with plastic wrap and let the dough rest on the counter until doubled in size, 45 minutes to 1 hour.

Once the dough has risen, lightly dust a work surface with 00 flour. Turn out the dough and punch it down with your hands to remove the air. Shape the dough into a ball. Return it to the bowl, cover, and let rest again until doubled in size, 30 minutes to 1 hour.

Once the dough has risen a second time, turn it out and punch it down again. Divide the dough into 6 equal portions (10 ounces/300 g each) and shape into balls. Place the dough balls in a well-oiled large, flat plastic container, leaving some space between them. Drizzle the balls with olive oil, cover with a lid, and place in the fridge overnight. (Fermenting the dough in the fridge slows down the yeast activity, allowing the dough to develop more flavour.)

Make the Sausage

In a large bowl, mix together the ground muskox, garlic, fennel seeds, salt, paprika, chili flakes, and black pepper. Shape the meat mixture into small meatballs (1/3 to 1/2 ounce/10 to 15 g each). Cover and keep refrigerated until ready to make the pizzas.

Assemble and Bake the Pizzas

Preheat your outdoor wood pizza oven to 700°F (370°C).

Remove the dough from the fridge. Lightly dust a work surface with 00 flour. Quickly pull a dough ball away from the rest of the dough and place it on the floured surface. (Pulling the dough fast helps unstick it from the container and the other dough balls.) Cover the remaining dough with the lid, plastic wrap, or a damp kitchen towel. Dust the dough with all-purpose flour and gently pat to flatten. Using your hands, stretch the dough into a 12-inch (30 cm) circle. Sprinkle semolina flour and all-purpose flour onto a pizza peel or rimless baking sheet. (The flour prevents the dough from sticking and the semolina acts as ball bearings so the dough can slide right off.) Carefully lift the stretched dough onto the peel.

Quickly ladle some of the tomato in the centre of the dough and use the back of a spoon to spread it evenly across the surface, leaving a 1/2-inch (1 cm) border. Scatter the provolone and mozzarella cheese over the sauce. Then evenly scatter the rapini and meatballs over the cheese.

Place the peel inside the hot oven and quickly pull it back towards you—the pizza will slide off and land on the hot stone. Bake for 2 to 3 minutes, until the dough is golden and blistered, rotating the pizza every minute or so, watching the side that went in first so it doesn't burn. Lift up the edges to check the bottom doesn't burn. Using the pizza peel, transfer the pizza to a wire rack. Season with more chili flakes, flaky sea salt, and a drizzle of olive oil as desired. Slice and serve immediately.

Repeat to assemble and bake the other pizzas.

Pulled Goose Leg Barbecue

Wild goose legs are incredibly tasty, but they are tough pieces of meat. These birds are constantly on the move, walking or swimming around in their never-ending search for food. In addition, these geese can live over the age of twenty, so those are going to be some tough thighs. Farmed birds have tough legs, too, but they usually break down after 2 to 3 hours of cooking, whereas wild goose legs can take anywhere from 5 to 7 hours. That flavour is well worth the wait, though! These smoked goose legs are intensely rich in flavour and have the texture of pulled pork.

SERVES 4 to 6

8 skinless, bone-in goose legs (4½ to 5 pounds/1.8 to 2.25 kg total)

2 tablespoons (30 mL) chili powder

1 tablespoon (15 mL) garlic powder

1 tablespoon (15 mL) kosher salt

2 teaspoons (10 mL) black pepper

3 quarts (3 L) chicken stock or game broth

1 cup (250 mL) lightly packed brown sugar

¼ cup (60 mL) apple cider vinegar

Leaves from 2 sprigs fresh thyme

4 to 6 hamburger buns, split

Barbecue sauce (optional)

Place the goose legs in a large bowl. Add the chili powder, garlic powder, salt, and pepper and toss to evenly coat.

Prepare your smoker at 200°F (93°C). Alternatively, prepare a charcoal or wood fire in an outdoor grill and let the flames die down with red embers visible. Set a grate over the fire. Alternatively, preheat a gas grill to 200°F (93°C).

Smoke the goose legs for 2 hours in the smoker or directly on the grill grate with the lid closed.

Transfer the goose legs to a cast-iron Dutch oven or large pot. Add the stock, brown sugar, cider vinegar, and thyme. Cover the pot with a lid or foil. Increase the smoker or grill heat to 300°F (150°C). Place the pot in the smoker. (If cooking over an open firepit, use a Dutch oven and place coals on top of the lid.) Continue cooking until the goose meat is tender and can be easily pulled from the bones, 3 to 4 hours. Check periodically to ensure the liquid has not reduced too much; if it has, add 1 cup (250 mL) of water and continue cooking until the meat is tender.

Once cooked, transfer the goose legs to a work surface. Pull the meat from the leg bones. Return the meat to the pot and stir into the sauce. Serve the meat on hamburger buns with barbecue sauce, if desired.

Roe Deer Caprese Salad

Roe deer is nicknamed "elf of the forest" because of its miniature size. But what they lack in height, they make up for in flavour. Roe deer is one the most flavourful meats I have ever tasted, and it pairs beautifully with the subtle flavours of fresh mozzarella cheese and ripe garden tomatoes. A good finishing balsamic is a must-have for this dish, as the sweetness in the vinegar complements the game flavour of the deer. I was lucky enough to travel to Italy to harvest this deer and was inspired by the simplicity of the cooking that focused solely on quality ingredients.

SERVES **4** AS AN APPETIZER OR **2** AS A MAIN

Prepare a charcoal or wood fire in an outdoor grill or firepit and let the flames die down with red embers visible. Set a grate over the fire. Alternatively, preheat a gas grill to 500°F (260°C).

Generously season the deer loin with salt and pepper. Preheat a large cast-iron skillet or plancha over the fire until hot. Add a splash of olive oil to the hot pan. Carefully add the loin and sear all over, 2 to 3 minutes per side. Remove the meat from the pan and let rest for 5 minutes. With a sharp knife, slice the meat crosswise into ½-inch (1 cm) slices.

To assemble the salad, on individual plates arrange the tomato, mozzarella, and venison slices, alternating and slightly overlapping them in a circle. Spoon the cherry tomato halves in the centre of the circle. Generously drizzle the salad with olive oil and aged balsamic vinegar. Top with the basil and season to taste with a sprinkle of flaky sea salt.

- 1 pound (450 g) boneless roe deer loin
- Kosher salt and freshly cracked black pepper
- Olive oil, for searing
- 2 large ripe organic tomatoes, thinly sliced
- 1 (250 g) ball fresh mozzarella or fior di latte, thinly sliced
- 1 pint (2 cups/500 mL) ripe organic cherry tomatoes, cut in half
- Good-quality extra-virgin olive oil, for drizzling
- Aged balsamic vinegar, for drizzling
- Handful of fresh basil leaves
- Flaky sea salt

Spit-Roasted Beaver with Birch Syrup and Blueberry Glaze

The beaver is an iconic symbol of Canada. It appears on our five-cent coin and was the first image ever on a Canadian postage stamp. It was also a valuable commodity in the fur trade and a primary source of sustenance long ago. The beaver has many meanings for people, but for me it's food. Not only do its dams, rivers, and streams create duck ponds for me to hunt, but its own meat supplies me with food. The meat tastes very beefy, and you would not be able to tell the difference between the two once cooked to perfection.

Beaver is traditionally smoked in Indigenous cultures, but I thought a slow spit-roast would be an appropriate preparation. The glaze, applied many times while the meat cooks, gives the beaver a rich molasses-like sweet, sticky coating. The birch adds a citrus note to the flavour, while the blueberries add more sweetness.

SERVES 10

Prepare a charcoal or wood fire in a firepit. Let the flames die down with red embers visible.

Prepare the Beaver

Lay the beaver belly side up. Run the spit through the opening in the pelvis and out through the jaw. Use the tie wire and pliers to fasten the beaver around the neck to the spit. Cut five 8- to 10-inch (20 to 25 cm) lengths of tie wire. Push one end of the wire through the meat on one side of the spine, push the other end of the wire through the meat on the other side of the spine, then twist the two ends of wire together around the spit and tightly fasten with pliers. Repeat with the remaining lengths of wire, evenly spaced in three other places down the spine and one for the tail, to securely attach the beaver to the spit.

Sprinkle the salt and pepper evenly on all sides of the beaver.

Make the Glaze

In a medium pot, bring the birch syrup to a simmer over high heat. Once simmering, add the blueberries and cook, stirring occasionally, until the berries are softened, 2 to 3 minutes. Using a hand blender or food processor, purée the mixture. Strain through a fine-mesh sieve into a small pot. Add the salt and pepper and stir.

Using butcher twine, tie the thyme at the bottom of the stems to a wooden spoon to use as a basting brush. Set aside.

Special Equipment

Metal tie wire

Spit for roasting, at least 4 feet (1.2 m) in length

Pliers

Butcher twine

1 whole beaver, gutted and skinned

½ cup (125 mL) Diamond Crystal kosher salt

¼ cup (60 mL) black pepper

Glaze

2 cups (500 mL) birch syrup

1 cup (250 mL) wild blueberries

1 teaspoon (5 mL) kosher salt

½ teaspoon (2 mL) black pepper

1 thick bunch fresh thyme with strong stems

recipe continues

Spit-Roast the Beaver

Position the spit about 3 feet (1 m) above the fire and spit-roast the beaver, using an electric or battery-powered unit to rotate the spit consistently. The heat should be around the 200° to 250°F (93° to 120°C) zone on a digital laser temperature gun. Cook the meat for 30 minutes before glazing. Continue to brush the beaver with some of the glaze every 30 minutes or so. The heat will reduce the glaze on the meat and make a sticky coating that keeps the meat moist. Plan for 4 to 6 hours of roasting time. It is very important to cook the beaver well-done to avoid parasites; cook until the internal temperature reaches at least 190° to 205°F (88° to 96°C) on a probe thermometer, at which point the meat will be incredibly tender and almost pull-apart. Once cooked, rest the beaver for at least 20 minutes before slicing. The tail is also very interesting to eat; however, it is thin tail bone surrounded by supple fat. If you like pork lardo, you will enjoy the tail.

Cold-Smoked Cured Swan Breast

Yes, you read that correctly—swan! When I was in culinary school, my mom mentioned to me that the queen of England claimed all the swans as hers and so you needed her permission to hunt swan, which were usually reserved for royal dinners. Well, that must mean they taste pretty good! In Canada hunting swan is illegal, but in the United States there is a season in several states for tundra swan. There are three species of swan in North America. The largest and native species is the trumpeter swan, with white feathers and a black beak. Then there is the mute swan, which has an orange beak. Mute swans are invasive and aggressive and push trumpeter swans from their habitat. (If you ask me, we should be able to hunt the invasive ones.) Then there's the smallest of the three, the tundra swan, with a black beak with its yellow band. I saw these beautiful birds in their nesting grounds in Nunavut while on a fishing trip one summer. They migrate south to winter in warmer climates. I drove to North Carolina to hunt mine and was blown away by the sheer numbers of swans I saw—entire farm fields full of giant white birds. These numbers wreak havoc on farmers' fields in multiple ways.

I originally thought these birds would have an incredible amount of meat, but to my surprise they aren't that much bigger than a Canada goose. This recipe uses the tender breast meat. Save the legs to make Pulled Goose Leg Barbecue (page 176).

Note: Cold-smoking leaves the meat still in its raw form. Some smokers can be fitted with a cold smoke baffle. If your smoker doesn't have a cold-smoke option, there are hacks to minimize the heat, usually involving ice. In a barrel smoker, where the heat and smoke come from the bottom, a pan of ice can be used to cool the smoke underneath the meat. With offset smokers, you may need to experiment with burning wood chips in a foil pouch to avoid overheating and cooking the meat.

MAKES **2** CURED SWAN BREASTS

Cure and Air-Dry the Swan

Season the swan breasts evenly with the salt, pepper, and juniper. Place the meat in a vacuum bag or large resealable plastic bag. Pour in the maple syrup and add the thyme and rosemary sprigs. Massage the meat in the bag, then vacuum-seal or close the bag. Place the bag in the fridge and cure for 1 week. If you are using a resealable plastic bag, flip the bag every couple of days.

After 1 week, remove the swan breasts from the bag and run under cold running water. Pat dry with a kitchen towel or paper towel. Place the breasts on a wire rack set in a small baking sheet and return to the fridge to air-dry for another week. The cured swan breast should feel firm to the touch.

2 skin-on, boneless swan breasts (about 2 pounds/900 g each)

¼ cup (60 mL) Diamond Crystal kosher salt or sea salt

1 tablespoon (15 mL) freshly ground black pepper

2 teaspoons (10 mL) freshly ground juniper berries

¼ cup (60 mL) pure maple syrup

2 sprigs fresh thyme

2 sprigs fresh rosemary

recipe continues

Cold-Smoke the Swan

See the Note on the previous page for setting up a cold smoker. Cold-smoke the swan directly on the grill for 20 minutes, then turn the smoker off and leave closed for 1 hour. Remove the swan from the smoker and refrigerate.

Vacuum-sealed cured and smoked meat can be stored for several months in the fridge or frozen for up to 1 year. Using an electric meat slicer or sharp knife, thinly slice the meat. Serve the smoked swan as an appetizer with bread or crostini. Mustard and pickles are great accompaniments to any smoked meat.

Grilled Wagyu Porterhouse Steak

A porterhouse steak is essentially a T-bone steak that is cut from the rear end of the short loin, whereas a T-bone steak is cut from the front of the short loin. Both have a T-shaped bone in the middle, but the porterhouse has a much larger tenderloin than the T-bone. A porterhouse has the best of both worlds: it has a striploin steak *and* a sizeable tenderloin. There's a bit of marrow at the top of the bone, which adds a lot of flavour during cooking. On top of that, this is wagyu, the Cadillac of cattle, a Japanese breed prized for its rich marbled meat. Here I guide you in grilling a perfectly cooked porterhouse with a foolproof technique.

SERVES 2 to 4

Place the steaks on a baking sheet and drizzle with the olive oil. Arrange the thyme and rosemary sprigs over the steaks. Cover and marinate in the fridge for 24 hours, turning after 12 hours.

Prepare a charcoal or wood fire in an outdoor grill or firepit and let the flames die down with red embers visible. Set a grate over the fire. Alternatively, preheat a gas grill to 500°F (260°C).

Bring the steaks to room temperature before cooking. Discard the thyme and rosemary sprigs. Season both sides of the steaks with a big pinch each of salt and pepper.

Brush the grill grate with olive oil to prevent sticking. Using metal tongs, press the steaks down on the grill and cook, without moving them, for at least 3 minutes, until deep grill marks are visible. Turn and cook for another 3 minutes or until the internal temperature reaches 120°F (50°C) on a probe thermometer inserted near the bone. Remove the steaks from the grill and place on a wire rack. Place 1 tablespoon (15 mL) of the butter on top of each steak and let rest for 10 minutes.

Cut the meat from the bone and slice. Plate the meat beside the bone and serve with flaky sea salt to garnish.

- 2 porterhouse steaks (about 1½ pounds/675 each)
- 2 tablespoons (30 mL) olive oil
- 4 sprigs fresh thyme
- 4 sprigs fresh rosemary
- Kosher salt and black pepper
- 2 tablespoons (30 mL) unsalted butter
- Flaky sea salt, for garnish

Elk Backstraps

These elk steaks are some of the finest wild meats I have ever tasted in my life. If you are lucky enough to get an elk tag, you are in for the adventure of a lifetime and a culinary treat. Elk live in the mountains at high elevations and can be very difficult to get to. They are massive animals, with adult bulls weighing 700 to 1100 pounds (300 to 500 kg). When harvesting an animal like this, be prepared to pack out about 250 pounds (100 kg) of deboned meat, no easy task. I was hunting in the early season and my bull was very fatty. They store fat in preparation for the rut, where they fight for territory and, more importantly, cows.

This recipe is great for a fast and light dinner. I like to leave a bit of the fat on the backstraps (striploins) for flavour, even though there is some tough silverskin underneath the fat on the loin. You can take it off or give it a try.

SERVES 4

1¾ pounds (790 g) boneless elk backstrap (striploin), cut into 4 steaks

Olive oil, plus more for drizzling

Sea salt and freshly ground black pepper

4 large heirloom tomatoes, sliced

Flaky sea salt

Aged balsamic vinegar, for drizzling

For garnish

Fresh flat-leaf parsley, torn

Amaranth sprouts

Cilantro sprouts

Brush both sides of the steaks with olive oil and season generously with sea salt and pepper.

Prepare a charcoal or wood fire in an outdoor grill or firepit and let the flames die down with red embers visible. Set a grate over the fire. Alternatively, preheat a gas grill to 500°F (260°C).

Place the steaks on the grill grate and cook, without moving them, for 3 to 4 minutes, until deep char marks are visible. Turn and cook for another 3 to 4 minutes, until the internal temperature reaches 125°F (52°C) on a probe thermometer. Remove from the grill and let rest for 10 minutes before slicing.

Season the tomatoes with flaky sea salt and pepper. Drizzle with the aged balsamic vinegar and olive oil. To serve, arrange everything on a large cutting board and garnish with the parsley and sprouts.

Elk Heart Skewers

Heart meat is best eaten fresh. I like to eat it the same day as the harvest because it's packed full of nutrients and isn't in rigor mortis like the meat from the muscles. Elk hearts are generally larger than deer and some cattle hearts, and I find there are large, thick veins and tough tissue that need to be removed. This is why I prefer to devein and cut the meat into cubes perfect for skewering and cooking over the fire.

I glaze this heart with yakitori sauce, a recipe given to us by my business partner and book photographer Jody's mother-in-law Noriko who is from Japan.

MAKES 12 to 15 SKEWERS

Special Equipment

12 to 15 (6- to 8-inch/15 to 20 cm) bamboo or wooden skewers

2 cups (500 mL) soy sauce
1 cup (250 mL) mirin
¼ cup (60 mL) sake
½ cup (125 mL) granulated sugar
Zest and juice of 1 orange
Zest and juice of 1 lemon
1½ pounds (675 g) elk heart
1 bunch green onions, white parts cut into 2-inch (5 cm) pieces, green parts thinly sliced and reserved for garnish
2 red radishes, very thinly sliced (I use a mandoline)

Soak the bamboo or wooden skewers in water for at least 1 hour to prevent them from burning.

In a small saucepan, combine the soy sauce, mirin, sake, sugar, orange zest and juice, and lemon zest and juice. Bring to a boil over high heat, stirring just to dissolve the sugar, until the liquid is reduced by half and is syrupy, 5 to 10 minutes. Remove from the heat and let cool to room temperature. The sauce should thicken slightly as it cools.

Trim away any fat and silverskin from the outside of the elk heart. Cut the heart in half lengthwise and cut out and discard any veins and tendons. Cut the cleaned heart meat into ¾-inch (2 cm) cubes.

Thread 3 pieces of heart meat onto each skewer, alternating with a white part of the green onion.

Prepare a charcoal or wood fire in an outdoor grill or firepit and let the flames die down with red embers visible. Set a grate over the fire. Alternatively, preheat a gas grill to 500°F (260°C).

Place a 3-inch (8 cm) strip of foil to one side of the hot grill to protect the exposed skewers from burning.

Brush the elk heart skewers with the cooled glaze. Place on the grill, with the handles of the skewers over the foil, and cook for 2 to 4 minutes, until dark char marks are visible. (The sugar in the glaze will cause the grill mark to be quite dark, which is desired for flavour.) Turn, and continually brush the meat with glaze while it is cooking. (This will cause the glaze to cook and to stick onto the meat.) Turn and repeat glazing until all sides are nicely charred.

Arrange the skewers on a plate and garnish with onion greens and radishes. Drizzle with more glaze and serve.

Elk Liver with Serviceberry Compote

My favourite part of hunting elk is hiking and experiencing the mountains where they live. Deer territory in my hometown is very flat and easily accessible by walking trails, but even four-wheeling into camp, I was definitely not physically prepared for what I was about to endure—miles upon miles of hiking steep hills in high elevation with lower oxygen levels. My solace came from many breaks along the way, profusely sweating and breathing heavily, foraging for serviceberries. Their flavour is similar to a slightly sun-dried blueberry, almost like a raisin but not quite as dry. The entire time I looked forward to cooking my elk with these tasty berries, and the best part to enjoy with something sweet is the liver.

Note: How moist your berries are depends on the weather and how long the berries have been in the sun. If your serviceberries seem very dry on the tree, you may need to add up to a cup of water to the compote to break down the berries before cooking.

SERVES 4

Serviceberry Compote
8 ounces (225 g) serviceberries

⅔ cup (150 mL) granulated sugar

Zest and juice from 1 lemon

Elk Liver
1 pound (450 g) elk liver

Salt and freshly ground black pepper

1 tablespoon (15 mL) vegetable oil

1 tablespoon (15 mL) butter

Nasturtium leaves and flowers, for garnish (optional)

Make the Serviceberry Compote

Prepare a charcoal or wood fire in an outdoor grill or firepit and let the flames die down with red embers visible. Set a grate over the fire. Alternatively, preheat a gas grill to 500°F (260°C) or cook indoors on the stovetop.

In a small saucepan, combine the serviceberries, sugar, and lemon zest and juice. Place the pot on the grill grate and bring to a boil. Move the pot to the side of the grill or to an elevated rack for indirect heat and simmer until the berries have softened and the berry liquid has reduced. The sauce should be thick but not as thick as jam. Remove from the heat and keep warm if using soon. The compote can be stored in an airtight container in the fridge for up to 1 week.

Sear the Elk Liver

Slice the liver horizontally into 4 equal portions ½ inch (1 cm) thick (about 4 ounces/115 g each). Season both sides with a pinch each of salt and pepper.

Preheat a large cast-iron skillet or griddle over the fire or grill.

Add the vegetable oil to the hot skillet or griddle. Add the liver and sear, without moving it, for 2 to 3 minutes to allow the meat to caramelize. Add the butter to the pan, then turn the liver and cook for another 2 to 3 minutes. Liver is best eaten rare to medium-rare doneness, but feel free to cook longer if desired. Remove the liver from the pan and let rest for 5 minutes.

Slice the seared liver. Serve with warm serviceberry compote spooned over top and garnished with the spicy nasturtium flowers and leaves, if using.

Elk Osso Buco

Osso buco comes from Lombardy, Italy. It is my absolute favourite way to cook shanks. Cutting the bones exposes the beautiful-tasting marrow that becomes a flavour in the stew but can also be scooped out with a small spoon or fork and eaten. It's rich and delicious and worth a try. The accompanying gremolata adds a bright citrusy fresh taste to the stewed flavours of the meat. Traditionally the braised shanks are served on a rich creamy saffron risotto. This is truly a decadent dish.

SERVES 4

Special Equipment
Hacksaw or reciprocating saw if you are harvesting the elk

Elk Osso Buco
2 pounds (900 g) bone-in elk shanks cut crosswise into about 1-inch (2.5 cm) thick pieces

1 tablespoon (15 mL) + 1 teaspoon (5 mL) kosher salt, divided

2 teaspoons (10 mL) black pepper

2 tablespoons (30 mL) vegetable oil

1 small white onion, diced

1 stalk celery, diced

1 medium carrot, peeled and diced

1 shallot, minced

3 cloves garlic, minced

1 cup (250 mL) dry red wine

1½ cups (375 mL) venison or beef stock

1½ cups (375 mL) tomato sauce

Leaves from 2 sprigs fresh rosemary, chopped

Leaves from 2 sprigs fresh thyme, chopped

Gremolata
Leaves from 2 sprigs fresh basil, chopped

Leaves from 2 sprigs fresh flat-leaf parsley, chopped

Leaves from 1 sprig fresh oregano, chopped

Zest of 1 lemon

Risotto
5 to 6 cups (1.25 to 1.5 L) venison stock (or dark beef or chicken stock)

2 tablespoons (30 mL) olive oil

2 cups (500 mL) arborio rice

1 large shallot, minced

1 stalk celery, minced

1 teaspoon (5 mL) kosher or sea salt

1 cup (250 mL) dry white wine

1 teaspoon (5 mL) saffron threads

1 tablespoon (15 mL) unsalted butter

2 tablespoons (30 mL) freshly grated Parmesan cheese

Make the Osso Buco

Prepare a charcoal or wood fire in an outdoor grill or firepit and let the flames die down with red embers visible. Set a grate over the fire. Alternatively, preheat a gas grill to 500°F (260°C).

Season both sides of the shanks with 1 tablespoon (15 mL) of the salt and pepper.

recipe continues

Preheat a large cast-iron Dutch oven or deep stainless-steel frying pan with a fitted lid over high heat. Add the vegetable oil to the hot pan. Using tongs, place the shanks in the hot pan and cook for 2 to 3 minutes per side or until golden brown. Add the onion, celery, carrot, shallot, and garlic and sauté until the onions are soft and translucent, 2 to 3 minutes. Deglaze the pan with the red wine and cook until the wine has evaporated, about 1 minute. Add the stock, tomato sauce, rosemary, thyme, and remaining 1 teaspoon (5 mL) salt and bring to a simmer. Cover with a lid. Using a small shovel or long metal tongs, pile hot coals on the top of the lid. Continue cooking for 1½ to 2 hours. The shank meat should be fork-tender but not falling off the bone when lifted. Keep warm while making the risotto or cool completely and store, covered, in the fridge for up to 1 week.

Make the Gremolata

In a small bowl, stir together the basil, parsley, oregano, and lemon zest. Cover and store in the fridge while making the risotto.

Make the Risotto

In a medium saucepan over medium heat, heat the stock.

In another medium saucepan over high heat, combine the olive oil and rice and toast the rice, stirring constantly, until it is light golden brown, 2 to 3 minutes. Add the shallot, celery, and salt and cook, stirring occasionally, until the shallot is soft and translucent, 1 to 2 minutes. Add the white wine and cook, stirring occasionally, until the wine is absorbed, 1 to 2 minutes. Stir in the saffron. Add 1 cup (250 mL) of the hot stock and cook, stirring occasionally, until most of the liquid has been absorbed. Continue ladling stock into the rice, 1 cup (250 mL) at a time, stirring until the liquid is absorbed before adding more, until the rice is tender with a little firmness in the centre. Remove from the heat and stir in the butter and Parmesan.

To serve, spoon the risotto into large shallow serving bowls. Place the osso buco on top, spoon some of the braising liquid and vegetables over the meat, and finish with a big spoonful of the gremolata.

Venison Patties

These patties are a delicious snack or lunch. Sweet and spicy ground venison filling is packed into a flaky pastry crust and served with hot sauce. The Toronto street food scene, where beef patties are sold in subway stations, Caribbean restaurants, and shops around the city, is the inspiration for this recipe that celebrates my home in Toronto, the city's beautiful multicultural food scene, and of course venison!

MAKES 4 to 6 PATTIES

Make the Filling

Preheat a large pot over high heat for 3 minutes. Add the vegetable oil and venison meat and cook, stirring occasionally, until browned, 4 to 5 minutes. Add the onion, garlic, Scotch bonnet pepper, thyme, curry powder, ginger, salt, and allspice and stir. Sprinkle in the flour and stir until incorporated. Add the stock and hot sauce and cook, stirring occasionally, until the mixture thickens, 6 to 8 minutes. Remove from the heat and cool in the pot until room temperature before shaping the patties.

Make the Dough

In a food processor, stir together the flour, curry powder, and salt. Add the butter and lard and pulse until both are incorporated with pea-size pieces of butter and lard visible. Do not overmix. (Alternatively, mix the dough by hand in a large bowl. Squeeze the butter and lard into the flour until small pea-size pieces are visible and the dough is crumbly.)

In a small bowl, mix the egg and cold water with a whisk or fork. Add the egg mixture to the flour mixture and pulse until the dough comes together in a ball. (If mixing by hand, stir in the egg mixture with a fork to incorporate, then squeeze the dough together into a ball.) Cover the dough with plastic wrap and let rest for 30 minutes.

Assemble the Patties, Brush with Egg Wash, and Bake

Prepare a fire in your wood pizza oven and let the flames die down with red embers visible. Heat the pizza oven to 400°F (200°C). Alternatively, if cooking indoors, preheat the oven to 400°F (200°C).

Line a baking sheet with parchment paper.

Filling

1 tablespoon (15 mL) vegetable oil
2 pounds (900 g) finely ground venison
1 small yellow onion, minced
4 cloves garlic, minced
1 small Scotch bonnet pepper, minced
Leaves from 4 sprigs fresh thyme
1 tablespoon (15 mL) curry powder
1 teaspoon (5 mL) finely grated unpeeled fresh ginger
1 teaspoon (5 mL) kosher salt
½ teaspoon (2 mL) ground allspice
¼ cup (60 mL) all-purpose flour
¾ cup (175 mL) venison or beef stock
1 tablespoon (15 mL) hot sauce

Dough

2 cups (500 mL) all-purpose flour
2 tablespoons (30 mL) curry powder
½ teaspoon (5 mL) kosher salt
¼ cup (60 mL) cold unsalted butter, cut into cubes
¼ cup (60 mL) cold lard
1 egg, beaten
¼ cup (60 mL) cold water

Egg Wash

1 egg, beaten
2 tablespoons (30 mL) water

Red Hot Sauce (page 127) or your favourite hot sauce, for serving

recipe continues

On a floured work surface, use a rolling pin to roll out the dough until about ⅛ inch (3 mm) thick. Using a 5-inch (12 cm) cookie cutter, cut out 4 to 6 circles of dough. (You can reroll the scraps once if needed, but rerolling further will make the dough tough.) Spoon the venison filling on one side of each circle. Using a pastry brush, brush the edges of the dough with egg wash. Fold the dough over the filling. Using your hands, pinch the edges together, then crimp with a fork to seal.

Place the patties on the prepared baking sheet and bake until the pastry is golden brown and the egg wash is shiny, 7 to 10 minutes. Serve with your favourite hot sauce.

Canned Moose Meat

Canned moose meat is a Newfoundland tradition that I learned about on my hunt there with friends. Pressure canning extends the shelf life of low-acid foods like meat and vegetables by sealing them in airtight containers and using heat to eliminate harmful microorganisms. Pressure canning employs higher temperatures than traditional water bath canning, so it eliminates the risk of botulism. This technique preserves flavour and nutrition while maintaining culinary traditions. Having canned meat on hand is great for a quick meal at home but even better when on the road on hunting and fishing trips or on snowmobile adventures. Simply place a jar into the coals beside the fire or pot and dinner is ready in 5 to 6 minutes. Tender and delicious, the meat can be eaten on its own or served over mashed potatoes or rice. It can also be used to make Canned Moose Poutine (page 205).

You can make this canned moose meat outdoors over a large propane burner or indoors on the stovetop. If you do not have a pressure canner, you can process the jars in a water bath but they will need to be kept in the fridge and consumed within 1 month.

MAKES **five** 4-cup (1 L) JARS

Cut the moose meat into 1-inch (2.5 cm) cubes. Firmly pack the meat into the mason jars (2 pounds/900 g meat per jar). Top each jar with ¼ cup (60 mL) stock, ¾ teaspoon (3 mL) pickling salt, a pinch of chili flakes, ½ teaspoon (2 mL) thyme, and a bay leaf, leaving 1 inch (2.5 cm) of headspace. Place a flat lid on the top of each jar, then screw the ring on top just until fingertip-tight. Follow the manufacturer's instructions to process. (My canner uses the 10-pound weight and once boiling cooks for 90 minutes.) When done, remove the canner from the heat and wait until the pressure returns to zero.

Pressure-canned meats can be stored in a cool, dark place for up to 1 year. Once opened, store in the fridge and consume within 1 week.

Special Equipment

Pressure canner

Five 4-cup (1 L) mason jars with 2-piece lids

---

10 pounds (4.5 kg) moose stewing meat

For each mason jar

¼ cup (60 mL) game broth or beef stock

¾ teaspoon (3 mL) pickling salt

Pinch of red chili flakes

½ teaspoon (2 mL) fresh thyme leaves

1 bay leaf

Canned Moose Poutine

Poutine has become part of Canada's national identity, and for good reason. It's simply delicious! Crisp, perfectly cooked french fries smothered in rich gravy and melted cheese curds is heavenly enough, but topped with flaky and tender canned moose, it's pure decadence. Just how exactly we are known for this dish I am not entirely sure. There are competing stories of who invented the dish, but the best information I found is that it originated in the province of Quebec in the 1950s when a customer at a fry shop asked for cheese curds to be added to his takeout fries and gravy, to which the owner exclaimed "Poutine!" which literally means "mess." Today the oozing melted curds and rich gravy are topped with everything you can think of—Montreal smoked meat, lobster, foie gras—but somehow it's always divine. Canned moose has a wonderful tender texture that's perfect for topping poutine!

The two-stage method is paramount when making french fries. Skipping the first "blanching" step will result in dark-coloured, limp fries that are still almost raw in the middle.

SERVES **4**

Prepare the Potatoes

Wash the potatoes. Cut the fries with a mandoline or french fry cutter. I like thick-cut fries (baton-size) but if you like thin matchstick fries, that works too—just reduce the cooking time slightly. Rinse the cut potatoes under cold running water to remove some of the starch and let drip-dry in a colander.

Meanwhile, Make the Gravy

Melt the butter in a medium saucepan over high heat. Add the flour and stir with a wooden spoon until the paste starts to turn brown. Switch to a whisk and slowly add ½ cup (125 mL) of the stock, whisking vigorously until thoroughly mixed with no lumps. Continue to add stock ½ cup (125 mL) at a time, whisking continuously until the gravy thickens and making sure not to burn the bottom. Remove from the heat. Reheat before serving.

French Fries

6 unpeeled russet potatoes

6 cups (1.5 L) vegetable oil or lard, for frying (duck fat is superb)

Kosher salt

Gravy (makes 4 cups/1 L)

4 tablespoons (60 mL) unsalted butter

½ cup (125 mL) all-purpose flour

4 cups (1 L) dark beef stock or game broth (or you can reduce amount to 3 cups/750 mL stock or broth + 1 cup/250 mL of liquid from the jar of canned moose meat)

For the Poutine

2 pounds (900 g) Canned Moose Meat (page 203; one 4-cup/1 L mason jar)

1 pound (450 g) fresh cheese curds

1 bunch fresh chives, chopped, for garnish

recipe continues

Make the Fries

Heat the vegetable oil in an extra-large pot to 325°F (160°C) on a deep-frying thermometer. Line a large baking sheet with paper towel.

Working in 2 batches if needed, drop the potatoes into the hot oil and fry for 2 to 3 minutes, until the potatoes are just soft enough that they break when pinched. Using metal tongs or a wire strainer, transfer the fries to the prepared baking sheet to absorb excess oil.

Increase the heat of the oil to 375°F (190°C) on a deep-frying thermometer. Drop the fries back into the hot oil and fry until dark golden brown and crispy, 3 to 4 minutes.

Meanwhile, in a small pot, heat the canned moose meat over high heat while stirring.

To serve, top the fries with moose meat and cheese curds. Smother with gravy. Garnish with chives.

Bear Curry

Black bear meat is one of the most underrated big game animals. There's a huge misconception that bear meat is awful and inedible. Bears, like all creatures, will taste like what they eat, so coastal bears or bears that live on a salmon-run stream that feast on fish may have a slight fishy taste, but I have yet to taste that. With proper cooking and the right recipes, bear can become one of your favourites too. Bear meat reminds me of lamb. Any lamb recipe you love can be made with bear, and especially spiced recipes like this curry.

It is important to cook bear meat well-done, to an internal temperature of at least 165°F (75°C), to kill any parasites. Since bears are opportunistic and sometime scavengers, they can carry the roundworms that cause trichinosis.

SERVES 4 to 6

Bear Curry

1 tablespoon (15 mL) ground coriander

1 tablespoon (15 mL) ground cumin

2 teaspoons (10 mL) cayenne pepper

1 teaspoon (5 mL) garam masala

½ teaspoon (2 mL) ground turmeric

1 tablespoon (15 mL) kosher salt

1 teaspoon (5 mL) black pepper

2 pounds (900 g) black bear stewing meat (from neck, hindquarter, or shoulder)

1 tablespoon (15 mL) ghee or unsalted butter

2 tablespoons (30 mL) vegetable oil

1 large yellow or Spanish onion, chopped (about 2 cups/500 mL)

4 cloves garlic

1 (1-inch/2.5 cm) piece unpeeled fresh ginger, sliced

3 cups (750 mL) chicken or vegetable stock

1 can (14.5 ounces/428 mL) diced tomatoes

½ cup (125 mL) plain full-fat yogurt, plus more for serving

2 cinnamon sticks

2 bay leaves

4 green cardamom pods

2 black cardamom pods

2 teaspoons (10 mL) whole cloves

1 teaspoon (5 mL) fenugreek seeds

Scented Basmati Rice

1½ cups (375 mL) basmati rice

2¼ cups (550 mL) water

1 cinnamon stick

2 green cardamom pods

2 black cardamom pods

2 teaspoons (10 mL) kosher salt

1 tablespoon (15 mL) ghee or melted unsalted butter

For serving

Plain full-fat yogurt

Mango pickle (optional)

Fresh cilantro leaves

Marinate the Bear Meat

In a large bowl, stir together the coriander, cumin, cayenne pepper, garam masala, turmeric, salt, and black pepper. Add the bear meat and mix to evenly coat in the spices. Cover with plastic wrap or transfer to a container with a tight-fitting lid and refrigerate overnight.

recipe continues

Make the Curry

The next day, prepare a wood or charcoal fire in an outdoor grill or firepit and let burn down until the flames subside and the coals are red hot. Set a grate over the fire. Alternatively, preheat an indoor oven to 300°F (150°C). Turn on your convection fan (the spices will smoke a little at first).

Remove the bear meat from the fridge.

Over the fire or on the stovetop, melt the ghee with the vegetable oil in a large cast-iron Dutch oven or large, heavy pot with a lid. Add the bear meat and cook, without stirring, for 2 to 3 minutes to let the meat and spices caramelize. Stir the meat and continue to brown on all sides. Add the onion, garlic, and ginger and cook, stirring occasionally, until softened, another 2 to 3 minutes. Add the stock, tomatoes, yogurt, cinnamon sticks, bay leaves, green and black cardamom pods, cloves, and fenugreek seeds. Bring to a simmer, cover with a lid, and place coals on top of the lid (if cooking outdoors) or transfer to the oven (if cooking indoors). Slowly braise the meat until cooked through and fork-tender, 3 to 4 hours. Check each hour for the first 2 hours, then every 15 to 20 minutes until tender. The curry will have reduced slightly and appear thick.

Make the Scented Basmati Rice

In a small pot, combine the rice, water, cinnamon stick, green and black cardamom pods, salt, and ghee. Cover with a lid and bring to a boil over medium heat. Once boiling, reduce the heat to low and steam the rice until the water has been absorbed, 5 to 6 minutes. Remove from the heat and let sit, covered, for another 5 to 6 minutes. Fluff with a fork.

To serve, divide the rice among plates. Scoop the curry over the rice. Top with yogurt and mango pickle, if desired. Garnish with the cilantro.

Bear Ragu with Smoked Cheddar Polenta

This recipe is special to me because it was quickly whipped together using ingredients we had at camp for a group of bear hunters who had never eaten bear before. In some areas overpopulated with bear, hunted meat doesn't legally have to be eaten because they are considered a nuisance and are primarily used for their fur. This gentle braise was cooked with neck and shank meat and was thoroughly enjoyed in disbelief by my new friends at bear camp. The tender braise on top of the smoky cheddar polenta is out-of-this-world good.

SERVES **4**

Prepare a charcoal or wood fire in an outdoor grill or firepit and let the flames die down with red embers visible. Set a grate over the fire. Alternatively, preheat a gas grill to 500°F (260°C).

Make the Bear Ragu

Preheat a large cast-iron pot or Dutch oven directly on the fire or coals for 3 to 4 minutes.

Season the bear meat with salt and pepper. Add the vegetable oil to the hot pot, then add the meat and sear over high heat to brown all sides. Add the onion, celery, carrot, and garlic and stir to combine. Cook over high heat, stirring occasionally, until the onions are translucent, 3 to 5 minutes. Add the red wine and cook until evaporated, 2 to 3 minutes. Add the stock, thyme, rosemary, bay leaves, and chili flakes and stir. Cover with a lid and cook over low heat off to the side of the fire, or hung above the coals, until the meat pulls away from the bone and is fork-tender, 4 to 5 hours. Remove from the heat and discard the thyme, rosemary, and bay leaves.

Make the Smoked Cheddar Polenta

When the bear meat is almost done, start the polenta. In a medium pot, combine the milk, cream, and salt. Bring almost to a simmer over high heat, then whisk in the polenta in a steady stream. Reduce the heat to medium and cook, stirring often, making sure to scrape the bottom of the pot to prevent scorching, until thick, 6 to 8 minutes. Whisk in the cheese and butter. Keep warm.

To serve, spoon the polenta onto plates. Top with the pulled bear meat and spoon some braising sauce over top. Garnish with rosemary and sliced jalapeños, if desired.

Smoked Bear Ragu

4 pounds (1.8 kg) bear neck and/or shank meat on the bone

1 tablespoon (15 mL) kosher or sea salt

1 teaspoon (5 mL) black pepper

2 tablespoons (30 mL) vegetable oil

1 small yellow onion, chopped

1 stalk celery, chopped

1 small carrot, peeled and chopped

4 cloves garlic, minced

1 cup (250 mL) dry red wine

8 cups (2 L) dark beef stock or game broth

4 sprigs fresh thyme

1 sprig fresh rosemary

2 bay leaves

1 teaspoon (5 mL) red chili flakes

Smoked Cheddar Polenta

2 cups (500 mL) whole milk

2 cups (500 mL) heavy (35%) cream

1 teaspoon (5 mL) kosher salt

1 cup (250 mL) instant polenta

1 cup (250 mL) grated smoked cheddar cheese

½ cup (125 mL) unsalted butter, cut into cubes

For garnish

Chopped fresh rosemary

Sliced jalapeño peppers (optional)

Game Barbecue

Wild BBQ

Cooking game over a fire shouldn't be intimidating. Like learning any other cooking technique, all it takes is common sense, practice, and the right recipe to master cooking game over the coals.

The major difference between game and farmed meat is that game has less fat. The animals are generally older than farmed animals, so the muscles have been used more, making them tougher in texture when eaten. There are ways to combat this and produce truly incredible meals and barbecue. Leaner meat needs a bit of tender care when cooking. Basting with juices released from the meat itself is a great way to keep the meat moist, as is brushing on a marinade or a barbecue sauce during cooking. After an initial smoking to flavour the meat, wrapping it in foil or parchment paper is a great way to seal in the juices so the meat gently steams itself and doesn't dry out. Fat can also be added on top or larded throughout the meat with a larding needle.

I have been a professional chef for over twenty-five years. To this day I am most excited by cooking over fire. Any event, gathering, or camping trip away, if I can cook over a fire, I'm happy. What's the difference between a professional chef and a talented home cook? Volume. Period. In some positions I have held working grill stations at restaurants, I would cook over 150 steaks of multiple cuts in a single dinner service, along with eight to ten prime ribs a day. Then there's cooking for weddings and banquets, ordering, teaching and training staff, and running the day-to-day operations. The title of "chef" is one I don't take lightly. I went to culinary school at nineteen years old with a baby at home, all while working full-time jobs as a cook. By the time I landed my first head chef job, I was twenty-seven years old with fourteen years of restaurant experience, five of those as a sous-chef working sixty to eighty hours a week for very low wages. It's a gruelling existence of relationship-killing, adrenaline-fuelled work, my days often starting at ten in the morning and ending at two the next morning. But that work is also fuelled by passion and an eagerness to learn and succeed. I was financially driven to support my young family that I never saw. The moral of the story is, I know a thing or two about food, flavour, and cooking meat, and I say nothing compares to cooking over a fire.

One of the most alluring aspects of fire is the transformative power of heat and smoke. Smoke and caramelization are the two main reasons why food cooked over fire tastes so good. From perfect brisket (page 228) to pull-apart ribs (pages 227 and 236), the possibilities are endless. Different types of wood offer different flavours from the smoke, and then there are different types of charcoal that impart entirely different flavours. Then there are the marinades, rubs, and sauces adding more and more layers of complexity and depth of flavour.

Cooking meat and fish on the bone also makes it taste better. It allows the marrow and collagen within the bones to melt and render into the meat or fish as it cooks. Bones and fat or fish skin act as natural insulators, retaining moisture inside and preventing drying out. Cooking evenly is another win: the bone helps distribute heat evenly and more uniformly throughout the flesh and imparts natural seasoning.

Smell is processed in the brain by emotional receptors, particularly those related to memory. Smells can trigger strong emotional responses, often associated with specific events, places, or people. The smell of wood burning and hog fat dripping onto the coals is enough to send my taste buds into a watery oblivion of anticipation. It reminds me of every single time I've cooked a hog over fire.

Whole Wild Boar Breakdown

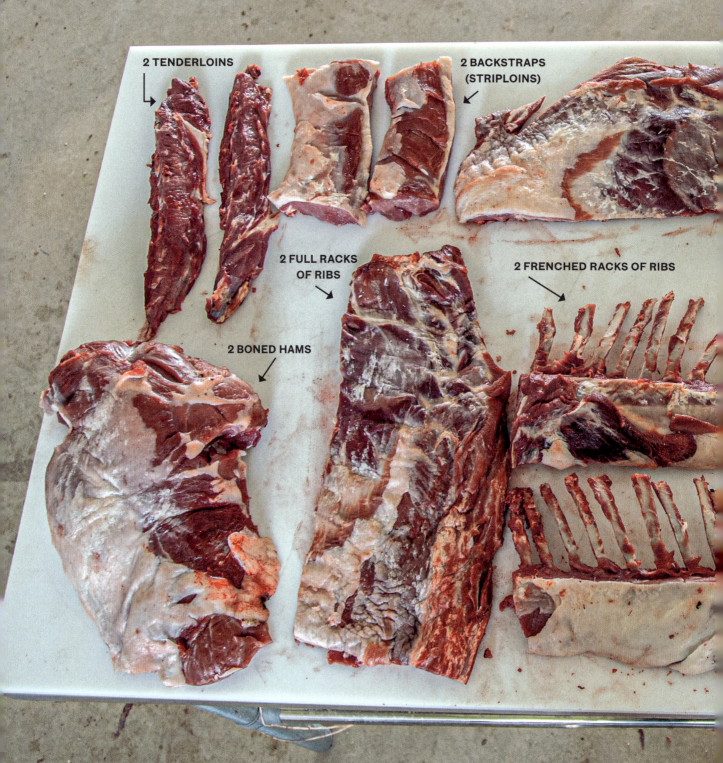

How to Roast a Pig

There are many ways to roast a pig. This is my way. Roasting a pig is a lot of fun and such a great showpiece for a barbecue with family and friends. Any butcher will be glad to order you a pig. They will even have near-exact weights for you to choose from. I find up to 100 pounds (45 kg) very manageable. Over that and things start to get tricky and lengthy. You need to plan the pick-up of your pig with the time of your event if you don't have a huge walk-in fridge or giant cooler. There are many types of grills and gadgets, but you don't need anything fancy. I once cooked a pig on scrap metal from a farm gate. I like to season the pig with salt and leave it overnight before cooking, so the salt has time to penetrate the meat and pull out some moisture from the skin. Plan for at least 6 hours of roasting time for a pig 60 pounds (27 kg) or less. Keep a metal shovel nearby, as it is very useful to move coals around if there are hot spots. Heavy-duty work gloves or leather welding gloves are handy for when it's time to turn the pig. And a fire extinguisher, just in case there is a grease fire.

STEP 1 Prepare a wood or charcoal fire in a large outdoor grill that will fit your pig or in a firepit. Let the flames die down with red embers visible.

STEP 2

Cut open the rib cage down the centre of the pig's chest. A butcher's cleaver, serrated knife, tinsnips, or large garden shears are all great tools for this job.

STEP 3

Remove large amounts of leaf fat from inside the abdominal cavity. This can be rendered down into leaf lard for later use. Not removing the fat can result in excess fat dripping into the fire and potentially catching fire.

STEP 4

Using a cleaver, butterfly or spatchcock the pig by chopping inside where the rib bones meet the spine. This allows the pig to open up flat so it cooks more evenly.

STEP 5

Attach the meat to the grill using tie wire at the leg joints. Then cut 4- to 12-inch (10 to 30 cm) lengths of wire, poke through the pig on each side of the spine, and tie around the centre of the grill to secure the pig when turning over.

STEP 6

Hoist the pig skin side up over the coals and cook for at least 1 to 2 hours before turning. Carefully turn the pig with another person helping. Baste the pig with a brush or a mop with water with a squeeze of lemon juice and a pinch of salt. If any spots on the pig are darker and more cooked than others, move away the coals with a shovel for a more even cook. The middle of the pig is the thinnest part of the animal, whereas the hindquarters and shoulders are the thickest parts. Move the coals to heat the thicker parts of the pig. You can even leave a space open in the middle of the coals if you feel the middle is cooking too quickly.

STEP 7

Once the pig is cooked to about 175°F (80°C) on a probe thermometer, lower the skin near the flames to crisp. Don't cook the pig past 185°F (85°C) or you risk drying out the meat. Let the pig rest for 20 minutes before slicing. You can use a chef's knife or cleaver, but you should be able to pull apart the joints at the shoulders and hams with your hands. Slice the meat and serve with pieces of the crispy skin.

Chopped Wild Boar Barbecue

The world of barbecue is a vast subject. Entire books have been written about it and the different styles of barbecue across the United States. Chopped barbecue is similar to pulled pork, except chopped results in a different texture and mouthfeel. I like to cook whole animals or large cuts of pork or wild boar to perfection, then cut off the bone and chop the meat into small pieces, whereas for me pulled pork is cooked until the meat is falling apart and can be pulled to shreds, resulting in a stringier texture. Both ways are delicious, and I love them equally. Slow-cooking meat whole on the bone yields incredibly flavourful and juicy meat and is a must-try if you haven't done it before.

For this recipe, I use a juvenile wild boar weighing about 35 pounds (16 kg). Keep in mind that half of this weight is bones, so you'll get about 18 pounds (8 kg) of meat. If you are using larger cuts, such as a whole back leg or shoulder, scale the weight by half. For a whole animal I don't wrap the meat, but if you are cooking a shoulder or hindquarter, once it reaches an internal temperature of about 160°F (70°C), about halfway through the cooking time, you can wrap the meat with foil or butcher paper for a juicier result.

SERVES 8 to 12

Smoke the Wild Boar

Prepare your smoker and let it burn for 15 to 20 minutes. Allow the flames to die down with red embers visible. You want to smoke at 225°F (110°C).

Combine the water, cider vinegar, and 1 tablespoon (15 mL) of the salt in a container and stir to dissolve the salt. Set aside; you'll use this mixture to baste the meat periodically while smoking.

Season the boar all over with the remaining ½ cup (125 mL) salt and the pepper, rubbing it into the meat with your hands.

Place the boar in the smoker and cook, maintaining the temperature at about 225°F (110°C). After 1 hour, brush the boar with the vinegar mixture. Continue to smoke, basting every 30 minutes. After 3 hours, start checking doneness. I like to smoke the meat until the internal temperature reaches 195° to 200°F (90° to 93°C) on a probe thermometer. Remove the meat from the smoker and let rest for 30 minutes before chopping.

Cut the smoked boar meat from the bones and chop into small pieces.

Meanwhile, Make the Coleslaw

In a large bowl, combine the cabbage and onion. Add the vegetable oil, cider vinegar, mustard, sugar, salt, and pepper and toss well.

Serve the chopped smoked wild boar on a cutting board or platter with the buns, barbecue sauce, mustard, pickles, and coleslaw.

Smoked Wild Boar

1 cup (250 mL) water

½ cup (125 mL) apple cider vinegar

½ cup (125 mL) + 1 tablespoon (15 mL) Diamond Crystal kosher salt or sea salt, divided

1 whole wild boar (about 35 pounds/16 kg)

¼ cup (60 mL) black pepper

Coleslaw

1 green cabbage, cored and thinly sliced

1 small white onion, thinly sliced

½ cup (125 mL) vegetable oil

¼ cup (60 mL) apple cider vinegar or white wine vinegar

1 tablespoon (15 mL) grainy mustard

2 teaspoons (10 mL) granulated sugar

1 tablespoon (15 mL) kosher salt

1 teaspoon (5 mL) black pepper

For serving

12 hamburger buns or Hawaiian rolls, split

Your favourite barbecue sauce

Ballpark mustard

Sweet pickles

Asado Roast Pig

Asado is a distinct style of cooking from South America, particularly Argentina and Uruguay, that involves cooking meat over an open flame. But the word also refers to the culturally important social tradition of people gathering to enjoy the aromas and sizzle of the slow-roasting dinner to come. The result after many hours of cooking is a tender, juicy, smoky piece of meat with a beautiful salty crust. Bright, zesty chimichurri is a favourite accompaniment.

Asado is typically hung over a fire on a 45-degree angle on a cross-like structure quite elevated from the flame so it cooks in more of an indirect manner. For pigs with the skin, I cook this way for 4 to 8 hours, depending on the size, then lower the pig quite close to the coals or flames for a very short time to crisp the skin. (See opposite page for building an asado setup—prefabricated rigs to my preference using rebar and tie wire.)

SERVES A PARTY OF 15 to 20

Special Equipment

Rebar (for the asado poles)
Metal tie wire
Pliers
Heavy-duty work gloves or leather welding gloves
Shovel (for moving coals)
Fire poker
8 cement cinder blocks
Butcher twine
Large wooden spoon

1 whole pig (40 to 50 pounds/ 18 to 23 kg), split down the middle (see pages 218–221)
1 cup (250 mL) + 1 tablespoon (15 mL) Diamond Crystal kosher salt, divided
4 cups (1 L) water
1 lemon
1 thick bunch fresh thyme or rosemary with strong stems, for basting
1 batch Chimichurri (page 161), for serving

Rub 1 cup (250 mL) of the salt into the skin and meat of the pig.

Prepare a charcoal or wood fire in a firepit. (I prefer wood for asado.) Let the fire burn while you set up the pig on the rebar. The pig will cook with indirect heat, so some flame from the fire is good. It doesn't have to be all coals.

Attach the pig to the rebar with tie wire at the hock and fore shank leg joints and the neck. Cut 4 pieces of tie wire about 16 inches (40 cm) long. Push the wire through the skin close to the spine and through the meat until it pokes out the other side. Poke it back through the pig on the other side of the spine to tie the pig to the rebar post. Repeat in 3 other spots down the back of the pig. Hoist the cross and position the pig skin side up over the fire on a 45-degree angle.

Roast the pig for 1 hour, and then turn.

Pour the water into a medium bowl. Cut the lemon in half and squeeze into the water. Add the remaining 1 tablespoon (15 mL) salt and stir. Using butcher twine, tie the bottom of the herb stems to a wooden spoon to use as a basting brush.

After roasting the pig for 1 hour, thoroughly baste the pig with the lemony water. Continue cooking, basting the pig on both sides every 30 minutes. Rotate the pig every hour or so and flip or rotate based on the meat's colour and internal temperature. The pig is done when a probe thermometer inserted into the thickest part reaches 175°F (80°C). Plan for at least 8 hours of cooking time. You can make it go faster by placing the pig closer to the flames, but I prefer low and slow. Once the temperature has been reached, lower the pig closer to the fire to crisp the skin. Once crispy, remove the pig from the fire and let rest skin side up for 30 minutes before slicing. Serve with chimichurri.

Building an Asado Setup

Building an asado setup is very easy. You can buy fancy prefabricated rigs, but it is so cheap to make it yourself. I have seen people use untreated wood, but I prefer to use rebar: a ¾-inch (2 cm) thick piece of rebar for the main beam and ½-inch (1 cm) thick rebar for the lateral crossbars. My friends have welders and they helped me weld the pieces together in about 5 minutes, but I have also used rebar tie wire and tied the beams on the post with pliers. This type of rebar setup costs less than fifty dollars to make and will last a long time. The setup can be hammered into the ground or propped up with cinder blocks or more rebar in an opposite 45-degree angle.

Birch-Syrup-Glazed Bison Short Ribs

Short ribs from beef, or in this case bison, are massive compared with pork ribs and are delicious with a dry rub and smoked. If you braise your ribs and have never tried a dry rub, I promise you will never go back to braising or boiling ribs ever again. So much flavour is packed in between the bones, and the fatty meat breaks down into supple pull-apart heaven. The birch syrup in the glaze has a dark molasses quality but is sweeter and has a hint of citrus. Birch syrup is common in northern and Indigenous communities. It's made the same way as maple syrup but is not as sweet, and it's fun to cook with because of its distinctive flavour. Brushing the glaze on the ribs while they're cooking reduces the glaze and leaves a sticky sauce while keeping the meat juicy.

Tip: Butchers can usually cut short ribs to a specific thickness.

SERVES 4 to 6

Prepare a charcoal or wood fire in an outdoor grill or firepit and let the flames die down with red embers visible. Set a grate over the fire. Alternatively, preheat a gas grill to 225°F (105°C) or prepare a smoker at 225°F (105°C).

Brush the ribs with the birch syrup. Generously season with salt and pepper. Place the ribs on the grill grate and cook for 2½ hours, brushing with more birch syrup every 30 minutes, until the internal temperature reaches 160°F (70°C) on a probe thermometer. Remove the ribs from the grill or smoker and wrap tightly in butcher paper or foil.

Increase the heat to 275°F (135°C). Return the wrapped ribs to the grill or smoker and cook until the internal temperature reaches 200°F (93°C) on a probe thermometer. The meat should pull off the bone but not fall apart when handled. If it doesn't, cook for another 30 minutes or until the internal temperature reaches 205°F (96°C). Remove from the grill or smoker. Brush with more birch syrup and let rest for 10 minutes in the wrap or foil. Slice and serve garnished with sour pickles.

Special Equipment

Butcher paper or foil

---

4 crosscut bone-in bison short ribs, 3 inches (8 cm) thick (5 to 7 pounds/2.25 to 3.2 kg total)

½ cup (125 mL) birch syrup

Salt and black pepper

Sour pickles, chopped, for garnish

Bison Brisket

Brisket can be overwhelming to think about. There are so many recipes and methods available and everyone has their own opinions on "barbecue." Brisket is easy to cook, and I am going to teach you my foolproof technique for you to cook for your family and friends at your next cookout. Bison brisket is a little smaller and thinner than a beef brisket, but the technique and doneness temperature are the same. I think the bison version tastes superior and has a bit of an earthier taste than beef, but that's just me. I have cooked hundreds of briskets and I find the best way is to smoke with a dry rub. I have done many side-by-side comparisons with wet brine, and the dry rub always comes out juicier.

When it comes to wood, there are so many types to choose from and it really comes down to your taste. There are fruitwoods, which are milder and sweeter, while oak, mesquite, maple, and hickory are more pronounced and have more depth of flavour. The woods to avoid are softwoods with a lot of resin, such as pine and cedar. That said, if I am pit-smoking, I will sometimes use a little bit of cedar for a flavour accent when finishing, but inside an offset smoker it would definitely be too harsh.

SERVES 10 to 12

Special Equipment

Butcher paper or foil

---

1 whole bison brisket (10 to 12 pounds/4.5 to 5.4 kg)

½ cup (125 mL) Diamond Crystal kosher salt

½ cup (125 mL) black pepper

Using your hands, rub the salt and pepper into the meat. Let sit, uncovered, in the fridge for at least 4 hours or ideally overnight.

Prepare your smoker at 200° to 225°F (93° to 110°C). I like to put a small pan with water in my smoker to create a bit of steam to help keep the meat juicier, but it is optional.

Smoke the brisket directly on the grill until the internal temperature reaches 165°F (75°C) on a probe thermometer, 6 to 8 hours. Once the brisket hits 165°F (75°C), the internal temperature will "stall" and stop increasing, sometimes for several hours. At this stage, wrap the brisket in butcher paper or foil and increase the smoker temperature to 275°F (135°C). (Wrapping the brisket helps keep it juicy, and after 6 to 8 hours it has enough smoke flavour.) Check the brisket 2 hours after wrapping. The brisket usually takes another 3 to 4 hours after wrapping, but it depends on the meat and your smoker. If you like a firmer brisket that's great for thinly slicing for sandwiches, you might want to finish cooking around 195°F (90°C), but if you want meat that's almost pull-apart tender, I recommend finishing at 205°F (96°C). Once the brisket is done to your liking, remove it from the smoker and let rest for 30 minutes before slicing. You can rest it in an empty cooler still in the wrapping to keep it warm.

Unwrap and slice to desired thickness.

Smoked Wild Boar Shoulder

Slow-smoking a wild boar is a labour of love that will reward you with succulent barbecue perfection. In this recipe, I use deboned shoulders, but you can smoke on the bone if you prefer—it will just take a little longer. It's best to marinate the shoulder meat with a dry rub overnight before the long and gentle smoke. Halfway through the cooking process I add barbecue sauce and beer to help keep the meat juicy and tender. Wild boar tends to be a little tougher than farmed pork, so it needs an occasional baste of sauce with a mop or brush during the smoking.

SERVES 10 to 12

Prepare the Wild Boar

Tie the boar meat with butcher twine at 1-inch (2.5 cm) intervals. This will ensure more even cooking.

In a small bowl, stir together the salt, brown sugar, black pepper, sweet paprika, garlic powder, onion powder, cayenne pepper, cinnamon, and juniper. Rub the dry rub mixture all over the boar shoulders. Place the meat in a large container, cover, and refrigerate overnight.

Make the Barbecue Sauce

In a small saucepan, combine the ketchup, maple syrup, red wine vinegar, Worcestershire sauce, brown sugar, smoked paprika, and cayenne pepper. Whisk to dissolve the brown sugar and bring to a simmer over high heat. Cook for 5 minutes, stirring occasionally. Remove from the heat, transfer to a container, and cool to room temperature. Store in the fridge, covered, until ready to use.

Smoke the Wild Boar

Prepare your smoker at about 225°F (110°C).

Place the boar shoulders in the smoker directly on the grill and cook for 2 hours before checking. Add wood to the fire to maintain the heat. Once the internal temperature reaches 160°F (70°C) on a probe thermometer, place the shoulders on a foil-lined baking sheet. Tightly cover the pan with foil and continue to smoke, mopping with the barbecue sauce every hour or so, until the internal temperature reaches 190°F (88°C) on a probe thermometer. (If you want to pull the shoulder, continue cooking past 200°F/93°C to a maximum of 210°F/100°C.) Remove the meat from the smoker and let rest for 20 minutes before slicing.

Slice the boar and serve with your favourite sides or in butter rolls for sandwiches.

Special Equipment

Butcher twine
Basting mop

2 boneless wild boar shoulders (8 to 10 pounds/3.5 to 4.5 kg total)
½ cup (125 mL) Diamond Crystal kosher salt
½ cup (125 mL) lightly packed brown sugar
¼ cup (60 mL) black pepper
¼ cup (60 mL) sweet paprika
2 tablespoons (30 mL) garlic powder
2 tablespoons (30 mL) onion powder
1 tablespoon (15 mL) cayenne pepper
1 teaspoon (5 mL) ground cinnamon
1 teaspoon (5 mL) freshly ground juniper berries
1 (473 mL) can of lager or ale

Barbecue Sauce

2 cups (500 mL) ketchup
½ cup (125 mL) pure maple syrup
¼ cup (60 mL) red wine vinegar
2 teaspoons (10 mL) Worcestershire sauce
¼ cup (60 mL) lightly packed brown sugar
1 tablespoon (15 mL) smoked paprika
1 teaspoon (5 mL) cayenne pepper

Smoked Cougar Ham

When I first heard that cougar meat tastes like pork, I knew I had to try it. Mountain lions are like ghosts in the forest and are not easy to hunt. Hunting with dogs and trapping are the most successful ways to harvest a big cat. Cougars are fierce machines of an animal and do not have the same fat content of a farmed or even feral pig, but the meat is incredibly delicious and does indeed taste like lean pork. Naturally, I knew I had to smoke a ham (back leg) in true barbecue fashion.

Cougars eat other animals and scavenge for food, so they can have parasites not seen by the human eye. It's very important to cook to the given temperatures.

Special Equipment

Butcher paper or foil

---

5 pounds (2.25 kg) boneless cougar hindquarter

1½ cups (375 mL) hoisin sauce

½ cup (125 mL) mirin

¼ cup (60 mL) rice vinegar

2 tablespoons (30 mL) sesame oil

½ cup (125 mL) granulated sugar

1 tablespoon (15 mL) five-spice powder

1 tablespoon (15 mL) sweet paprika

1 tablespoon (15 mL) kosher salt

1 teaspoon (5 mL) black pepper

Marinate the Meat

Place the cougar meat in a large plastic or stainless steel container with a tight-fitting lid.

In a large bowl, whisk together the hoisin sauce, mirin, rice vinegar, sesame oil, sugar, five-spice powder, paprika, salt, and pepper. Pour three-quarters of the marinade over the meat (reserve the remaining marinade in an airtight container in the fridge until needed). Cover with the lid and marinate in the fridge, turning the meat in the container every other day. (You can marinate overnight, but the meat will not have the same cured texture and will not be infused with the spices.) Cure for at least 1 week. (Alternatively, you can vacuum-seal the meat for a faster marinating time and more even cure. Vacuum-seal and marinate in the fridge for 4 days.)

Smoke the Ham

Prepare your smoker at 225°F (110°C). Smoking can be done with an offset smoker, pellet smoker, or barrel smoker, or by hanging above a firepit. Light your wood fire and let the flames die down with red embers visible.

Remove the ham from the container or vac bag. Reserve the residual marinade. Smoke the meat directly on the grill, brushing on the residual marinade every 45 minutes, until the internal temperature reaches 110° to 120°F (43 to 50°C) on a probe thermometer.

This next step is important to achieve a moist ham. Remove the ham from the smoker and wrap it in butcher paper or foil with the reserved quarter of the marinade and continue cooking until the internal temperature reaches 165°F (75°C) on a probe thermometer. Remove the ham from the smoker and let rest in the butcher paper or foil for 15 minutes before slicing. Serve with your favourite barbecue sides.

Elk Smash Burgers

I must credit my friend Daniel Haas for this recipe; he introduced me many years ago to making these burgers at home. Smash burgers are the perfect way to use ground elk, or any of your favourite ground game, as literally "smashing" or pressing the patty into flaming hot steel caramelizes the juices, crisping the outside and resulting in an intensified flavour and perfectly cooked burger. Everything gets cooked on a griddle pan, including the buns, so it's all about the crispy texture. If you've never tried a smash burger, now's your time. Bonus points if it's chanterelle season and you pick your own for toppings.

MAKES **8** BURGERS

Prepare a charcoal or wood fire in your grill or firepit and let the flames die down with red embers visible. Set a grate over the fire. Preheat a large cast-iron griddle or plancha over high heat for at least 10 minutes or until very hot. Alternatively, preheat a gas grill to 600°F (315°C).

Divide the ground meat into 8 equal portions (3 ounces/85 g each) and shape into balls.

Add a splash of vegetable oil to the hot griddle or plancha. Add the onions, chanterelles, thyme, and a pinch of salt and cook, stirring often, until the onions are soft, golden brown, and caramelized. Remove from the griddle and let cool to room temperature.

Working in batches, place 4 balls of elk meat on the hot griddle and season with a pinch each of salt and pepper. Working with one ball at a time, use a burger press (or the bottom of a small pot with a piece of wax paper on top of the meat to prevent sticking) to press each ball into a ¼-inch (5 mm) thick patty. Cook until brown on the bottom and caramelizing and crispy around the edges, 1 to 2 minutes. Flip and cook for 1 more minute. (The smash burgers are thin and do not need a lot of cooking time on the hot griddle.) Melt the cheese on the patties, then remove from the pan. Repeat to cook the remaining burgers.

Meanwhile, butter the cut sides of the buns. While the burgers are cooking and if there is room on the griddle, place the bun halves buttered side down on the hot surface and cook until golden brown, 1 to 2 minutes. (If there is no space, toast the buns once the burgers are off the heat.)

Assemble the burgers on the bottom of the buns. Top with the caramelized onion and chanterelle mixture and your favourite toppings. Close with the other bun half.

1½ pounds (675 g) ground elk (or other game or red meat)

Vegetable or canola oil, for frying

1 large yellow onion, thinly sliced

2 cups (500 mL) chanterelle or other wild mushrooms, brushed clean (large mushrooms torn in half)

Leaves from 2 sprigs fresh thyme, chopped

Kosher or sea salt and freshly ground black pepper

8 slices cheddar cheese

8 hamburger buns, split

Softened butter, for the buns

Toppings (optional)

Sliced dill pickles

Sliced tomatoes

Mayonnaise

Mustard

Ketchup

Bear Ribs

Black bear meat is one of those things that got a bad rap in the old days and ruined it for a lot of hunters. Yet it is one of the tastiest game animals I have ever eaten. Like any wild game, their flavour is a product of their diet, and in theory bears hunted near urban areas where they are close to a dump or landfill, or coastal bears that eat a lot of fish, may not have the best flavour, but all the bears I have ever hunted (ten plus) have tasted exceptional. Their rich, oily, gamy meat is comparable to a mix of beef and lamb, and when prepared correctly it is delicious.

All bear meat needs to be cooked well-done, past 165°F (75°C), to kill parasites, particularly those that cause trichinosis.

Reserve the drippings from the ribs and blend with your favourite homemade or store-bought barbecue sauce.

SERVES 4 to 6

Special Equipment

Foil or butcher paper

½ cup (125 mL) sweet paprika

1 tablespoon (15 mL) garlic powder

1 tablespoon (15 mL) onion powder

1 teaspoon (5 mL) ground coriander

1 teaspoon (5 mL) cayenne pepper

2 full racks bear ribs (from 1 bear; about 4 to 5 pounds/1.8 to 2.25 kg total)

½ cup (125 mL) pure maple syrup

1 tablespoon (15 mL) kosher salt

1 teaspoon (5 mL) black pepper

Fresh oregano leaves, for garnish (optional)

Marinate the Meat

In a small bowl, stir together the paprika, garlic powder, onion powder, coriander, and cayenne pepper.

Brush the ribs with the maple syrup. Season the ribs all over with the dry rub mixture, salt, and black pepper, and use your hands to rub the spices into the meat. You can marinate the ribs, covered, in the fridge overnight or smoke them right away.

Smoke the Ribs

When ready to smoke the ribs, prepare your smoker at 250°F (120°C). If cooking indoors, preheat the oven to 250°F (120°C). (Alternatively, the ribs can be cooked hung above a fire or on a grill in a firepit. Prepare a charcoal or wood fire and let the flames die down with red embers visible.)

Smoke the ribs until the internal temperature reaches 140°F (60°C) on a probe thermometer, about an hour. Wrap the ribs in foil or butcher paper and continue cooking until the internal temperature reaches 180°F (82°C) on a probe thermometer, another 1 to 1½ hours. At this temperature the meat should easily pull apart. Remove the ribs from the smoker or oven and let rest, tightly wrapped in the foil or butcher paper, for 15 minutes before slicing. The drippings can be brushed on the ribs or blended into your favourite barbecue sauce. Garnish with the oregano (if using) and serve.

Spit-Roasted Porchetta

Porchetta is a delicious classic Italian roast pork that is so incredibly easy to make. Traditionally, a whole suckling pig is deboned, rolled, and roasted, but the variation with pork belly is considerably easier and faster to prepare. Garlic, herbs, and spices make this dish come alive, but the real treat is the crispy puffed skin. If you see a porchetta at a festival or event and the skin looks flat and leathery, don't bother—it will be chewy and tough. I'll teach you how to perfect it the first time you make it.

Porchetta can be served on a bun or as a plated roast. Rapini sautéed with a squeeze of lemon and a sprinkle of red chili flakes is a perfect side dish for dinner.

Note: Use a mortar and pestle or spice grinder to crush the black peppercorns and fennel seeds.

Prepare the Pork Belly

Place the pork belly skin side down on a cutting board. Using a sharp knife, score the meat in a diamond pattern, making cuts halfway through the meat and about ½ to 1 inch (1 to 2.5 cm) apart. (This makes it easier to roll the meat and helps the marinating process. Do not pierce the skin.) Rub half of the salt into the meat.

Sprinkle the garlic, peppercorns, fennel seeds, thyme, rosemary, and chili flakes over the meat. Rub the seasonings into the meat. With a long side facing you, roll up the pork belly and tie it tightly with butcher twine every inch (2.5 cm) to secure the roast into a round form. Refrigerate, uncovered, overnight to allow the skin to dry out and the meat to slightly cure.

Spit-Roast the Pork Belly

Prepare a charcoal or wood fire in an outdoor grill or firepit and let the flames die down with red embers visible. (Alternatively, if you do not have a mechanical spit roaster or rotisserie machine, preheat a wood pizza oven or an indoor oven to 450°F/230°C.)

Bring a kettle full of water to a boil. Remove the roast from the fridge, then prick the skin all over with a sharp meat fork at least 50 times. (This will allow fat to escape while cooking. Some people score the skin, but I find too much moisture and juices from the meat soften the skin too much and it doesn't puff up after cooking.) Place the meat on a wire rack set in the sink and slowly pour the boiling water all over the skin. (This will shrink and tighten the skin and help it to crisp.) Pat dry with paper towel or a kitchen towel. Drizzle the porchetta with olive oil and rub it all over the skin. Season with the remaining half of the salt.

Special Equipment

Butcher twine

Spit

½ rind-on, boneless pork belly (6 to 8 pounds/2.7 to 3.5 kg)

⅓ cup (75 mL) Diamond Crystal kosher salt, divided

6 cloves garlic, minced

1 tablespoon (15 mL) black peppercorns, crushed

1 tablespoon (15 mL) fennel seeds, crushed

1 tablespoon (15 mL) finely chopped fresh thyme

1 tablespoon (15 mL) finely chopped fresh rosemary

2 teaspoons (10 mL) red chili flakes

Olive oil, for drizzling

recipe continues

If using a spit: Run your spit lengthwise through the middle of the meat and set up the spit roaster over the fire. Depending how high the meat is above the coals, the porchetta will take anywhere from 4 to 6 hours to cook. Once the internal temperature reaches 160°F (70°C) on a probe thermometer, it is time to crisp and puff the skin. This can be done by lowering the spit very close to the coals. The skin will puff almost instantly in direct heat. (Alternatively, using metal tongs, grab a large coal from a wood log and hold it near the skin. You will hear the skin crackle and pop and see it puff.)

If using a wood pizza oven or indoor oven: Place the meat on a rack in a roasting pan and transfer to the oven. Roast at 450°F (230°C) for 30 minutes, then reduce the temperature to 300°F (150°C). Once the internal temperature reaches 160°F (70°C) on a probe thermometer, it is time to crisp and puff the skin. Turn the broiler to high or increase the pizza oven to 700°F (370°C). If using a broiler, use metal tongs to turn the roast so the skin crisps on all sides. The crisping will not take long.

Once the skin is puffed on all sides, remove the roast from the spit or oven and let rest for 30 minutes before slicing. Use a sharp serrated knife or bread knife to cut through the crispy skin.

Vegetables by Fire

In today's world of dwindling time, we're offered pre-peeled garlic, pre-husked corn, and plastic-wrapped everything. But most vegetables don't need to have their outer protective layer removed and do not need all that plastic. Vegetables and some fruits can be cooked just the way they are, skin and all. They actually taste better this way.

Hardy root vegetables can be cooked directly in or under the coals because of their protective skin. Potatoes, sweet potatoes, beets, parsnips, carrots, onions, squashes, and so on, are perfect for cooking this way because of their density: they steam themselves inside their skin when cooked in the fire. They benefit from the long cooking times that are needed to soften their tough structure. Their time in the fire imparts smoke and earthy flavour while caramelizing their natural sugars. For example, the outer leaves of cabbage are its own protective "foil," and as you'll see in this chapter, something magical happens when a cabbage is cooked whole (see page 251).

One of the most attractive aspects of cooking vegetables over fire is the simplicity. Softer vegetables like asparagus, bell peppers, zucchini, mushrooms, corn, and greens can be cooked much faster over fire. Simply drizzled with oil and seasoned, they are ready for a hot and fast sizzle on a grill, where the flames and heat from coal come in direct contact with them, leaving a sweet smoky char. Grilled vegetables are perfect for any meal when time isn't a luxury. I love to grill a steak and a bunch of asparagus and zucchini all at the same time—a complete meal is ready in 15 minutes.

Even with a small backyard in Canada's largest city, we find room for a small vegetable garden. With creative planning we grow a few things that last us the whole year. Squash, for instance, is a climbing vine and easy on space when grown on a trellis. We plant four or five butternut squash plants at the edge of our garden and they climb the fence instead of taking over the whole garden. We usually harvest more than twenty huge butternut squash every year, and they will last us until the following June. Squash is a low-maintenance vegetable to grow and cook. With its hard outer skin, it can be cooked directly in the coals or even underneath the fire (see page 260). One tip to storing squash is to not keep it in the fridge, which will cause it to develop mould spots—a mistake I made our first year growing it. Instead, store it in a cool, dark place.

Garlic is another great vegetable to grow—it's low maintenance, easy to grow, and can last all year in a dark, cool basement. Plant it in late fall, covered with mulch, and it'll be the first thing out of the ground in the spring. It's usually ready to harvest by July, and the space can then be used for quick-growing plants like radishes, lettuces, and herbs. Garlic is another example of something you want to roast whole in its skin. Something magnificent happens when garlic is roasted. Thick and creamy roasted garlic has that umami taste that is heightened when cooked over an open fire.

Cooking vegetables over the fire isn't just about the taste. It encompasses the visual and physical experience of watching them blister and blacken over open flames—a primal and hypnotic experience. In a time of increasing focus on technology and gadgets, cooking over the fire remains a timeless and superior way to prepare and enjoy the natural beauty and flavours of the humble vegetable.

Campfire Chanterelle Risotto

I cooked this dish at camp in Mississippi after finding more chanterelles in a single day than I have in my entire life. The forest floor was huge patches of golden yellow and orange. I dream of this memory often, as chanterelles are one of the best-tasting mushrooms. Rice is the perfect canvas to highlight the rich and earthy flavour of these choice edibles. Paired with loads of richness from butter and Parmesan cheese, this risotto satisfies the soul. Over the fire it takes on a little smokiness, beautifully rounding out this special dish.

Note: If your chanterelle mushrooms are very dirty, gently wash them with cold water and dry well with a kitchen towel.

SERVES 4 to 6

Prepare a charcoal or wood fire in an outdoor grill or firepit and let the flames die down with red embers visible. Set a grate over the fire. Alternatively, preheat a gas grill to 500°F (260°C). In a medium saucepan over medium heat, heat the stock. Preheat a large cast-iron skillet.

Heat 1 tablespoon (15 mL) of the olive oil in the hot pan. Add the rice and toast it in the oil, stirring constantly, until it starts to turn golden, 2 to 3 minutes. Add the remaining 1 tablespoon (15 mL) olive oil, mushrooms, and shallots and continue cooking, stirring, until the mushrooms have wilted and the shallots are translucent, 2 to 3 minutes. Add the garlic and cook for another minute. Deglaze the pan with the white wine and cook until most of the liquid has been absorbed. Stir in the thyme and a pinch each of salt and pepper. Add 1 cup (250 mL) of the stock and cook, stirring frequently, until most of the liquid has been absorbed. Continue ladling stock into the rice, 1 cup (250 mL) at a time, stirring until the liquid is absorbed before adding more. (You might not need all the stock.) Once only 1 or 2 cups (250 to 500 mL) of stock is left, start testing the grains of rice for doneness. When done, the rice should be al dente with a slight firmness in the centre but not hard. If the rice is still hard, continue adding the remaining stock. Adjust seasoning with a pinch each of salt and pepper, if needed.

Remove from the heat and stir in the butter, mascarpone cheese, and Parmesan. Spoon the risotto onto plates or into shallow bowls. Serve with more Parmesan on top.

- 8 cups (2 L) chicken or duck stock
- 2 tablespoons (30 mL) olive oil, divided
- 1 pound (450 g) arborio, carnaroli, or other short-grain rice
- 1 pound (450 g) chanterelle mushrooms, brushed clean and roughly chopped (about 2 cups/500 mL)
- 2 shallots, minced
- 4 cloves garlic, crushed
- 1 cup (250 mL) dry white wine
- Leaves from 4 sprigs fresh thyme
- Kosher salt and freshly cracked black pepper
- ¼ cup (60 mL) unsalted butter, softened
- 2 tablespoons (30 mL) mascarpone cheese, softened
- 1 cup (250 mL) freshly grated Parmesan cheese, plus more for serving

Fire-Roasted Cauliflower with Baba Ghanoush

Baba ghanoush is a Lebanese roasted eggplant dip. Eggplants are the perfect fire-roasting vegetable. Their earthy flavour comes to life with a little smoke, and the inside becomes beautifully creamy when cooked. Select smaller firm eggplant varieties, as they are more flavourful. The fire-roasted cauliflower adds a complementary earthy element to the sweet, charred flavour of the eggplant. This recipe is tasty as a spread for canapés, as a dip for pita, or as a vegetables side.

For fresh crunch and bright flavour, you can shave some pieces of raw cauliflower on a mandoline for garnish.

SERVES 4 to 6 AS AN APPETIZER

1 head cauliflower
Olive oil, for drizzling
Kosher salt

Baba Ghanoush

3 medium globe or Italian eggplants
4 cloves garlic, minced
¼ cup (60 mL) tahini
¼ cup (60 mL) olive oil, plus more for drizzling
Juice of 1 lemon
1 teaspoon (5 mL) kosher salt
Freshly cracked black pepper
Fresh mint leaves, for garnish

Fire-Roast the Cauliflower

Prepare a charcoal or wood fire in an outdoor grill or firepit and let the flames die down with red embers visible. Set a grate over the fire. Alternatively, preheat a gas grill to 500°F (260°C).

Drizzle the cauliflower with olive oil and season with salt. Place the cauliflower on an elevated rack on a grill or in a spot with indirect heat over the fire. Roast until the cauliflower is golden on the outside and can easily be pierced all the way through with a metal skewer, about 1 hour.

Remove the cauliflower from the heat. Cut into 1- to 2-inch (2.5 to 5 cm) pieces.

Meanwhile, Make the Baba Ghanoush

Place the eggplants on the grill over direct heat and char over the fire, turning every 3 to 4 minutes, until the skin is black and the eggplants are very soft. Depending on your heat, this will take 20 to 30 minutes. Remove from the heat and let cool.

Once cool enough to handle, peel off and discard the charred skin and transfer the flesh to a blender. Add the garlic, tahini, olive oil, lemon juice, salt, and a few cracks of pepper. Blend until smooth. Taste and adjust seasoning.

To serve, spread a large spoonful of the baba ghanoush onto a large plate. Arrange the fire-roasted cauliflower over top. Drizzle with olive oil and sprinkle with the mint.

Charcoal-Roasted Whole Cabbage

Something magical happens when you roast a whole cabbage in a fire. The outer leaves will be completely burnt but the inside will steam in its own juices and will taste like a sweet, smoked vegetable delicacy. The trick is to place the cabbage into the pit, pour charcoal all around the cabbage, and light it. Then go about cooking the rest of your meal on the coals. After 3 hours or so, your cabbage should be roasted to perfection.

This dish can also be served as a slaw. Cool the cabbage, then chop and mix with the ranch dressing.

SERVES 4 to 6 AS A SIDE

Roast the Cabbage

Place the cabbage in an outdoor grill or firepit. Pour the charcoal around and on top of the cabbage and light the fire.

Roast the cabbage until it can easily be pierced all the way through with a metal skewer, about 3 hours. Remove from the coals and let cool.

Once cool enough to handle, peel off the burnt outer leaves. Slice the cauliflower into 1-inch (2.5 cm) pieces or wedges.

Make the Ranch Dressing

In a small bowl, combine the mayonnaise, sour cream, garlic, parsley, chives, dill seeds, salt, and pepper. Whisk until smooth.

Drizzle the cauliflower with the ranch dressing and serve.

Special Equipment

10 pounds (4.5 kg) hardwood lump charcoal (if using briquettes, they burn quite fast so you will need 20 pounds/9 kg)

1 large green cabbage

Ranch Dressing

½ cup (125 mL) mayonnaise

½ cup (125 mL) sour cream

2 cloves garlic, crushed

1 teaspoon (5 mL) chopped fresh flat-leaf parsley

1 teaspoon (5 mL) thinly sliced fresh chives

½ teaspoon (2 mL) ground dill seeds

½ teaspoon (2 mL) salt

Pinch of freshly ground black pepper

Fire-Roasted Heirloom Carrots and Onions with Hummus

SERVES 4 AS A SIDE

Carrots take on a beautiful sweetness when they're roasted over a fire. Their natural sugars caramelize, and paired with smoke from the fire, they make a wonderful side dish or appetizer with roasted onions and hummus. Try to source bunched local organic carrots or heirloom varieties with their tops from a farmers' market or local store in the summer or fall months, as they will be much sweeter than bagged orange carrots from far away.

Fire-Roasted Heirloom Carrots and Onions

2 bunches multicoloured heirloom carrots

Olive oil, plus more for drizzling

Salt and black pepper

8 ounces (225 g) unpeeled shallots or cippolini onions

1 bunch green onions, thinly sliced, for garnish

Pinch of sweet paprika, for garnish

Hummus

1 can (19 ounces/540 mL) chickpeas, drained and rinsed

¼ cup (60 mL) tahini

Juice of 1 lemon

2 cloves garlic, minced

1 tablespoon (15 mL) kosher salt

Pinch of freshly ground black pepper

Prepare a charcoal or wood fire in an outdoor grill or firepit and let the flames die down with red embers visible. Set a grate over the fire. Alternatively, preheat a gas grill to 500°F (260°C).

Roast the Carrots and Onions

If the carrots have long green tops, you can tie them together and hang the carrots over the fire. Brush the carrots with olive oil and season with salt and pepper. Place the carrots and shallots over indirect heat, near or over the fire where it is still very hot but the flames or coals are not touching the carrots. Roast the carrots and shallots, turning every 10 minutes, until dark char marks appear, the carrots are slightly wrinkled, and the carrots and shallots can easily be pierced all the way through with a metal skewer, 1 to 2 hours. Caramelized sugars should leak from the shallots when pierced. The cooking time will vary depending on the thickness of the carrots and the heat of the fire source. You can move the carrots closer to the fire to finish roasting, if needed. The carrots and shallots can be cooked ahead of time and served cold or reheated to warm.

Once cooked, remove the carrots and shallots from the heat and let cool slightly. Remove and discard the skin from the shallots, then cut in half lengthwise and roughly chop. Cut off and discard the carrots' charred green tops and slice the carrots lengthwise.

Make the Hummus

In a high-speed blender, purée the chickpeas on high speed until smooth. Add the tahini, lemon juice, garlic, salt, and pepper and blend, scraping down the sides once or twice, until smooth, about 2 minutes.

To serve, spread the hummus in the middle of a plate and place the roasted carrots on top. Scatter the chopped roasted shallots around the plate. Garnish with the green onions, a drizzle of olive oil, and a dusting of paprika.

Charcoal-Roasted Beets with Yogurt Dressing

Beets have a high sugar content, which is why they are used to make white and brown sugars and even molasses. Roasting beets concentrates their sugars while preserving their earthy root vegetable flavour, and the smokiness from cooking over a fire adds to that earthiness. Beets can be roasted wrapped in foil or placed directly on the grill grate or very near to the coals. They can even be buried underneath the fire and baked solely from the indirect heat. Beets are incredibly easy to grow, and the green leaves are also tasty raw or cooked. If you have the space in your garden or even pots in a sunny window, beets are a great addition even for a novice gardener, and they'll last all winter if stored properly. If you are buying beets, look for ones with the leaves attached, as they are fresher and sweeter than ones with the greens trimmed off.

The sweet, smoky flavour of these beets paired with the tanginess of the yogurt makes a perfect appetizer or side dish to accompany any lunch or dinner.

SERVES **4** AS AN APPETIZER OR SIDE

Prepare a charcoal or wood fire in an outdoor grill or firepit and let the flames die down with red embers visible. Set a grate over the fire, if using.

Place the beets in a large bowl. Drizzle with olive oil, generously season with salt and pepper, and toss to coat. Wrap each beet tightly in foil and place them near the coals. Alternatively, don't wrap the beets and roast them directly on the grate over the fire. Roast the beets for about 1 hour, or until they can easily be pierced all the way through with a metal skewer. Remove the beets with metal tongs, unwrap if you used foil, and let cool.

While the beets are cooling, wash, pat dry, and chop the reserved beet greens. In a small bowl, whisk together the yogurt and cider vinegar, then season with a pinch of salt.

Once the beets are cool enough to handle, wearing gloves, peel off the skin with a paring knife or vegetable peeler. Cut the beets into ¼-inch (5 mm) thick slices. Place the roasted beets, beet greens, and shallot in a large bowl. Drizzle with the yogurt dressing and toss. Spoon the salad into bowls and serve. (Alternatively, divide the beet and shallot mixture among individual plates and serve drizzled with the dressing.)

Special Equipment

Work gloves

---

4 medium red beets with green tops, unpeeled, trimmed and washed (cut off and reserve the greens)

Olive oil

Salt and black pepper

¼ cup (60 mL) plain full-fat Greek or Balkan-style yogurt

¼ cup (60 mL) apple cider vinegar

1 shallot, thinly sliced

Fire-Roasted Sweet Corn

This dish reminds me of eating grilled street corn in Mexico or enjoying a cob at a local fall fair as a kid. Corn is an incredibly versatile ingredient that can be cooked in so many ways. Do not buy the prepackaged corn behind plastic wrap. It's just nowhere near as good. Instead, wait until the end of the summer months to buy local corn from the markets or better yet from roadside farm stands where the corn is so sweet you can eat it raw. Corn can be roasted husked for a more noticeable charred flavour or roasted still in its husk for a subtler smokiness. This recipe cooks the corn in the husk for a subtler flavour, but feel free to try it whichever way you enjoy, or try both!

The star of this dish is the corn, but it is transformed by freshly grated Parmesan cheese and tangy Tajín, a Mexican chili-lime seasoning.

SERVES 4 AS AN APPETIZER OR SIDE

- 4 husk-on sweet corn cobs
- Olive oil, for drizzling
- 1 small wedge of Parmesan cheese
- 1 teaspoon (5 mL) Tajín
- Kosher salt and black pepper
- Leaves from 2 sprigs fresh oregano, chopped

Prepare a charcoal or wood fire in an outdoor grill or firepit and let the flames die down with red embers visible. Set a grate over the fire. Alternatively, preheat a gas grill to 500°F (260°C).

Place the husk-on corn cobs directly on the grill grate or on an elevated rack or hang them over the fire. Cook for 5 to 10 minutes, depending on your heat source. (Hung over the fire might take a little longer.) The husk will darken to golden brown and have black char marks. Remove from the heat, peel back the husks, and drizzle the corn with olive oil. Generously grate the Parmesan over the corn. Sprinkle with the Tajín, salt, and pepper. Garnish with the oregano.

Charred Zucchini and Stracciatella Cheese

Stracciatella is a wonderful briny, sweet, and rich Italian fresh mozzarella cheese curd in fresh cream. It is what is stuffed inside the equally delicious and popular burrata cheese. It hails from Puglia, Italy, where fresh mozzarella was traditionally pulled into large strings and tied into thick knots. Any cheese that did not sell would lose its fresh, soft texture. This unsold cheese was torn or shredded (*stracciare* in Italian) and soaked in fresh cream, where it transformed into something beautiful. If you're a fan of burrata, this is the real star ingredient and possibly the most delicious by-product ever created. Today it's more commonly made with scraps from cow's milk mozzarella production, but if you can find old-school buffalo milk varieties, it's extra special.

The cheese's rich and creamy texture beautifully elevates the subtle flavour of zucchini, which comes alive when charred on a grill or in the fire. The skin is very flavourful when charred, but make sure you don't burn it. Burnt skin will leave a gritty texture in your mouth. Black spots or grill marks are all you want here.

SERVES 4 to 6

Prepare a charcoal or wood fire in an outdoor grill or firepit and let the flames die down with red embers visible. Set a grate over the fire. Alternatively, preheat a gas grill to 500°F (260°C).

Char the zucchini directly on the grill grate or very close to the coals just until black spots or char marks appear, 2 to 3 minutes per side. Be careful not to burn the skin. Remove from the heat and let cool slightly.

When cool enough to handle, cut the zucchini into 3-inch (8 cm) batons (but any shape will work). Shave a few pieces of zucchini for a slightly different texture; reserve for garnish. Transfer the batons to a medium bowl.

In a small bowl, whisk together the olive oil, white wine vinegar, and honey. Season with a pinch each of salt and pepper.

Drizzle the zucchini batons with the vinaigrette. Adjust the seasoning with salt and pepper, if needed. Arrange the batons on plates. Spoon the stracciatella cheese over top. Season the cheese with a small pinch of salt. Garnish with torn zucchini flowers (if using), the reserved shaved zucchini, and oregano. Drizzle with extra-virgin olive oil.

2 medium or large green zucchini

¼ cup (60 mL) olive oil

2 tablespoons (30 mL) white wine vinegar

1 teaspoon (5 mL) pure liquid honey

Kosher salt and black pepper

1 cup (250 g) stracciatella cheese

Zucchini flowers, for garnish (optional)

Fresh oregano leaves, for garnish

Good-quality extra-virgin olive oil, for drizzling

Fire-Roasted Whole Squash with Burrata Cheese

Whole squash has such a hard, thick skin that it's a fun vegetable to roast directly in the fire. The outer skin will blacken completely and will need to be removed, but what's inside is steamed smoky goodness. Butternut squash is quite sweet in flavour. A decadent addition of burrata makes this dish incredibly rich and smooth. Burrata cheese is mozzarella that is stretched thin and stuffed with mozzarella curd in cream called stracciatella. The chunky liquid deliciousness oozes out when the ball is cut. Burrata is typically sold in 125 g or 250 g balls, but stores don't always carry both sizes. If only the 250 g size is available, buy two portions and cut them in half.

SERVES 4 AS AN APPETIZER

Pickled Squash

2 cups (500 mL) water

2 cups (500 mL) white wine vinegar

¼ cup (60 mL) granulated sugar

1 tablespoon (15 mL) yellow mustard seeds

2 teaspoons (10 mL) kosher salt

1 teaspoon (5 mL) black peppercorns

1 small butternut squash, peeled and thinly sliced (use a mandoline, meat slicer, or vegetable peeler)

Fire-Roasted Whole Squash

1 medium butternut squash

4 (125 g) balls burrata cheese

Flaky sea salt and freshly ground black pepper

Good-quality extra-virgin olive oil, for drizzling

White balsamic vinegar, for drizzling

For garnish

Fresh basil leaves

Squash blossoms (optional)

Make the Pickled Squash

In a medium pot, combine the water, white wine vinegar, sugar, mustard seeds, salt, and peppercorns and bring to a boil over high heat.

Place the squash strips in a heat-resistant bowl. Pour the boiling pickling liquid through a fine-mesh sieve over the squash. Transfer to the fridge to cool completely before serving. The pickle can be stored in an airtight container in the fridge for a couple of months.

Fire-Roast the Squash

Prepare a charcoal or wood fire in an outdoor grill or firepit and let the flames die down with red embers visible. Set a grate over the fire. Alternatively, preheat a gas grill to 500°F (260°C).

Place the whole unpeeled squash next to the coals or directly beside the fire source. Roast, turning every 10 or 15 minutes, until the squash is black and burnt on the outside and can easily be pierced all the way through with a metal skewer, about 1 hour. Remove from the fire and let cool slightly.

When cool enough to handle, peel the burnt skin off the squash. Cut the squash in half lengthwise and scoop out the seeds with a spoon and discard. Cut the squash into wedges and arrange on plates. Place a ball of burrata in the middle and tear or cut to expose the cheese curd inside. Season to taste with flaky sea salt and pepper. Remove several pieces of pickled squash strips from the pickling liquid with a fork and arrange around the cheese. Drizzle with the extra-virgin olive oil and white balsamic vinegar. Garnish with the basil and squash blossoms, if using.

Campfire Brussels Sprouts and Bacon

After eating brussels sprouts cooked with bacon in the smokiness of a campfire, it's extremely hard to go back to eating them any other way. Tender and creamy on the inside with smoky, fatty, crispy outer leaves, these are just heavenly. This simple dish is near impossible to mess up. All you need is a fire and a large cast-iron skillet, and you are good to go.

SERVES 4 to 6

Prepare a charcoal or wood fire in an outdoor grill or firepit and let the flames die down with red embers visible. Set a grate over the fire. Alternatively, preheat a gas grill to 500°F (260°C). Preheat a large cast-iron skillet over the fire.

Add the bacon to the hot pan and cook, stirring often, to render the fat evenly, 5 to 6 minutes. Add the brussels sprouts and cook, without stirring, until caramelized on one side, 4 to 5 minutes. Stir in the shallot, garlic, and thyme. Season with a pinch each of salt and pepper, remembering that the bacon will be salted. Cook, stirring occasionally, until the brussels sprouts are carmelized and soft in the middle.

1 pound (450 g) thick-cut bacon, cut crosswise into ¼-inch (5 mm) strips

2 pounds (900 g) brussels sprouts (cut in half if large)

1 small shallot, minced

2 cloves garlic, minced

Leaves from 2 sprigs fresh thyme, chopped

Kosher salt and black pepper

Grilled Artichokes

Grilled artichokes have a nutty flavour often compared to almonds or hazelnuts, and the smokiness of the grill really brings out their natural grassy earthiness. This unique vegetable is such a treat and super easy to cook at home and enjoy off the grill with friends. If you've never eaten whole artichokes before, the outer leaves are tough and spiky but the inside of the fleshy leaves and the inner heart and stem turn wonderfully creamy. I prefer to serve mine cut in half with the outer leaves still on and grilled as an appetizer. Pull the leaves off and dip the white fleshy end into the aioli, then pull them through your teeth to enjoy the deliciousness. You'll be left with the heart, which is edible.

SERVES 4 to 6 AS AN APPETIZER

Lemon Aioli

1 egg

2 cloves garlic, crushed

1 tablespoon (15 mL) Dijon mustard

1 teaspoon (5 mL) sea salt

Pinch of freshly ground black pepper

1 cup (250 mL) olive oil

Zest and juice of 1 lemon, divided

Dash of hot sauce (optional)

Grilled Artichokes

3 artichokes

Kosher salt and black pepper

Make the Lemon Aioli

To a food processor, add the egg, garlic, mustard, salt, and pepper. Process until blended. With the processor running, slowly stream in the olive oil and blend until emulsified. Add the lemon juice and hot sauce (if using) and blend until combined. Taste and adjust seasoning as needed. Pour the aioli into a ramekin or small bowl. Sprinkle the lemon zest over the aioli and store, covered, in the fridge for up to 1 week.

Steam and Grill the Artichokes

Pour an inch or so of water into a large pot that will fit a bamboo steamer. Bring to a boil over high heat. Place the artichokes in the steamer. Set the steamer, covered with the lid, on top of the pot and steam for 15 minutes. Poke the base of the artichokes with a toothpick to see whether they are tender. If they are still tough, continue to steam, checking every 5 minutes, until tender. Remove from the steamer and let sit until cool enough to handle.

Once cool, slice the artichokes in half lengthwise. Season with a pinch each of salt and pepper.

Prepare a charcoal or wood fire in an outdoor grill or firepit and let the flames die down with red embers visible. Set a grate over the fire. Alternatively, preheat a gas grill to 500°F (260°C). Preheat a large cast-iron skillet over the fire.

Grill the artichokes cut side down for 3 to 5 minutes, or until they have dark char marks. Rotate 90 degrees and grill for another 3 to 5 minutes for a charred crisscross pattern. Using a small spoon, scoop out and discard the small fuzzy "choke" in the centre of the artichoke; this part of the artichoke is inedible.

Serve the grilled artichokes with the lemon aioli for dipping.

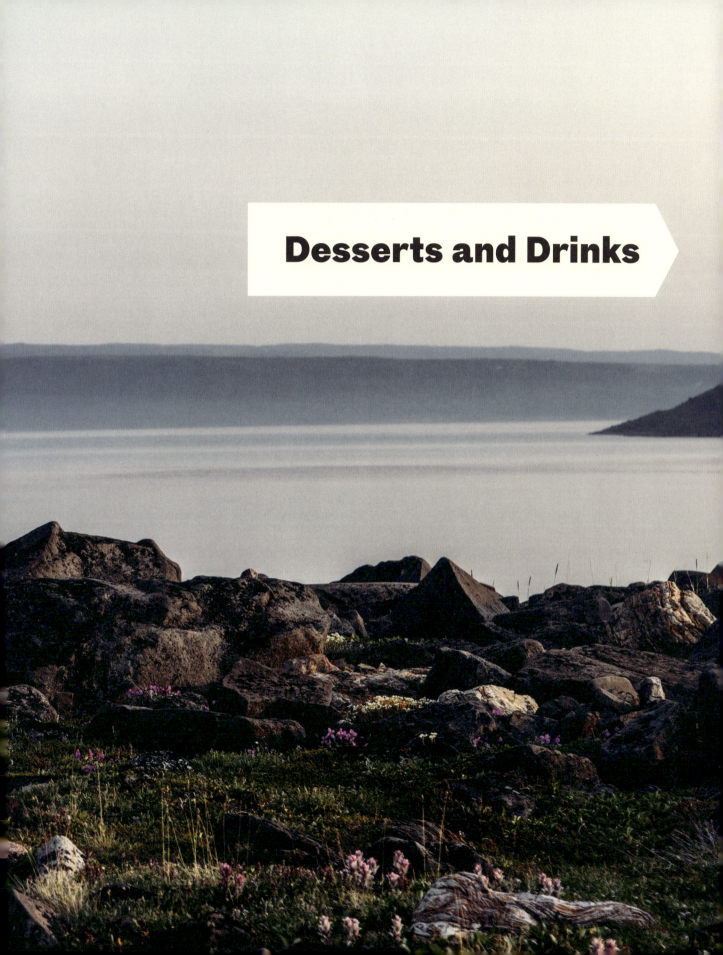
Desserts and Drinks

Sweets and Cocktails Fit for a Fire

Cocktails, like food, are always evolving. Sure, we have the classic martini, old-fashioned, and so on, but at the restaurant we are always innovating. Smoked citrus and garnishes and smoking the glass all create something special and different on our taste buds. When we start making our Applewood Smoke Barrel cocktail (featured in *The Hunter Chef Cookbook*), the whole dining room can smell the toasted smoke of cinnamon, and everyone starts looking for where that enticing smell is coming from. Then the bar gets flooded with orders for them. We can't help it—like moths to a flame, we are drawn to the fire and the smell of smoke. Cocktails crafted with care can enhance and be the highlight of any event. Can you smoke the glass, grill the fruit garnish, smoke the citrus to pair with the aromas of the spirit? Whiskeys, rums, scotches, and dark spirits work well because they are aged in charred barrels. Your whiskey or bourbon tastes so great partly because it's aged in smoky burnt wood!

Dessert, the grand finale to the meal, doesn't have to go off brand when it's cooked with fire. Peaches, pineapple, apples, even watermelon can be grilled. Natural sugars caramelizing over hot coals—there are so many possibilities. It doesn't have to get complicated. Pair them with ice cream or drizzle with honey or dust with cinnamon. I've baked pumpkin pie and strawberry pie in my smoker, as well as chocolate chip cookies and banana bread. You can make a pie or crumble over a fire in a cast-iron Dutch oven by placing some coals on the lid. Just because you are camping, dessert doesn't have to be boring. Have you ever made a s'more in a toaster oven? It's fun for the kids, but it's missing something without the smoke and experience of the campfire.

The art of pairing cocktails and dessert relies on harmonizing flavours. A bourbon with notes of vanilla will pair wonderfully with a grilled peach dessert or pecan pie, whereas a smoky mezcal may be better suited to grilled pineapple and smoked citrus wheels. This chapter explores cocktails and desserts perfect for pairing with any outdoor fire experience. They infuse the occasion with celebration.

Duck Fat Caramels

Caramel toffee is one of my favourite candies of all time, and when I learned that you could use animal fat in place of butter, I knew I had to develop my own recipe. These chewy and rich candies are easy to make at home and can be cut into any shape you want or rolled like the classic Tootsie Roll and wrapped in parchment or wax paper. The smell of the sugar caramelizing will make your mouth water in anticipation. Take these sweets with you on all your outdoor adventures. Experiment with bear lard or beef suet in place of the duck fat.

MAKES A
13 x 9-inch
(33 x 23 cm)
SLAB

Line a 13 x 9-inch (33 x 23 cm) baking sheet with parchment paper, leaving a 1-inch (2.5 cm) overhang on the sides, then spray with nonstick cooking spray or lightly oil or butter the parchment.

In a heavy medium saucepan, combine the sugar, corn syrup, duck fat, and butter. Cook over high heat, stirring occasionally, until the sugar is dissolved and the mixture is boiling. Maintaining a boil, and without stirring, pour the evaporated milk in a slow and steady stream into the boiling syrup. (The syrup must continue to boil while pouring in the milk. If the milk is added too quickly and the syrup stops boiling, the mixture can curdle.) Continue boiling, stirring constantly and scraping down the sides of the pan, until the temperature reaches 240°F (115°C) on a candy thermometer, 10 to 15 minutes. Check the temperature every 2 or 3 minutes.

Remove from the heat and stir in the vanilla and salt. Pour the caramel onto the prepared baking sheet. Set the sheet on a wire rack on the counter and let the caramel cool to room temperature. Transfer the caramel to the fridge to cool completely, at least 3 hours.

Lift the slab of caramel from the pan and place it on a cutting board. Let sit at room temperature for 15 to 20 minutes to soften for easier cutting. (If the caramel is too cold to cut, it may snap and break.) Using a sharp knife, cut the caramel into desired size, then wrap each piece in parchment or wax paper, twisting the two ends closed. Store the wrapped caramels in an airtight container in the fridge for up to 1 month.

- 4 cups (1 L) granulated sugar
- 2 cups (500 mL) corn syrup
- ½ cup (125 mL) rendered duck fat
- ½ cup (125 mL) unsalted butter
- 2 cans (354 mL each) evaporated milk, at room temperature
- 2 teaspoon (10 mL) pure vanilla extract
- 1 teaspoon (5 mL) sea salt

Chaga Ice Cream

Chaga is a type of mushroom that grows on birch trees in the colder climate of Canada and the northern United States and Europe. It isn't the kind of mushroom you can sink your teeth into. It is incredibly woody and has to be either boiled or ground into a powder. Look for birch trees with a charcoal-like black burl or large bulbous growth on the trunk and cut it off with a saw or hatchet. Chaga tastes very earthy and is full of medicinal properties. It pairs very nicely with sweet chai spices, and I love using it in this spiced ice cream recipe and hope you will too! Chaga mushroom powder is readily available at health food stores, most tea shops, and online.

SERVES 4 to 6

- 2 cups (500 mL) whole milk
- 2 cups (500 mL) heavy (35%) cream
- 1½ cups (375 mL) granulated sugar
- ¼ cup (60 mL) dark rum
- 2 teaspoons (10 mL) pure vanilla extract
- 4 star anise
- 3 green cardamom pods
- 2 cinnamon sticks
- 2 tablespoons (30 mL) chaga mushroom powder, plus more for dusting
- 10 large egg yolks

In a medium saucepan, heat an inch or so of water until simmering.

In another medium saucepan, combine the milk, cream, sugar, rum, vanilla, star anise, cardamom pods, cinnamon sticks, and chaga mushroom powder. Heat over medium heat until almost simmering, then immediately remove from the heat.

In a large bowl, whisk the egg yolks. Whisking constantly, gradually pour the hot milk mixture into the egg yolks in a slow and steady stream. (Adding all the hot mixture at once can cause the eggs to scramble, resulting in an eggy taste in the ice cream.)

Set the bowl with the hot egg mixture over the pot of simmering water (be sure the bowl is not touching the water). Continue to cook, stirring constantly and scraping the bottom of the bowl with a heatproof rubber spatula, until the custard thickens slightly and the temperature reaches 175°F (80°C) on a probe thermometer. Remove the bowl from the heat and let the custard cool to room temperature. Cover the surface with plastic wrap and transfer the custard to the fridge until cool, at least 2 hours. (If your ice-cream maker uses a frozen canister, chill the custard overnight.)

Strain the custard through a fine-mesh sieve into a medium bowl. Discard the spices. Pour the custard into an ice-cream maker and process according to the manufacturer's instructions. The ice cream can be stored in an airtight container in the freezer for up to 1 week. Scoop and serve dusted with chaga mushroom powder.

Grilled Peaches and Vanilla Ice Cream with Wildflower Honey and Black Walnuts

I live near a region known for its stone fruit, and every year I look forward to local peaches, sweet, flavourful, and bursting with juices. There are so many ways to enjoy them. I like to keep it simple and grill peaches and serve with ice cream. The char of the caramelized natural sugars paired with floral wildflower honey and the nuttiness of the black walnuts makes this an extraordinary dessert.

SERVES 4 to 6

Make the Vanilla Ice Cream

In a medium saucepan, heat an inch or so of water until simmering.

In another medium saucepan, combine the milk, cream, sugar, and vanilla. Heat over medium until almost simmering, then immediately remove from the heat.

In a large bowl, whisk the egg yolks. Whisking constantly, gradually pour the hot milk mixture into the egg yolks in a slow and steady stream. (Adding all the hot mixture at once can cause the eggs to scramble, resulting in an eggy taste in the ice cream.)

Set the bowl with the hot egg mixture over the pot of simmering water (be sure the bowl is not touching the water). Continue to cook, stirring constantly and scraping the bottom of the bowl with a heatproof rubber spatula, until the custard thickens slightly and the temperature reaches 175°F (80°C) on a probe thermometer. Remove the bowl from the heat and let the custard cool to room temperature. Cover the surface with plastic wrap and transfer the custard to the fridge until cool, at least 2 hours. (If your ice-cream maker uses a frozen canister, chill the custard overnight.)

Strain the custard through a fine-mesh sieve into a medium bowl. Pour the custard into an ice-cream maker and process according to the manufacturer's instructions. The ice cream can be stored in an airtight container in the freezer for up to 1 week.

Vanilla Ice Cream

2 cups (500 mL) whole milk

2 cups (500 mL) heavy (35%) cream

1½ cups (375 mL) granulated sugar

2 teaspoons (10 mL) pure vanilla extract

10 large egg yolks

Toasted Black Walnuts

½ cup (125 mL) chopped black walnuts

Grilled Peaches

6 peaches, cut in half and pitted

1 tablespoon (15 mL) butter, melted

For serving

¼ cup (60 mL) wildflower honey

Fresh thyme leaves (optional)

recipe continues

Toast the Walnuts and Grill the Peaches

Prepare a charcoal or wood fire in an outdoor grill or firepit and let the flames die down with red embers visible. Set a grate over the fire. Alternatively, preheat a gas grill to 500°F (260°C).

While the grill heats, toast the walnuts in a small pan on the grill grate, stirring occasionally, until golden, about 5 minutes.

In a large bowl, toss the peaches with the melted butter. Grill the peaches cut side down until dark grill marks form, 3 to 4 minutes. For a crisscross pattern, rotate the peaches halfway through grilling. (I only grill fresh and tender peaches on one side.)

Arrange the peaches grilled side up on plates. Scoop the vanilla ice cream on top. Drizzle with wildflower honey, sprinkle with toasted walnuts, and garnish with thyme, if using.

Stroopwafel S'mores

S'mores are the absolute greatest and simplest camping treat ever created, but you really need to make one with a stroopwafel. If you've never had a stroopwafel, it is a heavenly cookie of caramel sandwiched between two crisp, thin waffle cookies. The name means "syrup waffle" in Dutch, and they are usually eaten after warming on top of a hot mug of tea or coffee. The heat and steam soften the waffle and melt the caramel. It's divine on its own, let alone used to sandwich melted chocolate and these homemade cedar marshmallows.

MAKES **8** S'MORES

Make the Cedar Powder

Preheat the oven to 150°F (65°C).

Evenly spread the cedar leaves in a single layer on a baking sheet and dehydrate in the oven for 1 hour. Turn off the oven, prop open the door, and let the leaves cool in the oven. The cedar leaves should be crisp and break when pressed.

Transfer the cooled cedar leaves to a blender and pulse into a powder. Pass the cedar powder through a fine-mesh sieve into a container with a tight-fitting lid. The cedar powder will be vibrant green and taste and smell like the forest. It has a slight citrus taste too. The cedar powder can be stored in an airtight container at room temperature for up to 1 week.

Make the Marshmallows

Grease a 13 x 9-inch (33 x 23 cm) baking sheet with soft unsalted butter.

Pour the ½ cup (125 mL) cold water into the bowl of a stand mixer. Sprinkle the gelatine over the water and stir. Let sit until all the water is absorbed. Fit the mixer with the whisk attachment.

In a medium saucepan, combine the corn syrup, the ½ cup (125 mL) room-temperature water, and granulated sugar. Bring to a boil, stirring just long enough to dissolve the sugar. Once it reaches a boil, stop stirring or moving the pot (this would make the sugar crystallize) and continue cooking until the mixture reaches 240°F (115°C) on a candy thermometer, 6 to 8 minutes. Remove from the heat.

With the mixer on medium speed, pour the hot syrup into the gelatine mixture in a slow and steady stream, then increase the speed to high and continue whisking until the mixture has cooled, has doubled in volume, and is light and fluffy, 4 to 5 minutes.

Cedar Powder

A few handfuls of fresh cedar leaves (stripped off brown stems)

Marshmallows

½ cup (125 mL) cold water

3 envelopes (21 g each) unflavoured gelatine

1 cup (250 mL) light corn syrup

½ cup (125 mL) room-temperature water

1½ cups (375 mL) granulated sugar

Icing sugar, for dusting

Cedar Powder (recipe above), for dusting

For the S'mores

16 stroopwafel cookies

1 (100 g) 70% chocolate bar, cut into 8 pieces

Cedar Powder (recipe above), for dusting

Sea salt, for dusting

recipe continues

Scrape the mixture onto the prepared baking sheet and spread evenly with a wet spatula. Dust the top with the icing sugar and cedar powder. Let cool, uncovered, on the counter overnight.

The next day, using a greased knife or greased cookie cutters, cut the marshmallows into squares about the same size as your stroopwafels. Store the marshmallows in an airtight container at room temperature for up to 2 weeks.

Make the Stroopwafel S'mores

Build a campfire, or prepare a charcoal or wood fire in an outdoor wood pizza oven or in a grill or firepit. Let the flames die down with red embers visible. You can use a gas grill at 500°F (260°C) but the s'mores will not have the same flavour.

For each s'more, top 1 cookie with a piece of chocolate, then 1 marshmallow, and dust with cedar powder and a pinch of salt. Repeat with 7 more cookies. Heat your stroopwafels over the campfire on a grill or wire rack, or place the s'mores on a baking sheet and heat on the grill or in the pizza oven, until the chocolate melts and the marshmallows soften, 2 to 3 minutes. Remove from the heat, top with the remaining cookies, and sandwich together.

Smoker Strawberry Pie

Only in-season local strawberries should be used for this recipe. Strawberries imported from far away in the winter have almost zero flavour. Greenhouse strawberries also don't taste very good. At farmers' markets or specialty grocery stores, look for berries that were grown outside. They will be vibrant red and smaller in size, different shapes, and vibrant red throughout when cut. If the berries are white inside, they were picked before they were ripe. A wood oven, pellet smoker, or offset smoker are best for making this recipe, as the wood's subtle smoke flavour pairs incredibly with the sweetness of the pie. This recipe is inspired by and adapted from my wife's "aunt" Jane's recipe.

MAKES A 9-inch (23 cm) PIE

Make the Butter Pastry Dough

In the bowl of a stand mixer fitted with the paddle attachment, combine the flour, butter, lard, and salt. Mix on low speed until the mixture has just formed into a paste. Do not overmix. Add the cold water and mix on low speed just until incorporated. Do not overmix. Overmixing will cause the pastry to be tough and crunchy; you want it supple and flaky.

Turn the dough out onto a sheet of plastic wrap. Press the dough flat, fold half the wrap over top, and shape into a ½-inch (1 cm) thick disc. Wrap tightly and refrigerate for at least 1 hour and ideally overnight. This allows the gluten in the dough to relax, making it easier to roll out with less shrinkage.

Make the Strawberry Filling

Preheat your wood oven or smoker. The temperature should be between 350° and 400°F (180° to 200°C).

Wash the strawberries under cold running water. Pat dry, then remove the green stem and cut the berries in half. Reserve half of the prepped strawberries.

In a large saucepan, combine half of the berries and the sugar and bring to a boil over high heat. Continue boiling, stirring occasionally and crushing the berries with a masher, until the mixture starts to resemble a loose jam, about 6 minutes.

In a measuring cup, stir the cornstarch with the cold water until no lumps remain. Pour the cornstarch mixture into the pan and stir to incorporate. Stir in the lemon juice and vanilla, reduce the heat to medium, and simmer, stirring occasionally, until the jam is thick and has visible chunks of berries, another 2 to 3 minutes. Remove from the heat and let cool for 15 minutes.

Butter Pastry Dough

1¾ cups (425 mL/215 g) all-purpose flour, plus more for dusting

6 tablespoons (90 mL/85 g) unsalted butter, at room temperature

2 tablespoons (30 mL/25 g) lard, at room temperature

½ teaspoon (2 mL/2.5 g) kosher salt

3 tablespoons + 1 teaspoon (50 mL/50 g) cold water

Strawberry Filling

2 pints (4 cups/1 L) fresh strawberries

1 cup (250 mL) granulated sugar

1 tablespoon (15 mL) cornstarch

¼ cup (60 mL) cold water

1 tablespoon (15 mL) lemon juice

1 teaspoon (5 mL) pure vanilla extract

Whipped Cream

1 cup (250 mL) heavy (35%) cream

1 tablespoon (15 mL) granulated sugar

Fresh mint leaves, for garnish

recipe continues

Assemble and Smoke the Pie

On a lightly floured work surface, roll out the dough into a 12-inch (30 cm) circle. Loosely roll the dough over the rolling pin and transfer the pastry to a 9-inch (23 cm) pie plate. Gently press the dough into the pie plate and trim the overhang flush with the edge. Using a fork, gently prick the bottom of the pie shell all over in 1-inch (2.5 cm) increments. These small indents in the pastry will allow steam to escape and keep the pastry from rising.

Fold the reserved fresh strawberries into the jam mixture. Scrape the strawberry mixture into the pie shell and smooth it into an even layer. Cook the pie in the smoker or wood oven for 45 minutes to 1 hour. When the crust is golden brown and the centre of the pie jiggles only slightly when the pan is moved, the pie is ready. Remove from the smoker or oven and let the pie cool and set for at least 1 hour before slicing.

Make the Whipped Cream

In a medium bowl, beat together the cream and sugar until stiff peaks form.

Slice the pie and serve topped with whipped cream. Garnish with the mint.

Pawpaw Semifreddo

Semifreddo is a refreshing cold Italian dessert (it means "half frozen") and is a delicious way to incorporate fruit into your desserts. This recipe is very adaptable to any fruit that's in season, so feel free to experiment. Here I use pawpaw because it's delicious blended with cream with its super-soft banana-mango texture and flavour. Semifreddo is a great dessert if you don't have an ice-cream maker. It has the texture of ice cream but isn't churned—it is more of a mousse that is frozen while setting. See page 291 for more information about pawpaw, my favourite wild fruit.

Notes: The semifreddo is best made the night before so it has time to set in the freezer. Meringue crisps are very susceptible to humidity, so it's best to make the meringue the day they're needed or just before serving. If needed, store cooled meringue crisps in an airtight container. If it's humid, you can put some silica gel packs in the container to absorb the moisture.

SERVES **8**

Pawpaw Semifreddo

4 fresh pawpaw (you need 2 cups/500 mL pawpaw pulp)

2 cups (500 mL) granulated sugar, divided

1 cup (250 mL) heavy (35%) cream

1 teaspoon (5 mL) pure vanilla extract

¼ cup (60 mL) water

5 large eggs

Meringue Crisps

4 large egg whites

¼ cup (60 mL) granulated sugar

¼ teaspoon (1 mL) cream of tartar

Ground sumac or crushed dried edible rose petals, for dusting

Make the Pawpaw Semifreddo

Line a 9 x 5-inch (2 L) loaf pan with plastic wrap, leaving a generous overhang, and place in the freezer until ready to use.

Cut the pawpaw in half lengthwise and remove the seeds. Scoop the flesh into a small saucepan. Add 1 cup (250 mL) of the sugar. Bring to a simmer over medium heat and cook, stirring occasionally, until the sugar is completely dissolved, 4 to 5 minutes. Remove from the heat. Purée with a hand blender or transfer to a blender and blend until smooth. Scrape into a container, cool to room temperature, and store, covered, in the fridge until ready to use.

In a medium bowl, beat the cream with the vanilla until medium peaks form. Transfer to the fridge until ready to use.

In a small saucepan, combine the remaining 1 cup (250 mL) sugar and the water and bring to a boil, stirring occasionally, until the sugar is dissolved, 2 to 3 minutes.

Meanwhile, using an electric mixer, beat the eggs in a medium bowl on high speed until frothy, about 1 minute. While continuing to beat the eggs, gradually add the hot syrup in a slow and steady stream, beating until the side of the bowl feels cool to the touch and the mixture has doubled in volume, 6 to 8 minutes.

Scoop half of the chilled pawpaw purée into a small bowl (leaving the remaining pawpaw in the fridge until needed). Using a large spatula, fold the purée into the whipped cream in 3 additions, folding until each addition is incorporated before adding more.

recipe continues

Fold the beaten eggs into the cream mixture in 3 additions, folding with the spatula until each addition is incorporated before adding more. Pour the mixture into the chilled lined pan. Fold over the plastic wrap to cover tightly and freeze until firm, at least 8 hours or overnight. The semifreddo can be stored in the freezer for up to 1 month.

Make the Meringue Crisps

Position the racks in the upper and lower thirds of the oven and preheat to 150°F (65°C). Line 2 baking sheets with parchment paper.

In a stand mixer fitted with the whisk attachment, whisk the egg whites on high speed until frothy. With the mixer running, gradually add the sugar in a slow and steady stream. Add the cream of tartar and continue whisking until medium-firm peaks form, 2 to 3 minutes.

Divide the meringue evenly between the prepared baking sheets, using a long metal offset spatula to spread in an even layer. Sprinkle the meringue with sumac or crushed rose petals. Bake for 45 minutes to 1 hour, until the meringue is dry to the touch. Once completely dry, break into pieces. The meringue crisps can be stored in an airtight container for up to 5 days (see Note on previous page).

To serve, remove the semifreddo from the freezer and fold back the plastic wrap. Invert onto a cutting board. Using a large sharp knife, cut the semifreddo crosswise into ½-inch (1 cm) thick slices. Transfer the semifreddo to shallow bowls. Spoon the remaining pawpaw purée alongside, garnish with meringue crisps, and serve immediately.

Sumac Curd with Whipped Cream and Shortbread Crumbs

Wild staghorn sumac is one of my favourite natural lemon substitutes. It's fun to work with something that you can harvest yourself and let your imagination go wild. Anything with lemon can be replaced or enhanced with sumac. I love lemon curd; its rich and tangy sweetness is a perfect pairing with sumac and it's an easy dessert to make at home. If sumac doesn't happen to grow wild around where you live, substitute with the same amount of store-bought ground sumac.

Note: The curd will be light pink in colour. If you want a redder colour, add some beet powder with the ground sumac before cooking.

SERVES **6**

Make the Sumac Curd

In a medium saucepan, heat an inch or so of water until simmering.

In a medium bowl, combine the sugar, butter, lemon zest, lemon juice, sumac, and salt. Place the bowl over the simmering water and stir until the butter is melted. (Do not let the bowl touch the simmering water or the eggs will scramble.) Once the butter has melted, whisk in the eggs. Cook, whisking constantly, until the mixture resembles a thick custard, occasionally scraping the bottom of the bowl with a rubber spatula to ensure the eggs are not sticking to the bottom, 8 to 10 minutes. Using the rubber spatula, press the curd through a fine-mesh sieve into a clean bowl, making sure to press through all the liquid and scraping the underside of the sieve to get all the curd.

Pour the curd into six 1-cup (250 mL) mason jars, leaving space at the top for the whipped cream. Cover and cool in the fridge for at least 4 hours or ideally overnight before serving. The curd can be stored, covered, in the fridge for up to 2 weeks.

When ready to serve, Make the Whipped Cream

In a medium bowl, whisk together the cream and sugar until stiff peaks form.

Spoon a dollop of whipped cream on top of each jar of sumac curd. Top with crumbles of shortbread cookie.

Sumac Curd

1½ cups (375 mL) granulated sugar

⅔ cup (150 g) unsalted butter

Zest of 6 lemons

⅓ cup + 1 teaspoon (80 mL) lemon juice (from about 6 lemons)

6 tablespoons (90 mL) ground fresh sumac berries or dried ground sumac

Pinch of kosher salt

6 large eggs, beaten

Whipped Cream

½ cup (125 mL) heavy (35%) cream

¼ cup (60 mL) granulated sugar

Shortbread cookies, coarsely crumbled, for garnish

Dutch Oven Charcoal-Cooked Cherry Crumble

Cooking in a cast-iron Dutch oven with live charcoal is incredible fun and super easy. The only mistake I encountered when I first started cooking this way was using too many coals. Cast iron holds heat very well, so you need a lot fewer live coals than you think. A great tool is a digital laser temperature gun, readily available at kitchen stores or online.

This dessert is perfect for the summertime when cherries are in season—buy fresh local cherries because they always taste better. A cherry-pitting tool is inexpensive and time-saving, but you can also use a paring knife to halve and pit the cherries. Herbs are a great way to play with this recipe. I love earthy notes with stone fruit, especially thyme, but tarragon also goes wonderfully with cherries. For this recipe I used a 10-inch (5 quart) cast-iron Dutch oven. For easier cleanup, set a foil pie plate inside the Dutch oven.

SERVES 4

Special Equipment
Shovel or poker, if needed

Crumble
¼ cup (60 mL) cold unsalted butter, cut into small cubes
1 cup (250 mL) steel-cut oats
⅓ cup (75 mL) all-purpose flour
⅓ cup (75 mL) granulated sugar
Pinch of salt

Filling
1½ pounds (675 g) fresh sweet red cherries, pitted
⅓ cup (75 mL) granulated sugar
2 teaspoons (10 mL) cornstarch
Pinch of salt
Pinch of fresh thyme leaves (optional)

Vanilla ice cream, for serving
Fresh mint leaves, for garnish

Prepare a charcoal or wood fire in an outdoor grill or firepit and let the flames die down with red embers visible. Set a grate over the fire. Alternatively, you can use a wood pizza oven at 400°F (200°C).

Make the Crumble

In a medium bowl, combine the butter, oats, flour, sugar, and salt. Work the dry ingredients into the butter with your fingers or a pastry blender. The flour and oats will come together and the mixture will appear crumbly. Do not overwork or the crumble will be tough.

Prepare the Filling, Assemble, and Bake

Place the cherries in a medium bowl. Add the sugar, cornstarch, salt, and thyme (if using) and toss to combine.

Scrape the cherry filling into a cast-iron Dutch oven. Evenly sprinkle the crumble over the filling. Cover the Dutch oven with the lid and place directly on top of a few live coals (or in a pizza oven). If you have a fire going, use a shovel or poker to push some logs to the side. Place the Dutch oven where the fire was, then arrange a few coals on top. Check the crumble after 15 minutes. The cherries should be bubbling around the edges and the crumble topping should be golden brown. Depending on the heat, it will take 15 to 30 minutes.

Serve hot, topped with vanilla ice cream. Garnish with the mint.

Pawpaw Colada

Pawpaw is a wild fruit native to North America and it's one of my absolute favourites because it is the only tropical-tasting fruit that survives in the cold climate where I live. This wonderful fruit is shaped like a kidney bean and fits in your hand, and it tastes like a banana mashed together with a mango. It has large seeds that cling to the flesh, but the fruit inside is truly unique and it's worth the little effort to remove them. Pawpaw used to be considered a weed and much of the wild population was destroyed by farmers and development. There has been a huge push to reintroduce the trees back into nature. When I first started buying pawpaw from foragers, I had to agree to return the seeds so they could be planted back in the wild.

SERVES 4 to 6

Combine all the ingredients in a blender and blend until smooth. Pour into chilled highball or Collins glasses.

¾ cup (175 mL) white rum

¾ cup (175 mL) coconut cream

¾ cup (175 mL) pineapple juice

¼ cup (60 mL) banana liqueur

¼ cup (60 mL) añejo rum or golden rum

1 cup (250 mL) fresh pawpaw (from 1 or 2 pawpaw, peeled and seeds removed)

4 cups (1 L) ice cubes

Beet'tle Juice

MAKES ENOUGH BEET-INFUSED TEQUILA FOR 6 COCKTAILS

Beets have a tremendous amount of natural sugar that caramelizes wonderfully when they're cooked over charcoal. All those caramelized sugars work well paired with tequila. This fun and vibrant cocktail is a perfect variation for anyone who loves tequila.

Special Equipment
Work gloves
2 large mason jars with lids
Cheesecloth

Charcoal-Roasted Beet-Infused Tequila
4 medium red beets
2 cups (500 mL) blanco tequila

Pistachio Orgeat
½ cup (125 mL) shelled raw pistachios, plus more for garnish
1 cup (250 mL) water
1 cup (250 mL) granulated sugar
1 tablespoon (15 mL) brandy

For each cocktail
2 ounces Beet-Infused Tequila (recipe above)
¼ ounce mezcal
¼ ounce black currant liqueur (crème de cassis)
¾ ounce Pistachio Orgeat (recipe above)
1 tablespoon (15 mL) fresh lemon juice
10 or so ice cubes, for shaking and serving

Make the Charcoal-Roasted Beet-Infused Tequila

Prepare a charcoal or wood fire in an outdoor grill or firepit and let the flames die down with red embers visible. Set a grate over the fire. Alternatively, preheat a gas grill to 500°F (260°C).

Roast the beets in the charcoal fire (or on the hottest part of the grill if using a gas grill), turning every 30 minutes, until soft all the way through when poked with a skewer, 1 to 2 hours. Remove from the heat and let cool. Wearing gloves and using a paring knife, remove the skin. Slice the beets into ½-inch (1 cm) cubes.

Place the beets in a large mason jar. Pour the tequila into the jar and screw on the lid. Macerate in the fridge for 2 days.

Once macerated, strain the tequila (it will be red) through a fine-mesh sieve into another container, then pour back into the jar or a glass bottle and seal with a lid. Store the beet-infused tequila in the fridge for up to 6 months.

Make the Pistachio Orgeat

In a medium bowl, soak the pistachios in the water for 30 minutes. Strain, reserving the soaking water.

Place the pistachios in a food processor and pulse until coarsely ground. Add the reserved soaking water and pulse 2 or 3 times. Do not make a smooth purée. Leave the ground pistachios in the processor bowl to soak for 1 hour.

Strain the pistachios through a fine-mesh sieve lined with a few layers of cheesecloth into a medium saucepan. Gather the corners of the cheesecloth and squeeze out as much of the liquid as you can.

Add the sugar and heat over medium heat, stirring occasionally, until the sugar is dissolved, 2 to 3 minutes. (Do not boil or reduce.) Remove from the heat and let cool. Once cooled, stir in the brandy. Store the pistachio orgeat in a mason jar or glass bottle with a lid in the fridge for up to 1 week.

Make the Cocktail

In a cocktail shaker, combine the beet-infused tequila, mezcal, black currant liqueur, pistachio orgeat, and lemon juice. Add 6 ice cubes and shake for 15 seconds. Strain into a rocks glass over 4 or 5 ice cubes. Garnish with pistachios.

Wild Ginger Dark and Stormy

Wild ginger is much more floral and spicier than store-bought fresh ginger. It is a totally different plant. Early European settlers would dry the root and grind it into a powder for spice, but I find making a syrup with it much easier and very flavourful. If you are a fan of the classic Dark and Stormy cocktail, you must give this recipe a try.

Note: Wild ginger is a fun plant to forage, but there are mild toxicity concerns if consumed in large quantities.

MAKES ENOUGH SYRUP FOR **6** COCKTAILS

Make the Wild Ginger Honey Syrup

In a small saucepan, combine the honey, water, wild ginger, and lime zest. Bring to a boil, then reduce the heat and simmer for 5 minutes. Remove from the heat and let cool. Once cool, transfer to a mason jar and chill in the fridge overnight for a stronger infusion. Store in the fridge for up to 2 months.

Make the Cocktail

In a highball or Collins glass, combine the rum, wild ginger honey syrup, and lime juice. Add the ice cubes and ginger beer and stir again. Garnish with mint and candied ginger.

Wild Ginger Honey Syrup

½ cup (125 mL) pure liquid honey

¼ cup + 2 tablespoons (90 mL) water

¼ cup +2 tablespoons (90 mL) chopped fresh unpeeled wild ginger root

Zest of 1 lime

For each cocktail

2 ounces spiced rum

4 teaspoons (20 mL) Wild Ginger Honey Syrup (recipe above)

2 tablespoons (30 mL) fresh lime juice

4 to 5 ice cubes

4 ounces ginger beer

For garnish

Fresh mint sprigs

Candied ginger

Sumac and Sotol Margarita

Margaritas are known for that tangy zip of flavour, so when I tried sotol for the first time I immediately thought of pairing it with sumac for a new take on a margarita. If you haven't heard of sotol before, you aren't alone. It's something I just recently discovered myself. Sotol is in the same family as agave and grows wild in the dry, rocky conditions of the Chihuahuan desert of Mexico as well as in Texas, New Mexico, and parts of Arizona. Once harvested, it is usually roasted in large ovens, crushed, and left to ferment in open-air tanks before distilling. The spirit is very similar to tequila, although I find it a bit grassier and earthy tasting. It can also be barrel-aged for a smoky finish and amber colour. Look for Desert Door Texas Sotol if you are a tequila or mezcal fan. You won't be disappointed.

MAKES ENOUGH SUMAC SYRUP FOR **6** COCKTAILS

Special Equipment

Dehydrator (if making Smoked Lime Wheels)

Smoked Lime Wheels (optional)

1 lime, thinly sliced into wheels

Sumac Syrup

1 cup (250 mL) water

½ cup (125 mL) ground sumac

½ cup (125 mL) granulated sugar

For each cocktail

2 tablespoons (30 mL) ground sumac

Lime wedge, for rimming

1½ ounces Desert Door Texas Sotol (if unavailable, use mezcal)

½ ounce Grand Marnier or other orange-flavoured liqueur

1¼ ounces Sumac Syrup (recipe above)

¼ ounce fresh lime juice

1 cup (250 mL) ice cubes, for shaking

Make the Smoked Lime Wheels (if using)

Prepare your smoker at 165°F (75°C). Smoking can be done with an offset smoker, pellet smoker, or barrel smoker, or by hanging above a firepit. Light your wood fire and let the flames die down with red embers visible.

Arrange the lime wheels on a wire rack and smoke for 1 hour.

After smoking the lime, set a dehydrator to 150°F (65°C). Lay the smoked lime wheels on the dehydrator tray without overlapping. Dehydrate for at least 8 hours, until the lime wheels are completely dry and brittle. Store in an airtight container for up to 1 week.

Make the Sumac Syrup

Bring the water to a boil in a medium saucepan over high heat. Once boiling, add the sumac and sugar. Stir to dissolve the sugar, then remove from the heat. Allow the sumac to steep for 20 minutes. Strain through a coffee filter into an airtight container and let cool completely. Store in the fridge for up to 1 week.

Make the Cocktail

Rim a rocks glass with the ground sumac: pour the sumac onto a small plate. Wet the rim of the glass with the lime wedge, then dip it in the sumac to coat the rim evenly.

In a cocktail shaker, combine the sotol, Grand Marnier, sumac syrup, and lime juice. Add the ice cubes and shake for 15 seconds. Strain into the rimmed glass over ice. Garnish with a smoked lime wheel, if using.

Nocino (Black Walnut Liqueur)

This beautifully nutty and rich liqueur, with a flavour similar to Jägermeister but more refined, hails from the Emilia-Romagna region of Italy and is made from unripe or "green" walnuts before the shell is too hard to slice with a knife. This spinoff made with foraged wild black walnuts is popular in Canada and the United States. When collecting walnuts, pick them in June or early July before the shell is too hard. Experiment with the recipe to suit your taste by adding spices to enhance the delicate walnut flavour, but don't use too much and overpower the drink. The liqueur is best aged for at least 6 months, but a lot of home brewers prefer 1 year. I assure you it's worth the wait! Nocino is delicious on its own, chilled over ice, or splashed over vanilla ice cream.

Note: Wear gloves to peel the walnuts or your hands will be stained black for weeks. Learn from my mistakes!

MAKES 8 cups (2 L)

Wearing gloves, use a heavy-duty kitchen knife to slice the black walnuts into quarters. Place the nuts in a large stainless steel pot with a tight-fitting lid (or divide evenly between two 4-cup/1 L wide-mouth mason jars with lids). Add the vodka, espresso, cocoa nibs, cloves, and orange wedges. Cover with the lid and wrap the edge with plastic wrap to seal. (If using mason jars, screw the lids on tightly.) Label the container or jars with the date and place in a cool, dark place, either the back of a cupboard or a basement cold cellar, for 6 months. After 24 hours you will notice the liquid has turned a very dark yellowy green, almost black. Taste if you wish, but it will be very bitter and astringent. Make a note of the flavour, and then again after aging for a few months and then after 6 months. You will notice with time the flavour will soften and become smoother and the colour will darken.

After 6 months, mix in the maple syrup. Cover with 2 layers of cheesecloth or a coffee filter and secure with a rubber band or string. Let the nocino sit and "breathe" for at least 3 days or up to 1 week. This will further darken the liquid and smooth out the taste.

Strain through a coffee filter into a large bowl. Bottle the nocino in wine bottles and seal with a cork or twist cap. Store in the fridge for up to 6 months.

Special Equipment

Work gloves

2 (4-cup/1 L) wide-mouth mason jars with lids

Cheesecloth or coffee filters

Rubber band or string

---

1 pound (450 g) unripe (green) black walnuts

2 (26-ounce/750 mL) bottles vodka

1 tablespoon (15 mL) freshly ground espresso beans

2 teaspoons (10 mL) ground cocoa nibs

4 whole cloves

¼ unpeeled navel orange, cut into 2 wedges

2 cups (500 mL) pure maple syrup

Mead

Mead, an ancient honey wine, is the earliest recorded alcoholic drink humans made on purpose. This elixir has many forms and styles, but it is incredibly easy and fun to make at home. It is made by fermenting honey in water and flavouring with oranges, dried fruit, and spices. There is also a version with half honey and half maple syrup. It can be slightly fermented and enjoyed bubbly and sweet or fermented dry, aged, and enjoyed like wine. I prefer the sweeter effervescent version chilled on a hot summer day while barbecuing, but experiment and see what you like best. Use a local honey from a farmers' market or specialty shop and avoid commercial honey.

Notes: You can use active dry yeast or wine or champagne yeast. I find that wine or champagne yeast works better, and you need less, but active dry yeast works well, too. The cinnamon stick and cranberries are optional, but the raisins should always be added as a yeast nutrient. Alternatively, add 1 teaspoon (5 mL) of powdered yeast nutrient after whisking in the yeast.

MAKES 2.5 quarts (2.5 L)

Sanitize a 1-gallon (4 L) glass jug and all cutting boards and pots. It is important for everything to be clean when fermenting to avoid unwanted bacteria, which can ruin a project.

In a large pot, heat 6 cups (1.5 L) of the water over high heat until almost simmering. Add the honey and whisk until dissolved, then remove from the heat.

Add the remaining 6 cups (1.5 L) water to the pot and take the temperature of the water using a probe thermometer. Once the water has cooled to 80° to 90°F (27° to 33°C), vigorously whisk in the yeast until dissolved. (This is called pitching. Yeast needs oxygen to help with fermenting, and whisking the yeast incorporates air into the liquid.) Once the yeast is dissolved, pour the liquid into the jug using a funnel. Add the orange wedges, raisins, cranberries (if using), and cinnamon stick (if using). There should be about 1 inch (2.5 cm) of headspace below the neck of the jug to allow room for bubbling and swelling of the fruit during fermentation. Insert the rubber stopper into the jug and fill the airlock with water to the fill line. Place the jug in a dark, room-temperature or warm place to ferment for 24 hours.

Special Equipment

1-gallon (4 L) glass jug with screw cap

1 rubber stopper with airlock (available at wine- and beer-making stores or online)

Siphon hose

Probe thermometer

3 (26-ounce/750 mL) wine bottles or equivalent beer or spirit bottles

---

12 cups (3 L) water, divided

2 pounds (900 g) local natural honey

2 teaspoons (10 mL) active dry yeast (or 1 teaspoon/5 mL wine or champagne yeast)

1 unpeeled orange, sliced into wedges that will fit the neck of your jug

½ cup (125 mL) raisins

¼ cup (60 mL) dried cranberries (optional)

1 cinnamon stick (optional)

recipe continues

After 24 hours you will notice bubbling and air escaping out of the airlock. Monitor the fermentation every couple of days. After 1 to 2 weeks, the airlock should stop bubbling or slow considerably. This signals it's time to siphon the mead. If the airlock is still very active, the mead has not finished fermenting all the available sugars. (To make a totally dry mead with no sugar or sweetness, let ferment with the airlock for several months before bottling.) When siphoning, be careful not to place the siphon directly on the bottom of the glass jug. You will notice a small layer of dead yeast sludge at the bottom; this is safe to consume but has an off-flavour and is best left behind.

Once the mead is siphoned out, strain it through a fine-mesh sieve into sanitized wine, beer, or spirit bottles and refrigerate. It is important to note that at this point the mead is still fermenting and letting off gas, which can lead to bottles bursting. Refrigerating the mead heavily slows down fermentation, and I find a small effervescent quality enjoyable to drink and safe for the bottles.

How to Make a Euro Mount

A euro mount, or European mount, is a skull with the antlers attached and without the fur. It is fast and easy to make yourself or you can pay to have a skull mounted. Lifelike shoulder mounts usually start around $1,000 and go up depending on the size of the game harvested. Why do we keep these trophies? For me they spark a memory, a flashback to a time spent with a family member or friend. A reminder of climbing a mountain for five days before shooting my elk and a week at camp with friends sharing stories while cooking over the fire. My most prized trophy, of course, is the meat, and the antlers are a nice bonus. Here are step-by-step instructions for how to save a few hundred bucks and make something really cool that you will have forever.

STEP 1

Skin the skull: Using a knife, peel off the skin, cutting the membrane underneath the hide. Work around the bones and antlers until the skin is completely removed.

STEP 2

Boil the head: This is tricky if your animal is huge, but a large stockpot should work. Boil the head over high heat for 3 to 4 hours, until the tissue, tongue, and eyes can be easily pulled from the bones. Change the water and repeat if necessary.

STEP 3

Pressure wash the skull: Be sure to spray under the skull and spray out the brain from the natural hole in the back. Remove any cartilage in the nose. Sometimes the thin nose bones will fall out. These can be glued back on. Clean off any soft tissue. All that should be left is bones.

STEP 4

Whiten the skull: Brush the skull bone inside and out with peroxide cream and leave overnight. I avoid using bleach because it turns yellow over time. Leave the skull in a sunny window in cold weather or leave outside—the sun will react with the peroxide to whiten the bones. Wash and repeat if necessary. Let the skull dry for 2 to 3 days, and then it's ready to hang. It can be attached directly to the wall or to a piece of barnboard; hang it with a screw hook and picture wire.

Acknowledgments

Most of the outdoor photography in this book I took while exploring the great outdoors of Canada and the United States. Our two countries are home to some of the most beautiful lands on earth, but every trip I take, my favourite part is always the people I meet along the way. Hunting abroad I have made so many new friends and realized that these hunters are just like me. We share the same values and morals and can communicate without speaking the same language. These photos would not have been possible without you, the readers, supporting my obsession for adventure. Thank you.

To the fishing and hunting guides, this wouldn't have been possible without you. You know the land and the animals, and you put in the work to make these adventures possible for me and the rest of your clients. Thanks for sharing your passion with me: Corey Jarvis, 3 Rivers Adventures; Chuk Coulter, Plummer's Arctic Lodges; West Coast Fishing Club; Steve Johansen, Organic Ocean; Dave Clements, Three Forks Ranch; Brian Jarrell and Amy Shaffer, Branded Rock Canyon; Pat Bergson, Bows and Bullets Outfitting.

To the amazing folks that inspire me and help fuel my obsession with the outdoors: Daniel Haas, Neill Haas, Toxey Haas, and Vandy Stubbs at Mossy Oak; Iris Rossi, Bruno Beccaria, and George Wallace at Franchi/Beretta; Steve Corlett and Lana Calder at Vista Outdoors. Special thanks to Traeger Grills, Breeo, and Made with Meat for the best cooking equipment featured in this book.

A special thank you to the wonderful folks that read this book prior to publication and generously shared words of praise: Steven Rinella, Hank Shaw, Danielle Prewett, Malcom Reed, Chuck Hughes, and Curtis Stone.

To Jody Shapiro, for your talented photography skills and helping me stay organized.

To the dedicated staff at Antler, for your unwavering commitment and passion that drives our success every day.

Thanks to my editor, Andrea Magyar, and the team at Penguin Random House Canada for believing in me for a second book.

To my wife Ali, who lovingly stands by my constant travelling to bring home food for the year. It's probably cheaper to buy meat and fish from the store, but it's important to me that we eat off the land. I wish I could bring you and the kids with me on every trip and think about you every day I'm away from home.

To Annabelle and Zachary, I'm so proud of the young adults you have become.

To Marlow, you have so many adventures ahead of you! Sibelle, you are always in our hearts.

Photo Credits

AMBER DECELL 76, 107, 162, 163, 246

OWEN FINNAN ii–iii, viii, 3, 7 (bottom left), 191, 192, 195, 269, 308

DANIEL HAAS 234

ALI HUNTER 11, 46–47, 58, 219–221

MICHAEL HUNTER i, iv–v, vi–vii, xvi–xvii, 4, 7 (top right, bottom right), 12–13, 14–15, 18–19, 24, 28, 53, 54, 74–75, 79, 113, 114–115, 154, 210, 212–213, 216–217, 225, 242–243, 262, 266–267, 303, 310, 318, back cover

ROB KINNEY 8, 230

JACOB RICHLER 310

RYAN SCHNED x–xi

JODY SHAPIRO Front cover, 7 (top left), 23, 27, 31, 32, 35, 36, 39, 40, 45, 50, 57, 61, 62, 67, 68, 71, 72, 80, 85, 87, 88, 91–94, 95, 97, 98, 103, 104, 108, 110, 120, 123, 124, 129, 130, 132, 135, 136, 139, 140, 142, 147, 157, 158, 165, 166, 169, 170, 172, 177, 178, 180, 183, 184, 188, 196, 201, 202, 204, 209, 222, 226, 229, 233, 237, 238, 241, 249, 250, 253, 254, 257, 258, 261, 265, 270, 273, 274, 279, 280, 285, 286, 289, 290, 293, 294, 297, 298, 300, 305–307

PATRICK WALSH 20

Index

A

aioli
- Chili, 25
- Lemon, 264

almonds: Romesco Sauce, 101–102

antelope: Fire-Roasted Antelope Chops with Rosemary and Tzatziki, 156

appetizers and sides
- Boar Bacon Fig Poppers, 155
- Charcoal-Roasted Beets with Yogurt Dressing, 255
- Charcoal-Roasted Whole Cabbage, 251
- Fire-Roasted Cauliflower with Baba Ghanoush, 248
- Fire-Roasted Heirloom Carrots and Onions with Hummus, 252
- Fire-Roasted Sweet Corn, 256
- Fire-Roasted Whole Squash with Burrata Cheese, 260
- Fried Perch with Gribiche Sauce, 37
- Grilled Artichokes, 264
- Grilled Baitfish, 33
- Grilled Quail with Honey-Lime Glaze and Corn Salsa, 141
- Grilled Squid with Peperonata, 105
- Lobster Rolls on Squid Ink Buns, 83–84
- Pizza Oven Baked Clams, 89
- Roe Deer Caprese Salad, 179
- Smoked Carp, 30
- Whole Roasted Woodcock, 137

Arctic Char Torched with Soy and Honey, 38

Artichokes, Grilled, 264

Asado Roast Pig, 224

Asparagus, Grilled, 81–82

B

Baba Ghanoush, 248

bacon *see also* pork; sausages
- Boar Bacon Fig Poppers, 155
- Braised Collard Greens, 145–146
- Campfire Brussels Sprouts and Bacon, 263
- Potato Salad, 143
- Wild Boar Peameal Bacon, 167
- Wild Boar Peameal on a Bun, 168

Baitfish, Grilled, 33

Baked Salt-Crusted Trout, 70

barbecue
- Asado Roast Pig, 224
- Barbecued Pheasant with Alabama White Sauce, 143–144
- Bear Ribs, 236
- Birch-Syrup-Glazed Bison Short Ribs, 227
- Bison Brisket, 228
- Chopped Wild Boar Barbecue, 223
- Elk Smash Burgers, 235
- How To Roast a Pig, 218–221
- Pulled Goose Leg Barbecue, 176
- Smoked Cougar Ham, 232
- Smoked Wild Boar Shoulder, 231
- Spit-Roasted Porchetta, 239–240

Barbecue Sauce, 231

Barnacles, Gooseneck, 109

beans *see* chickpeas; green beans

bear
- Bear Curry, 207–208
- Bear Ragu with Smoked Cheddar Polenta, 211
- Bear Ribs, 236

beaver: Spit-Roasted Beaver with Birch Syrup and Blueberry Glaze, 181–182

beef: Grilled Wagyu Porterhouse Steak, 189

beets
- Beet'tle Juice, 292
- Charcoal-Roasted Beets with Yogurt Dressing, 255

bell peppers
- Grilled Squid with Peperonata, 105
- Red Pepper Butter Sauce, 65

Beurre Blanc, 43

birch syrup
- Birch-Syrup-Glazed Bison Short Ribs, 227
- Spit-Roasted Beaver with Birch Syrup and Blueberry Glaze, 181–182

bison
- Birch-Syrup-Glazed Bison Short Ribs, 227
- Bison Brisket, 228
- Bison Tomahawk Steaks with Chimichurri, 161
- Grilled Bison Tenderloin, 81–82

Blackened Catfish with Creole Sauce, 41–42

Blue Cheese Dipping Sauce, 127–128

blueberries, wild: Spit-Roasted Beaver with Birch Syrup and Blueberry Glaze, 181–182

boar, wild *see also* pork
- Boar Bacon Fig Poppers, 155
- Chopped Wild Boar Barbecue, 223
- Sausage-Stuffed Grouse with Maple Candied Yams, 159–160
- Smoked Wild Boar Shoulder, 231
- Wild Boar Peameal Bacon, 167
- Wild Boar Peameal on a Bun, 168

Braised Collard Greens, 145–146

brandy
- Beet'tle Juice, 292
- Whole Roasted Woodcock, 137

Brisket, Bison, 228

Broccoli Salad, 143–144

Brown Trout with Sweet Pea Risotto, 43–44

Brussels sprouts: Campfire Brussels Sprouts and Bacon, 263

Buffalo-Fried Quail, 127–128

Buns, Squid Ink, 83–84

Burgers, Elk Smash, 235

burrata cheese: Fire-Roasted Whole Squash with Burrata Cheese, 260

butter
- Beurre Blanc, 43
- Caper Butter Sauce, 59–60
- Compound Butter, 51
- Red Pepper Butter Sauce, 65
- Smoked Uni Butter, 81

C

cabbage
- Charcoal-Roasted Whole Cabbage, 251
- Coleslaw, 223

Campfire Brussels Sprouts and Bacon, 263

Campfire Chanterelle Risotto, 247

Candy, Coho Salmon, 69

Canned Moose Meat, 203

Canned Moose Poutine, 205–206

Caper Butter Sauce, 59–60

Caramels, Duck Fat, 271

Carp, Smoked, 30

carrots: Fire-Roasted Heirloom Carrots and Onions with Hummus, 252
catfish: Blackened Catfish with Creole Sauce, 41–42
cauliflower: Fire-Roasted Cauliflower with Baba Ghanoush, 248
Chaga Ice Cream, 272
chanterelle mushrooms
    Campfire Chanterelle Risotto, 247
    Elk Smash Burgers, 235
Charcoal-Roasted Beets with Yogurt Dressing, 255
Charcoal-Roasted Whole Cabbage, 251
Charred Zucchini and Stracciatella Cheese, 259
cheese see also specific cheeses
    Blue Cheese Dipping Sauce, 127–128
    Boar Bacon Fig Poppers, 155
    Campfire Chanterelle Risotto, 247
    Canned Moose Poutine, 205–206
    Charred Zucchini and Stracciatella Cheese, 259
    Fire-Roasted Whole Squash with Burrata Cheese, 260
    Grilled Oysters Rockefeller, 99–100
    Muskox Sausage and Rapini Pizza, 173–175
    Muskox in White Wine Cream Sauce with Orecchiette and Kale, 171
    Roe Deer Caprese Salad, 179
    Smoked Cheddar Polenta, 211
    Sweet Pea Risotto, 43–44
cherries: Dutch Oven Charcoal-Cooked Cherry Crumble, 288
chickpeas: Hummus, 252
chilies
    Chili Aioli, 25
    Maple Hot Sauce, 138
    Red Hot Sauce, 127
    Romesco Sauce, 101–102
    Venison Patties, 199–200
Chimichurri, 161
chocolate: Stroopwafel S'mores, 277–278
Chopped Wild Boar Barbecue, 223
clams, Manila: Pizza Oven Baked Clams, 89

cod: Ling Cod with Red Pepper Butter Sauce and Grilled Tomatoes, 65–66
Coho Salmon Candy, 69
Cold-Smoked Cured Swan Breast, 185–186
Coleslaw, 223
Collard Greens, Braised, 145–146
Compote, Serviceberry, 194
Compound Butter, 51
cookies: Stroopwafel S'mores, 277–278
corn
    Corn Salsa, 141
    Fire-Roasted Sweet Corn, 256
    Lobster Boil, 86
cornmeal
    Fried Perch with Gribiche Sauce, 37
    Wild Boar Peameal Bacon, 167
cougar: Smoked Cougar Ham, 232
cranberries, dried: Broccoli Salad, 143–144
Crane Steak au Poivre, 125–126
cream, heavy
    Chaga Ice Cream, 272
    Muskox in White Wine Cream Sauce with Orecchiette and Kale, 171
    Mussels in White Wine Cream Sauce with Grilled Baguette, 111–112
    Smoked Cheddar Polenta, 211
    Vanilla Ice Cream, 275
    Whipped Cream, 281–282, 287
    White Wine Cream Sauce with Herb Oil, 63–64
Creole Sauce, 41–42
Crispy-Skin Snow Goose, 133–134
Crumble, Dutch Oven Charcoal-Cooked Cherry, 288
cucumbers
    Cucumber Kohlrabi Slaw, 63–64
    Tzatziki, 156
Curd, Sumac, with Whipped Cream and Shortbread Crumbs, 287
Cured Salmon Roe, 55
Curry, Bear, 207–208

D

deer see venison
desserts
    Chaga Ice Cream, 272
    Duck Fat Caramels, 271
    Dutch Oven Charcoal-Cooked Cherry Crumble, 288

Grilled Peaches and Vanilla Ice Cream with Wildflower Honey and Black Walnuts, 275–276
    Pawpaw Semifreddo, 283–284
    Smoker Strawberry Pie, 281–282
    Stroopwafel S'mores, 277–278
    Sumac Curd with Whipped Cream and Shortbread Crumbs, 287
dips and spreads see also sauces
    Baba Ghanoush, 248
    Blue Cheese Dipping Sauce, 127–128
    Hummus, 252
    Olive Tapenade, 73
    Tzatziki, 156
doughs
    Muskox Sausage and Rapini Pizza, 173–175
    Smoker Strawberry Pie, 281–282
    Venison Patties, 199–200
Dressing, Ranch, 251
drinks
    Beet'tle Juice, 292
    Mead, 301–302
    Nocino (Black Walnut Liqueur), 299
    Pawpaw Colada, 291
    Sumac and Sotol Margarita, 296
    Wild Ginger Dark and Stormy, 295
duck
    Duck Fat Caramels, 271
    Smoked Duck Wings with Maple Hot Sauce, 138
    Smoked Pintail Duck, 131
Dutch Oven Charcoal-Cooked Cherry Crumble, 288

E

eggplants: Baba Ghanoush, 248
eggs
    Baked Salt-Crusted Trout, 70
    Chaga Ice Cream, 272
    Gribiche Sauce, 37
    Pawpaw Semifreddo, 283–284
    Sumac Curd with Whipped Cream and Shortbread Crumbs, 287
    Vanilla Ice Cream, 275
elk
    Elk Backstraps, 190
    Elk Heart Skewers, 193
    Elk Liver with Serviceberry Compote, 194
    Elk Osso Buco, 197–198
    Elk Smash Burgers, 235
Euro Mount, How to Make, 304–306

F

figs: Boar Bacon Fig Poppers, 155
Fire-Roasted Antelope Chops with Rosemary and Tzatziki, 156
Fire-Roasted Cauliflower with Baba Ghanoush, 248
Fire-Roasted Heirloom Carrots and Onions with Hummus, 252
Fire-Roasted Kelp-Planked Steelhead Trout, 29
Fire-Roasted Sweet Corn, 256
Fire-Roasted Whole Squash with Burrata Cheese, 260
fish, freshwater *see also* seafood
   Arctic Char Torched with Soy and Honey, 38
   Blackened Catfish with Creole Sauce, 41–42
   Brown Trout with Sweet Pea Risotto, 43–44
   Fire-Roasted Kelp-Planked Steelhead Trout, 29
   Fried Perch with Gribiche Sauce, 37
   Grilled Baitfish, 33
   Grilled Brook Trout, 25–26
   Grilled Lake Erie Whitefish, 34
   How To Cook a Whole Fish, 21–22
   Smoked Carp, 30
fish, saltwater *see also* seafood
   Baked Salt-Crusted Trout, 70
   Coho Salmon Candy, 69
   Cured Salmon Roe, 55
   Grilled King Salmon with Roasted Garlic Compound Butter and Sautéed Sweet Peas, 51–52
   Grilled Swordfish with Roasted Tomatoes and Olive Tapenade, 73
   Halibut with Cucumber Kohlrabi Slaw and White Wine Cream Sauce with Herb Oil, 63–64
   Ling Cod with Red Pepper Butter Sauce and Grilled Tomatoes, 65–66
   Pacific Albacore Tuna Donburi, 56
   Rockfish with Caper Butter Sauce and Pickled Shallots, 59–60
fowl
   Barbecued Pheasant with Alabama White Sauce, 143–144
   Buffalo-Fried Quail, 127–128
   Crane Steak au Poivre, 125–126
   Crispy-Skin Snow Goose, 133–134
   Goose Jerky, 122
   Grilled Quail with Honey-Lime Glaze and Corn Salsa, 141
   Smoked Duck Wings with Maple Hot Sauce, 138
   Smoked Pintail Duck, 131
   Whole Roasted Woodcock, 137
French Fries, 205–206
Fried Perch with Gribiche Sauce, 37

G

game, large
   Asado Roast Pig, 224
   Bear Curry, 207–208
   Bear Ragu with Smoked Cheddar Polenta, 211
   Bear Ribs, 236
   Birch-Syrup-Glazed Bison Short Ribs, 227
   Bison Brisket, 228
   Bison Tomahawk Steaks with Chimichurri, 161
   Boar Bacon Fig Poppers, 155
   Canned Moose Meat, 203
   Canned Moose Poutine, 205–206
   Chopped Wild Boar Barbecue, 223
   Cold-Smoked Cured Swan Breast, 185–186
   Elk Backstraps, 190
   Elk Heart Skewers, 193
   Elk Liver with Serviceberry Compote, 194
   Elk Osso Buco, 197–198
   Elk Smash Burgers, 235
   Fire-Roasted Antelope Chops with Rosemary and Tzatziki, 156
   Grilled Wagyu Porterhouse Steak, 189
   Mule Deer Tataki, 164
   Muskox Sausage and Rapini Pizza, 173–175
   Muskox in White Wine Cream Sauce with Orecchiette and Kale, 171
   Pulled Goose Leg Barbecue, 176
   Roe Deer Caprese Salad, 179
   Sausage-Stuffed Grouse with Maple Candied Yams, 159–160
   Smoked Cougar Ham, 232
   Smoked Uni Butter and Bison Tenderloin, 81–82
   Smoked Wild Boar Shoulder, 231
   Spit-Roasted Beaver with Birch Syrup and Blueberry Glaze, 181–182
   Spit-Roasted Porchetta, 239–240
   Venison Patties, 199–200
   Wild Boar Peameal Bacon, 167
   Wild Boar Peameal on a Bun, 168
game, small
   Hot Rabbit with Braised Collard Greens, 145–146
   Seafood and Rabbit Paella, 106
   Snacking Sticks, 121
garlic
   Chimichurri, 161
   Compound Butter, 51
   Lobster Boil, 86
   Romesco Sauce, 101–102
   Spit-Roasted Porchetta, 239–240
   Tomato Sauce, 173–174
geoduck
   Grilled Geoduck, 96
   How to Harvest and Prepare Geoduck, 90–94
   Sashimi-Style Geoduck, 95
ginger beer: Wild Ginger Dark and Stormy, 295
ginger, fresh
   Bear Curry, 207–208
   Mule Deer Tataki, 164
   Wild Ginger Dark and Stormy, 295
goat cheese: Boar Bacon Fig Poppers, 155
goose
   Crispy-Skin Snow Goose, 133–134
   Goose Jerky, 122
   Pulled Goose Leg Barbecue, 176
Gooseneck Barnacles, 109
Gravy, 205
green beans: Grilled Swordfish with Roasted Tomatoes and Olive Tapenade, 73
Gremolata, 197–198
Gribiche Sauce, 37
Grilled Artichokes, 264
Grilled Asparagus, 81–82
Grilled Baitfish, 33
Grilled Bison Tenderloin, 81–82
Grilled Brook Trout, 25–26
Grilled Cherry Tomatoes, 65–66
Grilled Geoduck, 96
Grilled King Salmon with Roasted Garlic Compound Butter and Sautéed Sweet Peas, 51–52
Grilled Lake Erie Whitefish, 34

Grilled Octopus with Romesco Sauce and Salsa Verde, 101–102
Grilled Oysters Rockefeller, 99–100
Grilled Peaches and Vanilla Ice Cream with Wildflower Honey and Black Walnuts, 275–276
Grilled Quail with Honey-Lime Glaze and Corn Salsa, 141
Grilled Squid with Peperonata, 105
Grilled Swordfish with Roasted Tomatoes and Olive Tapenade, 73
Grilled Wagyu Porterhouse Steak, 189
grouse: Sausage-Stuffed Grouse with Maple Candied Yams, 159–160

H
Halibut with Cucumber Kohlrabi Slaw and White Wine Cream Sauce with Herb Oil, 63–64
honey
    Arctic Char Torched with Soy and Honey, 38
    Grilled Peaches and Vanilla Ice Cream with Wildflower Honey and Black Walnuts, 275–276
    Grilled Quail with Honey-Lime Glaze and Corn Salsa, 141
    Mead, 301–302
    Wild Ginger Honey Syrup, 295
Hot Rabbit with Braised Collard Greens, 145–146
Hummus, 252

I
ice cream
    Chaga, 272
    Vanilla, 275

J
jalapeño peppers
    Chimichurri, 161
    Grilled Geoduck, 96
    Seafood and Rabbit Paella, 106
Jerky, Goose, 122

K
kale: Muskox in White Wine Cream Sauce with Orecchiette and Kale, 171
kelp: Fire-Roasted Kelp-Planked Steelhead Trout, 29
kohlrabi: Cucumber Kohlrabi Slaw, 63–64

L
lemons
    Gremolata, 197–198
    Lemon Aioli, 264
    Sumac Curd with Whipped Cream and Shortbread Crumbs, 287
limes
    Grilled Quail with Honey-Lime Glaze and Corn Salsa, 141
    Sumac and Sotol Margarita, 296
    Wild Ginger Dark and Stormy, 295
Ling Cod with Red Pepper Butter Sauce and Grilled Tomatoes, 65–66
liqueur: Nocino (Black Walnut Liqueur), 299
liver, elk: Elk Liver with Serviceberry Compote, 194
lobsters
    Lobster Boil, 86
    Lobster Rolls on Squid Ink Buns, 83–84

M
maple syrup
    Barbecue Sauce, 231
    Coho Salmon Candy, 69
    Goose Jerky, 122
    Maple Candied Yams, 159–160
    Maple Hot Sauce, 138
    Nocino (Black Walnut Liqueur), 299
Marshmallows, 277–278
mascarpone cheese: Campfire Chanterelle Risotto, 247
Mashed Potatoes, 81
Mead, 301–302
Meringue Crisps, 283–284
mezcal: Beet'tle Juice, 292
mirin
    Elk Heart Skewers, 193
    Pacific Albacore Tuna Donburi, 56
    Smoked Cougar Ham, 232
moose
    Canned Moose Meat, 203
    Canned Moose Poutine, 205–206
mozzarella cheese
    Muskox Sausage and Rapini Pizza, 173–175
    Roe Deer Caprese Salad, 179
Mule Deer Tataki, 164
mushrooms
    Campfire Chanterelle Risotto, 247

Chaga Ice Cream, 272
Elk Smash Burgers, 235
muskox
    Muskox Sausage and Rapini Pizza, 173–175
    Muskox in White Wine Cream Sauce with Orecchiette and Kale, 171
mussels
    Mussels in White Wine Cream Sauce with Grilled Baguette, 111–112
    Seafood and Rabbit Paella, 106

N
Nocino (Black Walnut Liqueur), 299
nuts *see* almonds; pistachios; walnuts, black

O
oats: Dutch Oven Charcoal-Cooked Cherry Crumble, 288
octopus, baby: Grilled Octopus with Romesco Sauce and Salsa Verde, 101–102
Oil, Spiced, 145–146
okra: Blackened Catfish with Creole Sauce, 41–42
Olive Tapenade, 73
onions: Fire-Roasted Heirloom Carrots and Onions with Hummus, 252
Osso Buco, Elk, 197–198
oysters: Grilled Oysters Rockefeller, 99–100

P
Pacific Albacore Tuna Donburi, 56
Paella, Seafood and Rabbit, 106
Parmesan cheese
    Brown Trout with Sweet Pea Risotto, 43–44
    Campfire Chanterelle Risotto, 247
    Grilled Oysters Rockefeller, 99–100
    Muskox in White Wine Cream Sauce with Orecchiette and Kale, 171
    Sweet Pea Risotto, 43–44
pasta: Muskox in White Wine Cream Sauce with Orecchiette and Kale, 171
Patties, Venison, 199–200
pawpaw
    Pawpaw Colada, 291
    Pawpaw Semifreddo, 283–284

peaches: Grilled Peaches and Vanilla Ice Cream with Wildflower Honey and Black Walnuts, 275–276
peas
   Grilled King Salmon with Roasted Garlic Compound Butter and Sautéed Sweet Peas, 51–52
   Sweet Pea Risotto, 43–44
peppers *see* bell peppers; chilies; jalapeño peppers
perch: Fried Perch with Gribiche Sauce, 37
pheasant: Barbecued Pheasant with Alabama White Sauce, 143–144
pickles
   Pickled Shallots, 59
   Pickled Squash, 260
Pie, Smoker Strawberry, 281–282
pistachios: Beet'tle Juice, 292
Pizza, Muskox Sausage and Rapini, 173–175
Pizza Oven Baked Clams, 89
Polenta, Smoked Cheddar, 211
pork *see also* bacon; boar, wild; sausages
   Asado Roast Pig, 224
   How To Roast a Pig, 218–221
   Sausage-Stuffed Grouse with Maple Candied Yams, 159–160
   Snacking Sticks, 121
   Spit-Roasted Porchetta, 239–240
potatoes
   French Fries, 205–206
   Lobster Boil, 86
   Mashed Potatoes, 81
   Potato Salad, 143
   Roasted Stuffed Potatoes, 125–126
Poutine, Canned Moose, 205–206
prawns: Seafood and Rabbit Paella, 106
provolone cheese: Muskox Sausage and Rapini Pizza, 173–175
Pulled Goose Leg Barbecue, 176
pumpkin seeds: Broccoli Salad, 143–144

Q
quail
   Buffalo-Fried Quail, 127–128
   Grilled Quail with Honey-Lime Glaze and Corn Salsa, 141

R
rabbit
   Hot Rabbit with Braised Collard Greens, 145–146
   Seafood and Rabbit Paella, 106
Ranch Dressing, 251
rapini: Muskox Sausage and Rapini Pizza, 173–175
Red Hot Sauce, 127
Red Pepper Butter Sauce, 65
ribs
   Bear Ribs, 236
   Birch-Syrup-Glazed Bison Short Ribs, 227
rice
   Blackened Catfish with Creole Sauce, 41–42
   Campfire Chanterelle Risotto, 247
   Pacific Albacore Tuna Donburi, 56
   Risotto, 197–198
   Scented Basmati Rice, 207–208
   Seafood and Rabbit Paella, 106
   Sweet Pea Risotto, 43–44
Roasted Stuffed Potatoes, 125–126
Roasted Tomatoes, 73
Roasted Turnips, 59
Rockfish with Caper Butter Sauce and Pickled Shallots, 59–60
roe: Cured Salmon Roe, 55
Roe Deer Caprese Salad, 179
Romesco Sauce, 101–102
rosemary, fresh: Fire-Roasted Antelope Chops with Rosemary and Tzatziki, 156
rum
   Chaga Ice Cream, 272
   Pawpaw Colada, 291
   Wild Ginger Dark and Stormy, 295

S
salads and slaws
   Broccoli Salad, 143–144
   Coleslaw, 223
   Cucumber Kohlrabi Slaw, 63–64
   Potato Salad, 143
   Roe Deer Caprese Salad, 179
salmon
   Coho Salmon Candy, 69
   Cured Salmon Roe, 55
   Grilled King Salmon with Roasted Garlic Compound Butter and Sautéed Sweet Peas, 51–52
salsas
   Corn Salsa, 141
   Salsa Verde, 101–102
sandwiches
   Elk Smash Burgers, 235
   Lobster Rolls on Squid Ink Buns, 83–84
   Wild Boar Peameal on a Bun, 168

sauces *see also* dips and spreads
   Barbecue Sauce, 231
   Beurre Blanc, 43
   Blue Cheese Dipping Sauce, 127–128
   Caper Butter Sauce, 59–60
   Chili Aioli, 25
   Chimichurri, 161
   Compound Butter, 51
   Creole Sauce, 41–42
   Gravy, 205
   Gribiche Sauce, 37
   Lemon Aioli, 264
   Maple Hot Sauce, 138
   Red Hot Sauce, 127
   Red Pepper Butter Sauce, 65
   Romesco Sauce, 101–102
   Tomato Sauce, 173–174
   White Wine Cream Sauce with Herb Oil, 63–64
sausages *see also* bacon; pork
   Lobster Boil, 86
   Muskox Sausage and Rapini Pizza, 173–175
   Pizza Oven Baked Clams, 89
   Sausage-Stuffed Grouse with Maple Candied Yams, 159–160
   Snacking Sticks, 121
sea urchins: Smoked Uni Butter and Bison Tenderloin, 81–82
seafood *see also* fish, freshwater; fish, saltwater
   Gooseneck Barnacles, 109
   Grilled Geoduck, 96
   Grilled Octopus with Romesco Sauce and Salsa Verde, 101–102
   Grilled Oysters Rockefeller, 99–100
   Grilled Squid with Peperonata, 105
   How to Harvest and Prepare Geoduck, 90–94
   Lobster Boil, 86
   Lobster Rolls on Squid Ink Buns, 83–84
   Mussels in White Wine Cream Sauce with Grilled Baguette, 111–112
   Pizza Oven Baked Clams, 89
   Seafood and Rabbit Paella, 106
   Smoked Uni Butter and Bison Tenderloin, 81–82
Semifreddo, Pawpaw, 283–284
Serviceberry Compote, 194
Shallots, Pickled, 59

Smoked Carp, 30
Smoked Cheddar Polenta, 211
Smoked Cougar Ham, 232
Smoked Duck Wings with Maple Hot Sauce, 138
Smoked Pintail Duck, 131
Smoked Uni Butter and Bison Tenderloin, 81–82
Smoked Wild Boar Shoulder, 231
Smoker Strawberry Pie, 281–282
S'mores, Stroopwafel, 277–278
snacks
    Coho Salmon Candy, 69
    Goose Jerky, 122
    Snacking Sticks, 121
    Venison Patties, 199–200
Sotol: Sumac and Sotol Margarita, 296
soy sauce
    Arctic Char Torched with Soy and Honey, 38
    Elk Heart Skewers, 193
    Goose Jerky, 122
Spiced Oil, 145–146
spinach: Grilled Oysters Rockefeller, 99–100
Spit-Roasted Beaver with Birch Syrup and Blueberry Glaze, 181–182
Spit-Roasted Porchetta, 239–240
squash, butternut
    Fire-Roasted Whole Squash with Burrata Cheese, 260
    Pickled Squash, 260
squid
    Grilled Squid with Peperonata, 105
    Squid Ink Buns, 83–84
steak
    Bison Tomahawk Steaks with Chimichurri, 161
    Crane Steak au Poivre, 125–126
    Elk Backstraps, 190
    Grilled Wagyu Porterhouse Steak, 189
    Smoked Uni Butter and Bison Tenderloin, 81–82
stracciatella cheese: Charred Zucchini and Stracciatella Cheese, 259
strawberries: Smoker Strawberry Pie, 281–282
Stroopwafel S'mores, 277–278
sumac
    Sumac Curd with Whipped Cream and Shortbread Crumbs, 287
    Sumac and Sotol Margarita, 296

swan: Cold-Smoked Cured Swan Breast, 185–186
Sweet Pea Risotto, 43–44
swordfish: Grilled Swordfish with Roasted Tomatoes and Olive Tapenade, 73
syrups
    Sumac, 296
    Wild Ginger Honey, 295

T

tahini
    Baba Ghanoush, 248
    Hummus, 252
tequila: Beet'tle Juice, 292
tomatoes
    Bear Curry, 207–208
    Creole Sauce, 41–42
    Elk Backstraps, 190
    Elk Osso Buco, 197–198
    Grilled Cherry Tomatoes, 65–66
    Roasted Tomatoes, 73
    Roe Deer Caprese Salad, 179
    Romesco Sauce, 101–102
    Seafood and Rabbit Paella, 106
    Tomato Sauce, 173–174
trout
    Baked Salt-Crusted Trout, 70
    Brown Trout with Sweet Pea Risotto, 43–44
    Fire-Roasted Kelp-Planked Steelhead Trout, 29
    Grilled Brook Trout, 25–26
tuna, albacore: Pacific Albacore Tuna Donburi, 56
Turnips, Roasted, 59
Tzatziki, 156

U

uni *see* sea urchins

V

Vanilla Ice Cream, 275
vegetables
    Campfire Brussels Sprouts and Bacon, 263
    Campfire Chanterelle Risotto, 247
    Charcoal-Roasted Beets with Yogurt Dressing, 255
    Charcoal-Roasted Whole Cabbage, 251
    Charred Zucchini and Stracciatella Cheese, 259
    Fire-Roasted Cauliflower with Baba Ghanoush, 248
    Fire-Roasted Heirloom Carrots and Onions with Hummus, 252
    Fire-Roasted Sweet Corn, 256
    Fire-Roasted Whole Squash with Burrata Cheese, 260
    Grilled Artichokes, 264
venison
    Mule Deer Tataki, 164
    Roe Deer Caprese Salad, 179
    Snacking Sticks, 121
    Venison Patties, 199–200
vodka: Nocino (Black Walnut Liqueur), 299

W

walnuts, black
    Grilled Peaches and Vanilla Ice Cream with Wildflower Honey and Black Walnuts, 275–276
    Nocino (Black Walnut Liqueur), 299
Whipped Cream, 281–282, 287
White Wine Cream Sauce with Herb Oil, 63–64
whitefish: Grilled Lake Erie Whitefish, 34
Whole Roasted Woodcock, 137
wild boar *see* boar, wild
Wild Ginger Dark and Stormy, 295
wine, white
    Muskox in White Wine Cream Sauce with Orecchiette and Kale, 171
    Mussels in White Wine Cream Sauce with Grilled Baguette, 111–112
    White Wine Cream Sauce with Herb Oil, 63–64
wings: Smoked Duck Wings with Maple Hot Sauce, 138
Woodcock, Whole Roasted, 137

Y

Yams, Maple Candied, 159–160
yogurt
    Bear Curry, 207–208
    Charcoal-Roasted Beets with Yogurt Dressing, 255
    Tzatziki, 156

Z

zucchini: Charred Zucchini and Stracciatella Cheese, 259